CHANGING COUNTRIES

Changing Countries

THE EXPERIENCE AND ACHIEVEMENT OF
GERMAN-SPEAKING EXILES FROM HITLER
IN BRITAIN, FROM 1933 TO TODAY

EDITED BY MARIAN MALET AND ANTHONY GRENVILLE

LIBRIS

First published 2002

Copyright © Libris, 2002

All rights reserved

Libris
26 Lady Margaret Road
London NW5 2XL

A catalogue record for this book is available from the British Library

ISBN 1 870352 61 0

Designed and produced by Tony Kitzinger
Printed and bound by Biddles, Ltd, Guildford

CONTENTS

Introduction — vii

Brief Biographies of the Interviewees — xiii

1. Introducing the Refugees: Family Backgrounds before Emigration *by* Anthony Grenville — 1

2. Culture, Education, Politics and the Impact of Historical Developments before Emigration *by* Anthony Grenville and Irene Wells — 18

3. Departure and Arrival *by* Marian Malet — 45

4. Everyday Life in Prewar and Wartime Britain *by* Stefan Howald — 90

5. Internment *by* Jennifer Taylor — 127

6. Life as an 'Enemy Alien' *by* Stefan Howald — 152

7. Religion *by* Anthony Grenville — 161

8. Facing the Facts: Relations with the 'Heimat' *by* Charmian Brinson — 184

9. Postwar: The Challenges of Settling Down *by* Marietta Bearman and Erna Woodgate — 217

Afterword — 247

Glossary and Abbreviations — 249

Notes on Contributors — 253

Index — 254

Introduction

This book is based on the life stories of a group of people who have not yet received the full recognition they deserve: the refugees from Germany, Austria and Czechoslovakia who fled from Nazism in the years after 1933 and made their home in Great Britain. They are remarkable for their strength in surmounting the traumas of persecution and exile, as well as for their achievements in their adopted homeland, which was and continues to be greatly enriched by their presence.

The Oral History Project, of which this book is a product, started in 1994 as the result of an initiative by members of what was then the London Research Group for German Exile Studies and is now the Research Centre for German and Austrian Exile Studies. The initial impetus was the realisation that time was running out for the preservation of the memories of the former refugees from Nazism in Great Britain. The overall aim of the Oral History Project is to preserve original reminiscences, to enlarge our stock of source material and to make it available for further research. More specifically, we think that the material gathered will enhance our understanding of the relationship between refugees and host country.

The contribution this book makes to our historical understanding of the refugees from Hitler in Britain differs from that of all the existing literature on the subject. As it covers the whole range of the refugees' experience, it extends beyond the narrower canvas of those studies that deal specifically with such areas as the mass internment of aliens, for example François Lafitte's 1940 classic *The Internment of Aliens*, or the Kindertransports, such as Barry Turner's *... And the Policeman Smiled*, or Bertha Leverton and Shmuel Lowensohn's *I Came Alone: Stories of the Kindertransport*. This book's focus on the personal experiences of individual refugees also differentiates it from studies of British Government policy towards the refugees like Bernard Wasserstein's *Britain and the Jews of Europe 1939–1945*, A.J Sherman's *Britain and Refugees from the Third Reich 1933–1939*, and more recently Louise London's *Whitehall and the Jews 1933–1948*.

In this book, interviews with refugees are subjected to academic analysis and reflection, which differentiates it again from the many personal memoirs and autobiographical works by such refugee authors as Judith Kerr (*Out of the Hitler Time: One Family's Story*) or those by Trude Levi (*A Cat Called Adolf*) and Martha Blend (*A Child Alone*) which appeared in the Library of Holocaust Testimonies series published by Vallentine Mitchell. Similarly, the volume *Strangers at Home and Abroad* edited by Adi Wimmer reproduces a series of memories of Jewish men and women who left Austria due to the advent of Nazism, but offers no analysis. There have been few academic books, indeed, devoted to the refugees from Hitler who fled to Britain. Two of these, *Second Chance: Two Centuries of German-Speaking Jews in the United Kingdom* edited by Werner E. Mosse and *Exile in Great Britain: Refugees from Hitler's Germany*, edited by Gerhard Hirschfeld, are collections of scholarly essays dealing with specific areas of refugee involvement with British society, and as such are quite different from this book. Marion Berghahn's *Continental Britons: German-Jewish Refugees from Nazi Germany*, the only existing study based on extensive interviews with former refugees, is now some twenty years old, and its findings, based on a highly academic anthropological approach, are by now due for revision; thorough as it is, Berghahn's book remains that of a scholarly outsider, a liberal-minded German of the post-war era who is, however, not always able to capture the complexities of the integration of a group of German-speaking Jews into their new British environment.

On the basis of a detailed programme of prepared questions, we recorded thirty-four interviews with refugees from a wide range of backgrounds: the result of personal contacts and recommendations as well as varying interests within our group. The transcribed material, amounting to some 1,000 pages, consists of differing elements of oral source material. There is direct lived experience (first-hand accounts), there is specific oral tradition (memories passed on, family stories, secondhand knowledge), and there is story-telling (constructed, organised forms of narration). Each one of these elements is valid in its own right, but needs special, carefully weighted deliberation.

INTRODUCTION

This book gives voice to invaluable human experiences. Furthermore, we believe that it has three specific distinguishing characteristics. It ranges widely over the refugees' lives, but it also provides in-depth analysis; it presents a broad and varied mix of interviewees with a strong emphasis on less well-known people; and it focuses on the question of assimilation. The first two of these, taken in conjunction, give our study some claim to be representative, albeit not in a strictly statistical sense, since our selection of interviewees comes nearer to a cross-section of the refugees from Hitler than do existing studies concentrating on specific professional, artistic or political groups within the emigration. The third distinguishing mark, the issue of assimilation, has not only shaped our interviews, but is also a constant theme throughout the book, whether explicitly or more indirectly.

The book follows a broadly chronological approach into which are interwoven several thematic strands. It traces the origins of the refugees, their departure and arrival, and investigates prewar, wartime and postwar experiences. Special attention is given to subjects like work and professional careers, education, language, everyday life in exile, and questions of religion, political attitudes and relations with the former 'Heimat' (homeland).

'Getting behind stereotype and generalisation,' says Dr Robert Perks of the British Library's National Sound Archive, 'is one of the most challenging aspects of Oral History.' It is also one of the most rewarding: obtaining new, concrete, detailed evidence which adds colour and life to an abstract thesis. However, the process of interpretation tends in the opposite direction: towards generalisation. We have tried in this book to find a balance between common experience and individual fate.

There is an ongoing debate on the question of exile and Diaspora as well as its reverse side, assimilation and integration. Assimilation, the adjustment of a people into another culture, was the subject of frequent debate within Central European Jewry in the first part of the twentieth century. It became urgent once again for our refugees after their arrival in Great Britain. Should they conserve or even forge an identity in whose name they were persecuted, or should they start to integrate as individuals into their new host community? We have tried to go beyond declarative statements and to show what assimilation means in reality, in everyday life. The process of integration is certainly not a clear-cut one, with time of successful completion neatly indicated. Linguistic competence, for instance, is embedded in the reality of social relationships. One must also bear in mind that assimilation is not a one-way street. Naturally, the interviewees tend to be modestly silent about their contribution to their new 'Heimat'. But this book is living proof of their commitment to British society.

The working group behind this project consists of eight colleagues: Marietta Bearman, Charmian Brinson, Anthony Grenville, Stefan Howald, Marian Malet, Jennifer Taylor, Irene Wells and Erna Woodgate. Alexandra Gründel and Jane Ennis kindly carried out three of the interviews on our behalf. The chapters were written and are attributed individually. The Oral History Project was conducted through the Research Centre for German and Austrian Exile Studies, itself located at the Institute of Germanic Studies, School of Advanced Study, University of London. Our tapes and transcripts are stored at the Institute and are available for use by other scholars. We would like to thank the Institute, and especially William Abbey, its librarian, for assistance generously given; for financial support we wish to express our gratitude to *German Life and Letters*, the Association of Jewish Refugees in Great Britain and Dresdner Kleinwort Benson; we are grateful to Dr Robert Perks of the National Sound Archive and Dr Trevor Lummis, formerly of the University of Essex, for advice and guidance on Oral History matters. Above all, however, we want to thank the interviewees, to whom this book is dedicated.

'So we went, changing countries more often than our shoes.'

Bertolt Brecht, 'To Posterity', 1938

Brief Biographies of the Interviewees

Hilde Ainger, née Salomon. Born 1917, Guben/Neisse, into Jewish family; father lawyer. Left Germany on her own and out of conviction, 1934, before schooling completed, for au pair job in Bristol. Held several domestic jobs. Finally married Englishman 1939. Able to arrange parents' move to Britain. Brought up family in north London, where she still lives.

Alec Armstrong, born Hans-Ludwig Baehr, 1907, into non-Jewish family. Trained as architect at Bauhaus in Weimar and Dessau under teachers such as Moholy-Nagy, Breuer, Gropius. Forced to emigrate 1934 to Denmark, then 1936 to Britain, as opponent of Nazi regime. Interned in Australia, later served in Pioneer Corps. After war had distinguished career in architecture, town planning and teaching. Lives in north London in retirement.

Hilde Auerbach, born 1908 Berlin; father successful Jewish theatrical agent, mother non-Jewish. HA Lutheran. PhD in Economics in Germany, which included year researching in England (1931–32). After Hitler's accession to power left for au pair post in England because of Social Democrat convictions. Took English degree after war and pursued teaching career in Bath where she still lives.

Lotte Berk, born Liselotte Heymansohn, 1913 Cologne into well-off assimilated Jewish family; father in clothing trade. Studied dance; performances 1930 onwards with English dancer Ernest Berk. Married him 1933 and they fled 1935 to England. Work as model and dancer. 1959 established own dance studio and fitness technique. Lives and still works in north London.

Eugen Brehm, born 1909 in Ulm/Donau into non-Jewish working-class family. 1929 became member of Gruppe revolutionärer Pazifisten. 1930 bookshop assistant Berlin; member of Sozialistische Arbeiterpartei (SAP). Brief arrest 1933, after which illegal work for SAP. Fled 1935 to Prague where worked as journalist until early

1939 when he emigrated to London. Soon began to work for BBC Monitoring Service, where he remained until retirement. Died November 1995.

Hans Brill, born 1930 Vienna into well-to-do Jewish family with thriving business. Forced to emigrate 1938 with family to Britain, to London then South Wales. Joined Royal Navy as a cadet, but broke off successful career in submarines to read for degree at Oxford. Subsequently went into academic life as art historian and librarian then lecturer. Died July 2001.

Josephine Bruegel, née Liebstein. Born 1914 in Neustadtl, present-day Czech Republic; father secular Jewish doctor. After rather disjointed education, began to study medicine in Prague. Emigrated 1939 to England and took work as nurse. Married fellow refugee and countryman, historian Wolfgang Bruegel. Qualified 1942 as doctor. They returned post-war to Prague, but soon came back to Britain where JB worked many years as doctor. Lives in north London.

Alfred Dörfel, born 1911 Leipzig into non-Jewish working-class family. Trained as lithographic printer. Member of German Communist Party. Arrested briefly 1933 and afterwards went to Prague, where acted as Party courier. Arrived February 1939 in Britain. Interned in June 1940 then deported to Canada, returning 1941 to take up work as printer. Lives in north London. Has retained German nationality.

Ernst Flesch, born 1928 Vienna into Jewish family. Arrived Britain January 1939 on Kindertransport; educated in Scotland then moved 1943 to London. Worked for photographer and became very involved in Young Austria (see Glossary). After the war trained and made career as teacher. Lives in north London. Is still an Austrian citizen.

Klary Friedl, née Heilmann, born 1912 Košice, Slovakia into well-to-do Jewish family. Worked as beautician in Bratislava, later in

Prague. Emigrated 1939 to Britain after husband had been granted entry on business grounds. Lived in London doing variety of jobs. Helped husband build up his import/export business with Hungary and continued after his death. Lived in Kew. Died 1996.

Dorothea Galewski, born 1926 Berlin into Jewish family; father lawyer. 1929 family moved to Breslau. Family arrived April 1939 in Britain with transit visa for Ecuador and were still in London at outbreak of war. DG attended poor schools in London. After war worked in Germany for American Army and for Nuremberg War Crimes Trials. Upon return to London, career in travel agencies, including 11 years in South Africa. Lives in south London where she helped found local branch of University of the Third Age.

Peter Gellhorn, born 1912 Breslau to Gentile mother and Jewish father, well-known architect; parents divorced and at age eleven moved to Berlin with mother. Studied piano and later conducting at Hochschule für Musik. Emigrated 1935 to Britain where built career as musician, conducting Carl Rosa Opera Company, at Covent Garden, Glyndebourne and for BBC. Interned in war on Isle of Man. Lives in London.

Mimi (Wilhelmine) Glover, née Grünfeld, born 1909 Vienna into Jewish family; father antiquarian bookseller. For family reasons, MG had to pay her way through later school years and through university, gaining Doctorate early 1938. Emigrated shortly after to Britain, then brought over mother and sister. Worked at various domestic jobs, also as teacher. Married sculptor 1945. Lived in northwest London. Died 1998.

Ruth Herring, née Hoppe. Born 1910 in Glogau/Oder into Christian family; father businessman. Gained Doctorate at Königsberg University before arriving 1934 in Britain to continue education. Later worked as Language Assistant in girls' boarding- school. From 1936, after brush with Nazi authorities on visit home, became 'voluntary refugee'. Marriage 1940 to fellow-refugee; interned at Holloway prison then Isle of Man, where she ran school in Married Camp.

After release resumed teaching career. Committed Quaker. Lives High Wycombe, Buckinghamshire.

Margarete Hinrichsen, née Levy. Born 1919 in Bad Polzin (Pomerania) into old-established Jewish landowning family. Educated locally and in Breslau. Sent to England 1937 to learn language. Father killed during Kristallnacht; she stayed in England, studying and working. Met and married another refugee. Lives in north London.

Renée Hubert, née Riese. Born 1916 Wiesbaden into very comfortable assimilated Jewish family; both parents doctors. After father temporarily arrested Spring 1933, family emigrated via Switzerland to France (Lyons, then Paris) where RH completed secondary studies, then entered Sorbonne. *Assistante* in school in Chichester 1936. Awarded degree Paris 1939, then took teaching post in Norfolk. Caught in Britain because of war, and continued teaching there before being able to join family in USA in 1944, where she completed education and pursued academic career in American universities. Now in retirement in Newport Beach, California, where continues to do research.

Peter Johnson, né Wolfgang Josephs, born 1916 Berlin into Jewish family; father manufacturer who, foreseeing difficulties, organised his son's emigration to London in 1933, financed his education there and arranged his apprenticeship in fur trade. Mother joined him in London. PJ interned and deported to Australia, released to join Pioneer Corps, then worked as interpreter in Occupied Germany. Later returned to fur trade. Lives in north London.

Nelly Kuttner, née Mueckenbrun, born 1905 Vienna into Jewish family in dressmaking business. Trained as milliner, obtaining Meisterbrief (diploma) at age of twenty, then set up own business. Left Austria as result of Kristallnacht. Mixed experiences as domestic servant in London before being able to restart what became a very successful millinery business in Maida Vale. Met and married another refugee from Vienna. Died January 2000.

BIOGRAPHIES

Christel Marsh, née Christiane Christinneke, born 1917 Magdeburg. Father Gymnasium teacher and Lutheran theologian. After completing Abitur 1936 became apprentice in bookshop/publishing house in Halle/Saale where met future (English) husband. Member of Confessional Church. Denounced as anti-Nazi by colleague and interrogated by Gestapo but allowed to leave for England to marry fiancé. Lived in Oxford and then London. Died April 2000.

Hanne (Johanne) Norbert-Miller, née Nussbaum, born 1916 Vienna into Jewish family with theatrical connections; father businessman. Attended Reinhardt-Seminar and pursued acting career in Austria until Anschluss. First unsuccessful attempt to enter England 1938 followed by work in film industry in Paris; admitted to Britain August 1939, where family now settled. Continued to work as actress in London (in refugee theatre, then for BBC); 1946 married fellow-refugee and actor, Martin Miller. Died 1999.

Eva Pollard, née Schäfer, born 1912 Breslau into well-to-do Jewish home. Attended commercial college, then worked in father's office and as translator in Berlin. Came to England 1939 on domestic visa. Married refugee lawyer who had set up insurance business as not allowed to practise law. EP assisted in business. Died January 1999.

Helga Reutter, née Rostal, born Vienna 1914 into prosperous Jewish family; father owned clothing factory. Forbidden to attend university, but learned dressmaking. Fiancé preceded her to England 1938. Brought her family over, married and subsisted on domestic and similar jobs whilst husband in army. Also worked in father's tailoring business. Lived in Bayswater, London. Died 2000.

Eric Rose, born Adolf Rosenberger, 1924, in Breslau into Zionist family. As father's attempt to emigrate legally to Palestine in late 1930s unsuccessful, he obtained post as agent in London. ER arrived with mother 1939; attended school but arrested and interned on sixteenth birthday; when released continued education, obtaining degree. Chose manufacturing career. Lives in retirement in west London where he pursues academic studies.

CHANGING COUNTRIES

Elizabeth Rosenthal, born 1927 Berlin; parents Jewish professionals and committed Communists. Father, engineer, moved to Moscow in early 1930s to find work and died there during war. ER left for England on Kindertransport 1939, mother following soon after. After schooling and teacher training, ER taught in schools, and later studied for PhD in French Literature. Finally headed Modern Languages Dept in Teacher Training College. Retired and lives in Richmond, Surrey.

Stella Rotenberg, born 1916 Vienna into Jewish middle-class family. Forced to give up medical studies at Anschluss; emigrated to England via Holland. Married Czech refugee doctor. Worked in war as medical assistant and accountant. Settled in Leeds after war. From 1940 wrote poems, but first publication only in 1972. Since then, several more publications and growing recognition. Still lives in Leeds.

Adelheid Schweitzer, née Schoenewald, born 1913 Giessen into Jewish medical family, grew up Bad Nauheim, emigrated June 1933 to Britain after dissolution, on racial grounds, of Mannheim Interpreters' School where she had been training. Worked in London for German-Jewish import/export firm. In wartime worked part-time in welfare field; following death of husband in 1952, qualified then worked as psychiatric social worker. Lives in north London.

Hans Seelig, born 1930 Mannheim, only son of Jewish furniture wholesaler. 1939 sent to Sweden on Kindertransport; arrived August in Britain to join parents who had obtained permission to settle there. After school and before university did National Service. Obtained scholarship to Oxford to read Modern Languages. Teaching career in secondary then higher education. Unmarried. Retired, lives in Hemel Hempstead, Hertfordshire. Chairman of Club 1943.

Hanna Singer, née Cohn, born 1928 Halle/Saale into assimilated Jewish family; father in banking, later estate agent; parents divorced 1933. Sister emigrated to England; Hanna and twin brother came 1939 on Kindertransport and mother followed. Parents decided to remarry but father imprisoned in France and deported. Educated in Britain, obtained university degree and had career in teaching. Married to Peter Singer. Lives in London.

Peter Singer, born 1923 Nuremberg to Jewish dentist parents. Sent 1933 to be educated in Turin on account of Nazi accession to power, but soon returned home as very unhappy. Sent 1936 to England with two other boys, via private arrangement, to continue education. After completing schooling, trained and worked in aircraft production. Worked for Americans in Germany after war. Back in Britain, held different engineering posts, then became director of manufacturing company. Lives in retirement in London. Husband of Hanna Singer.

Eva Sommerfreund, née Oplatek, born 1917 Vienna into wealthy assimilated Jewish family with strong Czech connections who moved in literary/artistic circles. Was member of well-known female close-harmony singing group but career as singer and actress cut short by occupation of Prague by Germans. Emigrated with first husband to France, then after adventurous escape via South of France and Gibraltar reached Britain 1940. Worked and acted in refugee theatre in London where met second husband. Lived for some years in Panama with third husband before settling again in London.

Gertrud Wengraf, née West. Born 1915 in Lundenburg (now Břeclav), Moravia, into Jewish family. Father, industrial chemist, lost job after First World War and family moved to Vienna in straitened circumstances when GW aged 13: her 'first emigration'. Studied at university, active in Socialist youth movement, where met future husband, Jewish art dealer. Married and left Austria right after Anschluss, settling in south London where soon had child. Husband able to start picture dealing and finally to open gallery. Husband's business prospered. Still lives south London.

Ilse Wolff, née Zorek, born 1908 Glatz (Silesia) into Jewish middle-class family. Grew up in Berlin, attended commercial college. From 1924 worked as secretary. 1933 joined office of Reichsvertretung deutscher Juden. Emigration 1939 with husband to London. 1939–66 on staff of Wiener Library (from 1947 as Chief Librarian). Second marriage to Oswald Wolff; took over his publishing house on his death in 1968. Worked as publisher and editor until 1985. Died February 2001.

Walter Wolff, born 1926 Berlin into assimilated Jewish family. Father owned photographic business. Arrived Britain aged 12, attended Quaker school. Mother to Britain on domestic visa. Trained as chemist and worked most of life for large pharmaceutical firm in Britain and abroad. Lives in west London.

Erika Young, née Fallaux, born 1927 Vienna into old-established, well-to-do Catholic family. Arrived 1938 Britain where educated in convent school of same order as her school in Vienna. Mother emigrated just before war, and died 1941, father died in Austria during war. EY worked mainly in publishing and as freelance journalist. Married in 1961. Lives in Richmond, Surrey.

CHAPTER ONE

Introducing the Refugees: Family Backgrounds before Emigration

Anthony Grenville

1. Introduction

It may be helpful to begin with some basic information about the thirty-four interviewees. As might be expected of a group whose ages when interviewed ranged from sixty-six to ninety, the women (23) outnumber the men (11). Many of them were in their later teens when Hitler came to power in Germany in 1933, or in the first half of their twenties for those who experienced Nazi rule after the annexation of Austria (1938) or the occupation of Czechoslovakia (1939); there is also a significant group who were still children, including three who came to Britain on Kindertransports.[1] Ten of the refugees were children of fourteen or less when they emigrated, and four were aged sixteen or seventeen. The other twenty all left as young adults of twenty or above; only two were over thirty.

Eight of the refugees were married, engaged or firmly settled with their partner before their departure. Two of these, Ilse Wolff and Eva Sommerfreund, subsequently divorced, but both remarried other refugees, twice in Eva Sommerfreund's case. Three more got married in England to refugee partners whom they had previously met in Germany. At least eight others married other refugees in England, including Peter and Hanna Singer, husband and wife. The picture that emerges is of a tight-knit group with strong internal cohesion and loyalties. Those who married English partners seem often to have been those who left young and underwent their socialisation in Britain, like Eric Rose and Erika Young; the exception is

1. See Glossary and Abbreviations, p. 249.

Christel Marsh, who had met and become engaged to an Englishman before she left Germany.

As one would expect, there is a heavy preponderance of Jews among the refugees, twenty-eight, as against six non-Jews who left Germany for political, ethical or religious reasons;[2] though most Jews fled Germany for racial reasons, some were also political opponents of the Nazis. Among the Jews are included three half-Jews, who were defined as Jewish by the Nazis, even though in each case the mother was non-Jewish, making them non-Jews in the eyes of the Jewish community. Of the six non-Jewish refugees, three profess no faith, two are Protestant, and one Catholic. Alfred Dörfel, Eugen Brehm and Hans-Ludwig Baehr (who changed his name to Alec Armstrong when he was sent to France on D-Day) are left-wing activists who belong to the category of political refugees. Christel Marsh, a member of the anti-Nazi Bekennende Kirche (Confessional Church), opposed the regime on moral and religious grounds, though the immediate reason for her leaving Germany was a personal one: she had an English fiancé. Erika Young also had a family background that predisposed her to rejection of National Socialism, though in her case it was the instinctive revulsion of Catholic Austrian conservatives against the Nazis that led her parents to send her to England. Ruth Herring left Germany for what can best be termed ethical reasons: she refused to sign a document designed to incriminate her doctoral supervisor in the eyes of the authorities. Unlike the Jews and left-wingers, who were predestined to persecution under Hitler, these people, clearly acting against the pattern set by those from similar backgrounds, freely chose not to conform to the regime's demands.

There are twenty-two Germans among the refugees, including Eric Rose, whose parents, though long resident in Breslau, retained their Austrian nationality, and hence their immunity from Nazi excesses, until Austria was annexed to the Reich. Five of the six non-Jewish refugees are from Germany. There are eight Austrian nationals and four Czechoslovaks. However, reflecting the tradition of mobility between the Czech crownlands of Habsburg days and

2. Non-Jews happen to be over-represented in this study: one would normally not expect more than 10%, statistically speaking.

1. FAMILY BACKGROUNDS BEFORE EMIGRATION

Vienna, two of the Czechs, Gertrud Wengraf, whose family moved from Lundenburg/Břeclav in Moravia to Vienna when she was thirteen, and Eva Sommerfreund, who was brought up mostly in Vienna, should be added to the Austrians. All four of the Czechoslovaks are Jewish, and all came from families that spoke German as well as Czech (or Hungarian in the case of Klary Friedl, deep in Slovakia). These national differences play only a very minor role as factors determining the interviewees' experience of life under Nazi rule and in exile. The experiences of Jews resident in big cities, by far the largest group among the interviewees, are remarkably similar, whether they lived in Berlin, Vienna, or Prague, once they confronted the reality of persecution and the problems and ruptures of exile. What this group had in common as German-speaking Jews from a Central European culture far outweighed any differences in nationality, and this chapter treats them accordingly.

2. *Patterns of residence*

Striking differences emerge between the residential patterns of Jews and non-Jews. The latter often grew up in smaller towns, Christel Marsh in Magdeburg, Ruth Herring in Glogau an der Oder, Eugen Brehm in Ulm; only Erika Young and Alfred Dörfel grew up in large cities, Vienna and Leipzig respectively. The Jews were far more concentrated in a small number of major urban centres. Nine grew up in Vienna, including all seven Austrian Jews, as well as Gertrud Wengraf and Eva Sommerfreund, who spent the first few years of her life in Prague. Six grew up in Berlin, including Peter Gellhorn, who moved there aged eleven from Breslau. Three grew up in Breslau, including Dorothea Galewski, who moved there from Berlin aged three. Two grew up in or near Frankfurt am Main, and one in Cologne. Three-quarters of the Jewish refugees, twenty-one of twenty-eight, thus lived in five of the eight large cities where the Jewish population of Germany and Austria tended strongly to concentrate; only seven came from smaller towns.

The residential pattern of the interviewees bears out trends that have been amply documented, especially the heavy concentration of the educated and prosperous Jewish professional middle classes in

Berlin for Germany and, above all, in Vienna for Austria. That the great majority of the Jewish interviewees came from exactly this assimilated, secularised background will be shown below. In the German cities and in Vienna, there was a remarkable concentration of Jews in certain bourgeois occupations: trade, commerce, banking and the professions, especially law and medicine. It should, however, be noted that the composition of the urban Jewish communities changed, as immigrants from the East ('Ostjuden'), who were often poor, Orthodox and strangers to German culture and language, flooded in. In Vienna, the mass of these impoverished and still backward people congregated in the Leopoldstadt (Second District), where they formed what was virtually a second Jewish community very different from the secularised, assimilated 'Western' Jews. The over-representation of Jews in middle-class and independent occupations should not blind one to the existence of large numbers of poor Jews. Despite their numbers, poorer Jews, 'Ostjuden', and those from humbler social and occupational strata are notable by their absence among our interviewees. That the latter stem almost exclusively from prosperous, middle-class, urban Jewish backgrounds points to important conclusions regarding the type of people who were best placed to make their escape from Nazi Germany.

3. Family background

A detailed analysis of the interviewees' lives must begin in the family home, with their parents. Here there is, as might be expected, all manner of diversity. Some of the families were well established in their native areas, like Margarete Hinrichsen's father's family in Bad Polzin; Josephine Bruegel's father's family, resident in the Pilsen area of Bohemia since 1600; Christel Marsh's father, who was descended from a long line of teachers from the Altmark, north-west of Magdeburg; or Adelheid Schweitzer's parents, who could trace their family trees in the Kassel area back at least to the mid-eighteenth century. Others were newcomers from afar, like Lotte Berk's father, who had fled the pogroms of Russia and arrived via Holland in Cologne; Klary Friedl's father, who had walked from Poland to Switzerland at the age of thirteen to learn his trade as a

1. FAMILY BACKGROUNDS BEFORE EMIGRATION

clockmaker and jeweller, then set up independently in business in the Slovakian town of Košice; or Eva Sommerfreund's mother, 'a total mixture of the [Habsburg] Monarchy', born in Sofia to a Viennese father and a Sephardic, Ladino-speaking mother from Belgrade who was enchanted, on arriving in Uruguay as an exile, to re-enter the Spanish-speaking world that her family had left centuries before.

Particularly mobile, indeed internationally so, are those families with pronounced Communist sympathies. Alec Armstrong had a bilingual mother born in France and a Russian-speaking father whose support for the Bolsheviks took him to Russia. Elizabeth Rosenthal's father came to live in Berlin when his father sent him from what was then Russian Poland to be educated at a 'Party school' in Germany for the children of committed left-wingers; in the 1930s her grandparents were living in Moscow, where her father joined them in 1931. Alfred Dörfel's father, on the other hand, a working man who was to become a dedicated Communist, simply moved from the Vogtland, on the Czech/Saxon border, to Leipzig, a case typical of millions of Germans who were drawn to the great cities by the prospect of employment in the factories created by Germany's breakneck industrialisation.

Given the great migration of Jews from the East to cities like Vienna and Berlin, it is no surprise that they show a high degree of mobility. A typical Jewish success story is that of Helga Reutter's father, who came from Poland to Vienna at the turn of the century, owned his own clothing factory, and married the daughter of a wealthy grain merchant from Bielitz/Bielsko, Silesia. Gertrud Wengraf's family, by contrast, fell victim to historical developments. When her father was called up in the First World War, her mother was forced by food shortages to leave Vienna and went to live with her mother in Lundenburg/Břeclav, Moravia; but after the war her father, unable to keep the family, moved to Vienna, where he was reduced by the Depression to living with his family in one room in his mother's flat and selling goods on the street.

Mimi Glover's grandparents, who had moved to Vienna from Czechoslovakia on her father's side and from Hungary on her mother's, exemplify a very common pattern of Jewish migration in the late nineteenth century. Ernst Flesch's parents were also typical examples of these modest new arrivals in the Imperial capital:

> My mother came from the country. She was born in Lower Austria, her father was Hungarian-speaking Slovakian, her mother from a very old Austrian German-speaking family who were, I think, in the clothing business in quite a big way. They supplied uniforms to the Imperial army and things like that. But my father's people were from Moravia. They had come to Vienna in the previous generation. He was already born in Vienna, so I'm sort of third-generation Viennese, as it were. Before that they came from Moravia and were 'Provinzjuden', in business in a very small way, greengrocers or something like that.

By contrast, Eva Sommerfreund's paternal grandfather was a major industrialist and an adviser to President Masaryk at the peace talks at Saint Germain, where the postwar treaty with defeated Austria was signed in 1919, and Hans Brill's father worked as a young scientist under Marie Curie and Ernest Rutherford and corresponded with Niels Bohr.

Nelly Kuttner's father came to Vienna as a child from Bielitz/Bielsko, and her mother from Moravia as a baby. But both integrated into Viennese life, coming, like many middle-class Jews, to love the city where they had made their home and to feel deeply rooted in their assimilated milieu:

> I must say – it's very silly to say, it sounds very chauvinistic – they felt very much . . . 'we are real Viennese people', you see, they felt that. They didn't feel a mixture, they felt . . . there was no need to think about it, my father was not born in Vienna, but he was a real Austrian and my mother felt very Viennese, she went to school and everything in Vienna.

This unquestioning confidence in the security of their integration into Gentile society is deeply poignant, in the light of what was to befall the Austrian Jews, whose love of their homeland and pride in their native cities was as heartfelt as those of their German counterparts. The spell cast over the assimilating Jews by the German-speaking cities, which seemingly opened out before them a sunlit

1. FAMILY BACKGROUNDS BEFORE EMIGRATION

vista of social, economic and cultural opportunity, was to prove a false enchantment that darkened into rejection and persecution.

Disparities in wealth and origin are matched by differences in childhood experiences. Many of the refugees look back fondly on a happy, secure childhood with their parents. Eva Pollard (born 1912 in Breslau) remembers 'a very happy uneventful childhood' before 1933, with the all-embracing normality, as it seemed to middle-class children, of a large house, wealthy parents, servants, nice holidays and non-Jewish friends at school. 'My early childhood memories are really very happy,' says Walter Wolff (born 1926, Berlin):

> We lived a relatively comfortable life, without being wealthy. We had holidays in a country house which we shared with friends of ours. I went to a German primary school quite near to where we lived . . . in a district called Wilmersdorf. We had a comfortable flat, we had – as most people did – live-in domestic help, my parents had a very good social life, with many friends, and quite a large number of relatives as well – some of them Jewish, a lot of them non-Jewish.

Josephine Bruegel (born 1914, Neustadtl, Sudetenland) looks back affectionately: 'My father was a doctor there, and I had a very lovely childhood, a very secure, lovely childhood.' The closeness of Nelly Kuttner's (born 1905, Vienna) relationship with her parents resonates throughout her interview, along with her awareness of its destruction in the Holocaust. Margarete Hinrichsen (born 1919, Bad Polzin, Pomerania) speaks of a happy childhood, marred at most by the teasing she endured for a time as a result of her squint. But the summer sporting pastimes she so enjoyed were increasingly closed to her after 1933, when as a Jew she could not use the tennis courts or swimming-pool, the latter a particular irony since her father had been the principal donor to the town's pool; and in winter she dared no longer obliterate with her skates the swastikas carved by German children in the ice.

Events closer to home than the rise of Hitler could also cause disruption. Lotte Berk's mother died suddenly when she was still a child, while Christel Marsh and Josephine Bruegel lost their fathers as teenagers and Mimi Glover in her twenties. Peter Gellhorn's parents divorced when he was eight, Eva Sommerfreund's parents separated when her father returned to Prague from Vienna with another woman, and Peter Johnson's parents divorced. Hanna Singer's mother, who divorced her husband in 1933 when Hanna was five, hoped to remarry him if he too reached safety in Britain; but he was arrested in France and died in Auschwitz. Elizabeth Rosenthal's family, as Jews and Communists, became victims of both Hitler and Stalin; when anti-semitism cost her father his job in Germany in 1931, he went to the Soviet Union, only to be arrested during the purges of 1937 and sent to a prison camp, where he died. The last time that she heard her father's voice, as a child in Nazi Germany, was over a public telephone, and her survival with her mother in Britain has not dimmed her sense of loss: 'And we had to be glad to be alive. And so we are, but anyway we missed my father all our life.'

4. Professional and economic status

Very distinct patterns emerge from an examination of the occupational and economic status of the interviewees' families. There is clear information about the professions of twenty-nine of the refugees' fathers; one more, Ilse Wolff's, was killed in the First World War when she was still small. Outstandingly the most striking feature of the fathers' occupations is that they are almost exclusively concentrated in the commercial and professional middle classes and, even more specifically, in the categories of independent businessmen, lawyers, and doctors and dentists. This applies to both Jews and non-Jews, the one significant difference being that the only state employees are two of the five non-Jews, Christel Marsh's father, a teacher, and Erika Young's, a government lawyer, which sharply illustrates the barriers faced by Jews in obtaining public sector jobs.

There are no fewer than fourteen independent businessmen: Ruth Herring's father owned a ladies' clothing business, Klary Friedl's was a clockmaker/jeweller, Eric Rose's a wholesale wine merchant, Helga Reutter's owned a clothing factory, Hanne Norbert-Miller's had his own business dealing in 'technical articles' (unspecified), Peter Johnson's was part-owner of a large ready-made clothes business, Hans Seelig's was joint owner of a wholesale soft-

1. FAMILY BACKGROUNDS BEFORE EMIGRATION

furnishings business, Walter Wolff's ran a photographic business, Mimi Glover's was an antiquarian bookseller, Margarete Hinrichsen's ran the family estates and the agricultural and industrial enterprises situated on them, Hans Brill's ran the family's leather-goods factory, Hilde Auerbach's was a theatrical agent, Nelly Kuttner's made and sold 'coats and costumes' from home with his wife's help, and Lotte Berk's owned a chain of men's clothing shops. The fathers of Eva Sommerfreund, Gertrud Wengraf and Hanna Singer may also be included in this category.

There are ten members of the independent professions, a considerable representation. Three are lawyers, the fathers of Erika Young, Hilde Ainger and Dorothea Galewski; interestingly, the latter two both moved away from Berlin, to Guben an der Neisse and Breslau respectively, where they had more chance of obtaining a practice outside the capital with its seemingly inexhaustible supply of Jewish lawyers. There are three doctors, the fathers of Josephine Bruegel, Adelheid Schweitzer and Renée Hubert, whose wife, also a doctor, had a large private practice. Peter Singer's father was a dentist, as was his mother. Other professionals were Peter Gellhorn's father, an architect, Elizabeth Rosenthal's, an engineer and academic, and Christel Marsh's, a Gymnasium (grammar school) teacher.

Ernst Flesch's father is the sole representative of the lower-middle class. He was a clerical worker, however, and far from impoverished: though he lived in the working-class Tenth District of Vienna, he held the position of secretary of the local synagogue and was able to move to a larger flat when an insurance policy matured. Gertrud Wengraf's family experienced a degree of poverty when, after the demise of the father's factory, he took his family to Vienna, and was reduced to street-selling and his wife to selling underwear. Yet both Ernst Flesch and Gertrud Wengraf were well educated in Vienna and seem not to have tasted the grinding poverty of the proletariat in the hard years of the Depression. Nelly Kuttner's father also suffered a considerable drop in income and status when, after service in the First World War, he was unable to continue his previous well-paid job and had to resort to the home production of clothing; but by 1925 the family was living modestly but very contentedly in a very pleasant flat. By contrast, Mimi Glover's father struggled to make money from his antiquarian bookshop. Her family lived in conditions far worse than those of the comfortable bourgeoisie, but her father's brothers belonged to the wealthy upper-middle class and helped the family out.

Alfred Dörfel's father is the only one from the working-class, which, along with the lower-middle class (and in Austria the agricultural peasantry), composed the great bulk of the population. He was an industrial worker, a tuner in a large factory making musical-boxes. Yet the family was not poor; the father earned well as a skilled worker, made sure that all his sons learnt a trade as apprentices, and enjoyed reading Ibsen with a good cigar:

> I think they were very well off. They were very well settled...
> Father, as a tuner, was very well paid. They had all, except perhaps
> Fritz, they had all... say by 1910, before I was born, entered
> apprenticeships, it must have been a very wealthy... not wealthy,
> but a very well-off working-class family. They had a big flat and
> quite a cultural background.

The family's aspirations – several of the children were highly motivated achievers, in their political activities or their acquisition of an education – marked them out as potentially upwardly mobile, though this sat somewhat uneasily with their revolutionary proletarian convictions. Alfred Dörfel grew up in a home background which radiated the energy and intelligence, the adaptability and mobility that can often help a refugee overcome the problems of exile and integration into a new society.

The profile that emerges from this survey of the professional backgrounds of the parents of our interviewees, admittedly a small group chosen at random, differs significantly from that of the general population of both Germany and Austria, whether Jewish or Gentile, though it broadly reflects the social composition of the emigration from Central Europe to Britain.

Divorce and separation adversely affected the economic position of children who were then provided for by their mothers, as was the case for Peter Gellhorn and Eva Sommerfreund, though not for Peter Johnson, who lived with his father, and less so for Hanna Singer, who

1. FAMILY BACKGROUNDS BEFORE EMIGRATION

went to live with her grandparents. When the money from her industrialist father-in-law dried up at his death, Eva Sommerfreund's mother had to work as the manageress of a dressmaking salon, but this state of relative poverty covered only a short period of her daughter's otherwise affluent youth. Peter Gellhorn's mother, however, lived in very straitened circumstances; her situation was further exacerbated by the emotional side-effects of the divorce and the father's remarriage: 'She was really unhappy. I mean, poverty always accentuates all these things. I decided then I would never marry, because I felt there was enough in me of my father and I did not want to be responsible for leading a woman the life my mother had.' Nevertheless, the young Peter enjoyed a good education and was able to pursue his musical studies thanks to a combination of grants and generosity, living a life that was recognisably middle-class, if at a very modest level. This also applies to Ilse Wolff, whose widowed mother could not afford to let her go to university. Elizabeth Rosenthal's mother seems to have coped reasonably well financially when her husband went to work in Moscow, at least until Hitler came to power.

With the exceptions of Mimi Glover, Peter Gellhorn, Ilse Wolff, Gertrud Wengraf, Alfred Dörfel and Ernst Flesch, the refugees consistently paint a picture of comfortable prosperity in the pre-Nazi years, as might be expected from their parents' professional status. Renée Hubert's family, where both parents worked as doctors in private practice, arranged private French lessons for their children as a matter of course, as well as employing two maids, a secretary and a nurse. Klary Friedl's family enjoyed an affluent lifestyle, with a cook, a maid, a nanny and a French governess, the symbol of assimilation through culture and education into the higher reaches of the middle-class. She recalls vividly the rich furnishings of her parental home: 'We had a house, we had beautiful furniture, wonderful paintings, wonderful silver, Persian carpets, and all kinds of beautiful things.' Helga Reutter's family was 'very comfortably off, rich'; she had a governess to teach her French and attended the progressive and doubtless expensive Schwarzwaldschule:

> We had a cook and we had a parlour-maid who departed in the middle thirties, because everybody was suffering in the crisis and

also my father's business wasn't doing so well. So then we had a cook and a cleaner and a washerwoman, which for a family of three in a four-room flat seems rather a lot today. But this is how it was.

Lotte Berk's account is not untypical: 'Well, I came from a businessman's family, my father was a successful businessman... He married my mother there in Cologne and became successful in men's clothes. He had a chain of shops. So we were very well off, had servants, you know.' Hanne Norbert-Miller's father could afford to let her have private acting lessons. Even Nelly Kuttner's parents, who had suffered a sharp drop in their pre-1914 standard of living, were by the mid-1920s enjoying a comfortable style of life where culture ranked higher than the desire for money and material pleasures:

> We had a pleasant life, it was quite sufficient for us, nobody had a car, we didn't think that we had to have a car.... My parents went to the theatre; they had a very good life for that time, but there was not then the desire that you have to spend your holidays in Bermuda, we didn't know it existed, we didn't know it was on the map.

Of the middle-class interviewees whose parents were not affected by death or separation, only Mimi Glover paints a picture of continuing financial hardship, with grim living conditions in a severely sub-standard flat:

> Oh, it was terrible and it was cold, you couldn't heat that kitchen, the window couldn't be opened so there was only the door. Oh, it was quite terrible, you can't imagine that flat we had. It was very damp and I got rheumatism, I had rheumatic fever at one time, I was about seventeen, but the water ran down the walls and it was terrible.

There was strong parental pressure on the three children to start work at the earliest possible opportunity, so her stubborn battle over the years to finance her own education is among the earliest of the interviewees' triumphs over adversity, but by no means the least.

Erika Young came from a family accustomed to wealth:

> I remember being absolutely comfortable, going abroad for holidays, having every kind of lesson and things, but I know that, compared with my father's upbringing, he must have been – or his family must have been – much, much better off. They had an estate in the

1. FAMILY BACKGROUNDS BEFORE EMIGRATION

country, and the only thing I remember him saying about that was, a little bit nostalgically, talking about the aviary they had, and the eagle with clipped wings that sat on his pram.

Adelheid Schweitzer, while a guest of the Brooke family (of Brooke Bond tea), came to the conclusion that her family enjoyed a standard of living not far below that of her opulent hosts:

> They were very wealthy people, which I began to understand, but I wasn't impressed by it because in many ways the standard of living of that very wealthy class wasn't a lot different, except for owning cars, than our standard of living had been in Germany. We had central heating, we had a lot of servants, we ate extremely well, we travelled. My parents never owned a car. But as I say, I wasn't impressed with that wealth.

Hans Brill, whose father was a wealthy businessman, was often collected from school by the family chauffeur; his father dabbled in filmmaking, had a library that contained fifteenth-century incunabula and owned a picture collection that was outstanding enough to merit systematic plundering by the state galleries after the Anschluss.

Hilde Ainger, the daughter of the most prominent local solicitor, remembers:

> It was a very comfortable existence. We lived... we were obviously fairly well off, but lived modestly, you know, comfortably, but very modestly, you wouldn't have known. But on the other hand, in those days middle-class people had a servant, at least one maid, whether they were hard up or not, and we quite often had two maids, but do you know, it was... I never felt rich, we were not rich or poor, but it was all very comfortable.

However, she is not alone in stating that her family were far from comfortable when she was born (1917) and in the inflation years. But at those times almost all Germans, including most of the otherwise prosperous middle class, suffered hardships, and these were in no way incompatible with middle-class wealth and comfort in the 'normal', economically secure years. Much the same applies to the circumstances of Jewish families after 1933, when they were gradually squeezed out of German economic life; this would explain why some of the younger interviewees, like Dorothea Galewski, Hans Seelig and Hanna Singer, who remember less of life before 1933, give no evidence of the prosperity that one might have expected from their family backgrounds.

Eva Pollard, who paints an almost standard picture of a well-off, middle-class home, had to have cookery lessons before emigrating, as she had been forbidden to enter the kitchen, the servants' preserve. Josephine Bruegel came into a substantial private income after her father's death:

> In 1933 I didn't really know what I should do after my school-leaving exams, because there was a lot of unemployment, and I had a certain income, that is, the interest from the estate of my father and grandfather, so that I could live well without doing anything. So I had no need to do some office job or something like that.

Eva Sommerfreund's parents were able to indulge their cultural tastes, as long as her grandfather's money reached them, to employ servants and a nanny for each of their daughters, and to sport a brace of grand pianos. Margarete Hinrichsen's family was rich by any standards and lived in state on their Pomeranian property, driving out in a horse-drawn carriage:

> And there was a driver, and the groom who sat on top, and it was a great thrill if we were allowed to sit next to him, to hold the reins, but otherwise it wasn't really a great treat. But it was still, you know, it was very feudal. I mean, every morning the milk was delivered by horse-drawn cart. That was quite a big cart: the milk and the eggs and the butter, and the greens, the vegetables from the farm, and the flowers. That was always brought to the house, you see. And you took it absolutely for granted. I mean, that's how life was and that's how one lived life.

5. Social and residential status

Lotte Berk, who came from a very affluent home, was strongly aware of the social status conferred by wealth:

> I would almost call my father a nouveau riche, we never felt we were poor. And I became a great snob, too, as a child. When they wanted

to play with me, I asked, 'Do you have a maid?', and if they hadn't, I didn't really want to play with them.

Many interviewees express their consciousness of their middle-class status, though in more positive terms. Peter Johnson defines his family as belonging to the Berlin 'Mittelstand' (middle-class), while Hanne Norbert-Miller speaks of a 'very typical Viennese middle-class assimilated Jewish' family, and Eva Sommerfreund of a 'middle-class, good middle-class family'. Nelly Kuttner's parents were too conscious of their middle-class status to let their daughter start work as an apprentice sweeping floors, so they found her a more suitable place as a 'Lehrfräulein' (trainee) at a smart milliner's. Hans Brill's father, who had served in a cavalry regiment in the First World War, looked down with some amusement on the bulk of Viennese Jewry, secure in his cosmopolitan connections, cultured tastes and affluent upper-middle class lifestyle. Ruth Herring conveys something of her parents' pleasure that aristocrats patronised their business and that they mixed socially with the von Richthofen family on holiday, which would have cemented her father's status as one of the leading local middle-class 'Honoratioren' (dignitaries).

Hilde Ainger, born into a middle-class, professional Jewish family in Guben an der Neisse, was aware both of the respect in which her father, a leading lawyer, was held and of the snobbery that restricted her family's friends to professional people of the same class. Margarete Hinrichsen too notes that her family's wealth endowed them with an aura of social superiority over other Jewish families and prevented them from mixing outside a small circle of friends. Even Christel Marsh, who came from a family of relatively modest means, was strongly aware of the social gulf between a middle-class child like herself and some of her fellow pupils: 'I went to school in the neighbourhood school, where most of the children came from the slum area, and it certainly gave me the impression right from the start, although my parents were no snobs in any way, that we were a cut above the others.' The predominance of professional, prosperous, middle-class backgrounds among the interviewees is so marked that the two clear exceptions, Ernst Flesch, who emphasises his family's lower-middle class status, and Alfred Dörfel, stand out strongly.

Accommodation is a sure indicator of class status and wealth. The large majority of the refugees who give details of their accommodation lived in houses or flats that were spacious or at the very least comfortable. Ruth Herring's father had bought the large house in which his family lived and where his firm was also located; Eva Sommerfreund's family lived in a largish flat in the prosperous Ninth District of Vienna and Helga Reutter's occupied a substantial four-room flat in the neighbouring Eighth District. Eva Pollard recalls the large family house in Breslau, Walter Wolff a comfortable flat in Berlin-Wilmersdorf, and Lotte Berk a spacious flat in Cologne with three big rooms, one with a grand piano. Nelly Kuttner lived in 'a very pleasant flat in one of the main streets in Vienna which was really wonderful, Praterstrasse, which was at that time a very famous street'; indeed, she identifies envy of the standard of accommodation enjoyed by middle-class Jews amidst a desperate housing shortage as a potent factor in the virulence of Viennese anti-semitism. It is no accident that Mimi Glover, Ernst Flesch, whose family was poorly housed in a tenement block, and Gertrud Wengraf, once her family had had to move to one room in a flat in Vienna, are exceptions to the overall pattern.

Where city areas are given, the refugees tended predominantly to live in the better, more expensive districts, like Wilmersdorf and Charlottenburg in Berlin. Even Christel Marsh lived in a new suburb of Magdeburg, in 'a very nice, relatively modern flat' appropriate to the means of a Gymnasium teacher with three children and a wife who had stopped working. Significantly, Mimi Glover's prosperous uncles lived in the expensive First District of Vienna, whereas her father had to move to the outlying, working-class Nineteenth District (Sievering), where the grim conditions she endured throw into yet sharper relief the privileged situation enjoyed by most of the interviewees; and Ernst Flesch lived in the Viennese working-class area of Favoriten. Elizabeth Rosenthal's parents were well housed, first in the Berlin suburb of Mariendorf, then in a pleasant flat in a Socialist cooperative in the suburb of Britz, where the family's professional status could coexist harmoniously with their Communist convictions, without undermining the predominant impression of comfortable prosperity.

1. FAMILY BACKGROUNDS BEFORE EMIGRATION

The factors outlined here, family background, economic and social status, and patterns of residence and accommodation, delineate the refugees interviewed as a fairly homogeneous group already within their countries of origin. Particularly striking is the number coming from relatively affluent, professional, middle-class homes in the larger cities. These factors were mostly to extend into their lives as immigrants in Britain. The next chapter investigates the culture – in the broad sense of the term – in which the refugees grew up; here too clear patterns emerge.

CHAPTER TWO

Culture, Education, Politics and the Impact of Historical Developments before Emigration

Anthony Grenville and Irene Wells

1. *Culture*

Culture played an extremely important role in the lives of the refugees' families; indeed, it is arguably culture rather than religion that defines our interviewees as a recognisable group and endows them with an element of common identity in their adopted country. As will be shown in a later chapter, the Jewish religion alone is not the defining element that creates the sense of a distinguishable community among the refugees, or at least among their Jewish majority, given that these were the children of largely assimilated and secularised parents for whom religious faith was no longer at the heart of daily life. If such Jews had largely abandoned their traditional religion, but were still denied full acceptance into Gentile society, around which values could they build a new sense of their Jewish identity? The answer is to be found in the process of assimilation itself, which was first and foremost the assimilation of Jews into classical German culture, the culture of Goethe, Schiller, Beethoven, Kant and Lessing. German culture, the bearer of western civilisation, held out the promise of a new identity, that of emancipated, assimilated Jews, who espoused the progressive values of liberalism and humanism while still remaining conscious of their Jewishness, albeit in secularised form. As Steven Beller says, assimilation had become for them 'the continuation of Judaism by other means beyond the Jewish identity'.[3]

    3. Steven Beller, *Vienna and the Jews 1867–1938: A Cultural History*, Cambridge, 1989, p. 143.

2. CULTURE, EDUCATION, POLITICS BEFORE EMIGRATION

The assimilated Jews, standing between two religions and belonging fully to neither, found a partial substitute in 'Bildung', in liberal/classical German culture; hence their eagerness for education. Education assumed a special importance for middle-class Jews like our interviewees, for they saw it as the main vehicle of assimilation, the means by which Jewish families could climb the social ladder and, over two or three generations, could leave the world of trade and commerce for the academic and independent professions. The important role played by Jews in the cultural life of Germany and Austria, which was out of all proportion to their numbers in the population, is well known. In Vienna, culture was largely dominated by bourgeois Jews. The Jewish middle-classes were not only those who produced much of Austrian and German culture, but they also formed a prominent proportion of those who consumed it, as readers and as members of audiences at theatres, concerts and operas.

The importance that attached to culture is abundantly evident among the parents of the interviewees, as in Walter Wolff's family history:

> All our family on both sides . . . seemed to be in the arts or in journalism. My paternal grandfather was a journalist, and . . . was also associated with the impresario business which his brother had started in the mid-nineteenth century. In fact my great-uncle was the founder of the Berlin Philharmonic Orchestra, which before then was a band of musicians, and later was formed into what became one of the greatest orchestras in the world. . . On my mother's side, her father was a music critic for a Berlin newspaper. My father trained as an artist and became a photographer.

Renée Hubert, whose sister became a painter, is only one of several whose parents insisted that their children learn musical instruments and arranged private tuition for them in French, the pass-key to modern high culture. Peter Gellhorn's father was a well-known architect who became president of the Reichsverband bildender Künstler (National Union of Fine Artists); and Hilde Auerbach's worked in the theatre world.

A touching example of the aspiration of the commercially successful Jewish parent towards the sphere of the arts is the dream of

Lotte Berk's father, something of a parvenu businessman by his daughter's own account, that she should become a concert pianist. In the small town of Guben, Hilde Ainger remembers the prominence of culture and visits to the theatre in her parents' life. Eva Pollard, both of whose parents came from families with eminent musical connections, learnt of Brahms, Joachim and Sarasate as family connections. Her great-grandparents had founded the Breslau Philharmonic Orchestra, and she grew up in a household saturated in art and music:

> There was always music in the house, my mother sang very nicely and played the guitar, and we sang nursery-rhymes or folk-songs with her, and I, of course, had piano lessons, which I didn't enjoy very much, but one had the time. That way there was always music in the house... and also my parents, apart from the [antique glass] collection, were always very interested in art. When we went with my father to Venice, we went into every church, and in Breslau to the museum, Sunday mornings they took us to the Breslau Museum... So I grew up with music and art as, what shall I say, it was so natural, it wasn't anything to be discussed, it was just around us.

Klary Friedl's father, though he had had hardly any formal education, was 'always reading and studying' – a striking tribute to the hold of culture over assimilating Jews. He ensured that both her brothers were excellent musicians and imbued her with his love of music:

> He loved music very much. He was very, very musical and he went far to hear somebody, for instance, he loved Caruso very much – he went everywhere where he was singing, he went there to listen to him.... my first opera was when I was about seven years old and was sitting on his lap. We always had music in the house.

Helga Reutter also came from a very musical family, one of her two musician cousins being the violinist Max Rostal. For her birthdays her father gave her tickets for dress rehearsals of the Vienna Philharmonic, which sealed her lifelong love of concerts, opera and theatre. Eva Sommerfreund spent her childhood in exceptional proximity to the cultural life of Vienna. Her parents took full advantage of the city's cultural abundance, with music an integral

2. CULTURE, EDUCATION, POLITICS BEFORE EMIGRATION

part of the family's daily life, and they also moved in artistic circles: the radical journalist Egon Erwin Kisch was a family friend, her father numbered the writers Karl Kraus, Friedrich Torberg and Leo Perutz among his acquaintances, and the composer Alexander Zemlinsky discovered her gifts as a singer. As her mother had been a ballet dancer, her future career as a singer and actress was something of a foregone conclusion.

This love of culture and the life of the mind spread across the entire spectrum of the Jewish refugees' parents, regardless of disparities in wealth and status. Mimi Glover's father, who had opted for the impecunious life of an antiquarian book-dealer, loved to read the English classics. Hans Brill's father, by contrast a very affluent man, was also a book-lover with a fine library, an equally fine collection of pictures and a taste for the world of artists, all of which probably contributed to his son's eventual choice of career as an art historian. Peter Gellhorn describes his father thus: 'He was quite a well-known architect, a member of what was called the November Group, [an association of] artists of all kinds, [including] architects . . . a bit of a revolutionary group of avant-garde artists.' Despite their very different political background, Elizabeth Rosenthal's parents displayed similar likings, with an appropriately progressive tinge:

> My mother and father had very good connections with the artistic world. Elisabeth Bergner [a distant relation] got tickets. Karl Liebknecht's brother's wife Julie Goldstein [a family friend] was a musician, so they went to concerts, went to art exhibitions, and I got books from the translators of the 'Doctor Dolittle' books. . . Children were brought up on Doctor Dolittle and Selma Lagerlöf. So my mother knew the publishers of these good children's books and I had masses of excellent books. . . I had a very lovely artistic literary education. Whenever I think about it, I really had a very, very privileged childhood.

Her mother, who acquired both the Froebel and Montessori Certificates, had inherited her own mother's strong interest in progressive education; this she passed on to her daughter, who went on to build an academic career in the field of teacher training.

Hans Seelig's parents, whose income and lifestyle probably

approximated to the average of the Jewish interviewees' families, were again book-loving people who valued education highly. His mother's creative gifts enabled her to write and publish poetry and travel essays; both parents were highly musical, his father achieving an extraordinary standard of accomplishment, given that he had had no formal training:

> [My parents] were both musical, especially my father, he had an incredible ear, taught himself the violin and scraped away happily. I have a lovely record – can't play it any more, it's an old 78 of course – where he plays Beethoven's Spring Sonata with a friend who was in fact a professional performer, and at the end of it I could hear my father's voice saying 'fertig' ['that's it']. He had a tremendous ear for music – and memory, and I think I did inherit to a great extent that ear.

This is a moving tribute to the richness of culture that was the heritage of these refugees, a heritage they transferred to their adopted country.

Of the non-Jewish refugees, Alec Armstrong speaks of his parents' love of the German literary classics, and Alfred Dörfel's father created a family home marked by his passion for reading; one of his sons possessed two or three hundred books already as a young man, which was unique in the whole neighbourhood. Although the father worked as a tuner in a factory making musical-boxes, he seems to have developed no particular musical interests, nor did music play as great a part in the life of these families as it did in that of the music-loving Jewish families. One may surmise that the Dörfels' cultural aspirations were closely linked to their commitment to the cause of the working class and their belief in its ability to improve itself by self-education. In this sense, the left-wing refugees form a small group dedicated to reading and study, in their case for specific social and political reasons.

This exceptional richness of cultural experience continues with the interviewees themselves before emigration. Ilse Wolff is just one who was powerfully drawn to the world of the mind, even though her widowed mother's straitened circumstances obliged her to start work early:

2. CULTURE, EDUCATION, POLITICS BEFORE EMIGRATION

> I had to start my working life at the age of sixteen, and always tried to get jobs with some sort of cultural orientation, like working with journalists, as a secretary, and working with Electrola, a record company in Germany. And I also took extensive evening classes at the Humboldt University and tried to educate myself. And also, of course, chose my friends, who were very educated people.

She even founded and conducted a prize-winning choir. Similarly, Peter Gellhorn describes himself as a keen student:

> I was interested, I was reading books. I was interested in science. I went to listen to famous physicists, simply to be in the presence of a man of eminence and to hear what he had to say... Hindemith, whom I met in Berlin, who was friendly with my father, was a professor at the Akademie until he had to leave.

Anyone who has visited the homes of German-speaking refugees from Central Europe will have come to expect the bookshelves lined with the apparently obligatory editions of the classics. Our interviewees are no exception: Alec Armstrong proclaims his love of the German classics, Josephine Bruegel is equally at home with them in German, Czech or English, and Nelly Kuttner's husband so loved books that even in exile he would spend his last pennies in second-hand bookshops. Significantly, Gertrud Wengraf, who feels herself to be neither English, nor Austrian, nor Jewish, appears to find some cultural identity in her love of German literature; in Vienna, a shared love of culture drew her to her future husband:

> He was a writer and an art historian, without the academic qualification. His family were art dealers, and he worked in the family business. But he was mostly interested in artists, in music, and in painting... I met him because he had lectures in his flat, about Socialism, about Marxism, about art, and I went there, and I was very impressed.

Klary Friedl loved reading and studying. Visits to the cinema, theatre and opera formed part of her social routine, and she even had her own Hungarian-language radio programme, a five-minute slot called 'Verses in Prose'. Eva Sommerfreund, who went to her first opera at seven, the same age as Klary Friedl, and who, like Hans

23

Seelig, could read music before she could read books, developed a consuming passion for music which dominated her life. She points out that in Vienna it was quite natural for adolescents to go to concerts or operas three times a week, since their entire peer group did so:

> When we were in school, we had to go to the opera or the theatre because that's what we talked about at school. Whereas here they can't go to the opera so often or to concerts. We knew all about it, not because we were particularly highbrow, we were just naughty little brats as they are here too, but our interests were all the same, we all of us were interested in music, arts.

Elizabeth Rosenthal, who had been taken before she was three to *Hansel and Gretel* (prudently leaving before the appearance of the witch), was sent in February 1937, aged nine, to the progressive school Caputh, outside Berlin, where she enjoyed an outstanding education until the school was destroyed during Kristallnacht; for those twenty-one months, she lived in a cultural 'heaven on earth'.

Although from the very different background of the non-Jewish working-class, Alfred Dörfel expresses the same profound attraction to the life of the mind:

> I had a terrible urge to learn, to learn, to learn. I used to go with my meagre apprentice money, I used to go, perhaps nobody else of the boys did, booked tickets at the theatre and the opera. I saw Brecht, Mackie Messer, *Dreigroschenoper* and other plays and operas in Leipzig, and I learnt there. I was deep in Brecht.

His work for the Communist Party put an end to his formal education, but his remarkable dedication to self-education in the face of formidable obstacles is an enduring tribute to the hold of culture and learning over our refugees. Not a few of them were to go on to achieve success in cultural fields in Britain: Stella Rotenberg as a writer, Peter Gellhorn as a musician and Lotte Berk in modern dance are among the best known. This high level of culture is, as already indicated, not matched by a comparable devotion to religion. Culture and education emerge as common features more important in unifying the refugee community in exile than any deep sense of allegiance to the ancestral faith.

2. CULTURE, EDUCATION, POLITICS BEFORE EMIGRATION

2. Educational, academic and professional achievements before Nazi rule

Education plays an unusually important part in the life stories of the interviewees, where it is often recalled in considerable detail and indeed with some fondness. The number of our interviewees, twenty-one in all, who went to grammar schools ('Gymnasien') and other schools where the university entrance examinations could be taken, or who were only prevented from doing so by the Nazis, is remarkably high when compared to the handful who went to ordinary secondary schools. This striking level of educational achievement may indicate that those who were well educated had more mobility in an emergency, greater aptitude at coping with the requirements of Nazi bureaucracy, more openness of culture and more confidence in their ability to cope with foreign countries. Thanks in large measure to their relative wealth, they had more familiarity with entry and exit procedures and more experience of travel, as well as some knowledge of foreign languages, all of which gave them a headstart in the struggle to make their escape abroad.

Parental attitudes to education were strongly positive, time and again according it the highest priority. Elizabeth Rosenthal is a particularly clear case, but by no means exceptional: 'My father was a university lecturer and he had vowed that I would continue in the family tradition. It was all education and intellectual achievement, so they supported me.' Renée Hubert recalls the attention that her father lavished on his daughters' education, and Dorothea Galewski's father was ready to put his daughter's education before financial concerns, even when the family was in desperate straits in England. Hans Brill's family shows in exemplary form how education was used by assimilating Jewish families as the social escalator by means of which the generation of the parents, commercially successful, educated its children to a high level, enabling them to continue the process of integration by graduating from business to the learned professions:

> [My father] was in fact, I think, an interesting example of the
> adaptation of Jews to Austrian society. His father had set up in the

25

standard Jewish quarter of Vienna, the Zweiter Bezirk [Second District], a leather-goods factory making machine-belting which was exported all over the Austrian Empire, and his son – that's my father [who] evidently was intended for better things – he was sent to university and became a physicist. It was also very much, I think, part of the family attitude that he shouldn't go into the family business, and instead he went to work for Madame Curie in Paris, and he subsequently worked with scientists . . . Rutherford in Manchester, Ramsay at University College London.

The refugees appear to have absorbed this respect for education as a tool for self-improvement, and to have applied it to their children. Where else would Eva Pollard have encountered an old friend from Vienna, last seen in 1939 when they arrived together in England as young women, than at a parents' meeting years later at South Hampstead High School for Girls, that cradle of academic excellence for so many of the daughters of north-west London's Jewish community? In Mimi Glover's case, the urge to acquire an education seems like an inbred need. After threatening to jump into the Danube unless her parents let her stay on at school, she proceeded to pay part of her way through Realgymnasium (grammar school with emphasis on modern languages) by giving private lessons while herself still a schoolgirl, fitting her studies around a daunting daily routine:

> Well, all these four years, you only go to school in the morning, so I had private lessons and, after the private lessons, I went to the shop in the First District to father to help him. . . I went to auctions to sell books and he told me how much you can pay. I went to school, I did private lessons and I went to the shop, and my exercises I had to do on the tram, because from Sievering to Schottentor is half an hour and in half an hour I could do a lot, I mean, I read Dante's *Divine Comedy* on the tram.

Dedication on this scale is rare indeed.

Elizabeth Rosenthal paints an unusually detailed and vivid picture of her education. Her father had gone to the Soviet Union to work when other opportunities were closed to him, leaving his wife in considerable financial difficulties after 1933. Despite this, Elizabeth Rosenthal was sent to the liberal Jewish boarding-school, the

2. CULTURE, EDUCATION, POLITICS BEFORE EMIGRATION

Jüdisches Landschulheim Caputh, near Potsdam, at the age of nine and a half, when things became too difficult at her primary school in the Berlin suburb of Britz. She loved everything about the school: the gardens, the devoted teachers, the small class sizes, the progressive attitude to all aspects of education:

> Progressive in the best sense. The teachers were absolutely devoted and they were wonderful people . . . an exceptional staff. . . And there were only classes of ten, so you could have progressive education. . . The philosophy of Caputh was to make children confident in themselves, because Nazi Germany was pushing down the Jews and making people feel inferior, it was to develop themselves really. Feeling [good] about themselves, as well as giving them languages and appreciating the arts and literature and the sciences. The best possible education and the best sense of values, as well as liberal Jewish philosophy. . . And I had the happiest time. One of the most wonderful times in all my life [was] in that school . . . the lost paradise, we all called it.

But not even here could Jews find a safe haven. Elizabeth Rosenthal was still at Caputh at the time of the Kristallnacht, when the school was attacked and both children and teachers had to flee:

> So, one November morning we were sitting in our classroom. . . It was a dark day and there was a drizzle. And we had the electric light on, and suddenly there was a noise of glass breaking. . . Then the light went out and that was rather eerie. And then we were all told . . . to go into the hall. And in the hall all the children came from the different classrooms and the headmistress was there as brave as can be. And the Nazi stood there in his uniform and his boots and his Nazi expression and shouted: 'Raus, raus, Juden raus!' ('Out, out, Jews out!')

The headmistress managed to obtain ten minutes' grace for the children to collect a few of their things. They then left the school in groups, one adult to each group of children, the doctor carrying a toddler with pneumonia, and travelled by a roundabout route to Berlin, where the prescient head had arranged accommodation for such an eventuality.

Given the importance of education, the disruption caused by Nazi restrictions on the schooling of Jewish children was correspondingly great. First, Jewish children aged ten or over were compelled to leave the state schools and attend Jewish secondary schools, as Walter Wolff recalls:

> But by the time I was ten years old [1936], it was no longer possible for people from Jewish or half-Jewish backgrounds, as I was, to continue at state schools... It was then that my parents decided to send me to these particular [private] schools.

But despite these restrictions, the parents of this group of younger interviewees seem to have made determined efforts to secure them a good education, even when it was disrupted by enforced changes of school. Peter Singer attended a Jewish Reformrealgymnasium (grammar school with emphasis on sciences) in Nuremberg until 1936; Walter Wolff went to two private primary schools, then to a Gymnasium; and Eric Rose attended the co-educational Jewish Reformrealgymnasium in Breslau from 1934 to 1939 where, he notes, there was considerable emphasis on Hebrew, Jewish history and religion.

Dorothea Galewski, who came from a very assimilated home background, had a similar experience. Forced to switch from her Gymnasium to a Jewish Gymnasium in Breslau, she found much of the curriculum, consisting of specifically Jewish subjects, strange to her: 'I think we had religious instruction pretty well every day and, of course, observed the Jewish holidays, and that was really my first acquaintance with that style of life, because I was not brought up in the Jewish faith.' Renée Hubert, whose father was briefly imprisoned in 1933, had her schooling disrupted early; after her father's release, the family fled via Switzerland to France, where she was sent – initially as a boarder – to a lycée in Lyons. Here she experienced for the first time not only life in a boarding-school, but also 'lots of Catholicism' as well as the challenge of operating alone in a foreign language and culture. She did her *Baccalauréat* and thus prepared herself to undertake the university education of which the Nazis had deprived her in Germany. Hilde Ainger too left her classical grammar school before she could take her Abitur, though in her case freely, and emigrated to England in 1934, aged seventeen.

2. CULTURE, EDUCATION, POLITICS BEFORE EMIGRATION

Of the younger interviewees, Hanna Singer managed to go to a Gymnasium for a year, thanks to being able enough to skip a year at primary school. As she explains:

> Because from the latish 1930s on we were aware that things were difficult, maybe we'd leave, education became really important, so although one normally had four years at primary school, at Volksschule, I skipped a year, I did an entrance exam so that I could go to secondary school... slightly under age. This was very useful, because this happened in April 1938 and by November 1938, Jewish children couldn't go to school any more, and so I had a little bit of English. [I had] a wonderful form teacher who also taught English. The sort of thing I remember, when there was a big meeting of Hitler Youth and BDM [Bund Deutscher Mädel] girls, a sort of female version of the Hitler Youth, she said to me the evening before, 'Hanna, I know you like reading very much, why don't you just stay at home tomorrow with a book?'

Kristallnacht in November 1938, the climax of an escalating wave of harassment, also brutally affected Hans Seelig's education. He had also managed to skip a year at primary school, but was still too young to have finished there before the November pogrom, after which most Jewish children were prevented from attending school:

> I was not really aware of anti-semitism as such, but when I went to school from 1935 or '36 onwards, it soon turned out that I wasn't allowed to go to that school any more, and we were sent to a Jewish school, which was held in or near one of the synagogues in Mannheim... I started at a normal school; I think I was only there for about a year. I had in fact jumped one class, because I had taught myself to read about a year before I was due to start school; I taught myself to read music before that, even, at the age of three... So, yes, of course, I then began to experience a certain harassment from '36 onwards, I think I became aware of it then, and Kristallnacht was one of the worst occasions. When I got to school, [it] had been blown up, and the only children going home from school that day, at that time, were Jewish... So I was chased through the streets by the Hitler Youth.

In Vienna, where Nazi measures only took effect in March 1938, Ernst Flesch was able to attend a Gymnasium for about a year before emigration. Jewish schoolchildren had not been the target of state-sponsored harassment in Austria, but that changed abruptly when the full rigour of Nazi discrimination was imposed after the Anschluss. Hans Brill recalls:

> I had no trouble about being Jewish at school, although I did hear of other children who had. I suppose my first awareness that something was wrong was when I was told to listen . . . when Schuschnigg [the Austrian Chancellor] gave his last broadcast, and I remember [the sound of] him being marched away, the feet on the floor. And then I remember the order to put out the Nazi flags, and the sort of general fuss. And, of course, one didn't go out into the street at that point.

Moving on to the activities of those interviewees who were already young adults before emigration, one is again struck by their level of intellectual achievement, an indicator of considerable future career success in exile. A brief résumé of their academic achievements yields impressive results. Ruth Herring and Hilde Auerbach both completed doctoral dissertations in Germany, in Königsberg and Heidelberg respectively. Alec Armstrong trained as an architect, including a spell at the legendary Bauhaus. Mimi Glover was awarded her doctorate at Vienna University in January 1938, the final stage in her single-minded pursuit of her education. Entirely dependent on her own resources, she financed her studies by giving private lessons and by achieving high enough marks to be exempted from paying tuition fees. Ingeniously combining academic prowess with financial advantage, she opted for a course in French art that secured her a scholarship to spend two months in Paris, then returned there for a further year as a tutor, which enabled her to work on her dissertation at the Bibliothèque Nationale.

A number of the interviewees had their courses of study cut short by the Nazis, who moved rapidly to ban Jews from universities, with considerable disruption of potential high achievement. Gertrud Wengraf, who was in her third and final year studying history and geography at Vienna, had to leave the university after the Anschluss; if she had not lost a year as a result of spending four weeks in

2. CULTURE, EDUCATION, POLITICS BEFORE EMIGRATION

prison as a member of a Socialist youth movement after the uprising of February 1934, she would have finished her studies. That Gertrud Wengraf ever reached university represented a triumph of natural ability over adverse circumstances. Born in Moravia, she went first to a German-medium school, but had to transfer abruptly to a Czech-medium school, though she spoke no Czech, when rising Czech nationalism after 1918 forced the closure of the German school; the family returned to Vienna when she was thirteen, and she had to relearn German to study in a Gymnasium. Josephine Bruegel, who was studying medicine at the German University in Prague, had one semester left when Hitler occupied Czechoslovakia in March 1939, and Stella Rotenberg had done two years of her medical course at Vienna when she was forced to interrupt it. Unusually, she was already aware of the precarious nature of her position as a Jewish student under the pre-Hitler regime, partly as a result of the police raids she witnessed at the university; during one of these, a fellow Jewish student advised her to keep her hands in her coat pockets, to prevent anything compromising being slipped into them.

It was not only Hitler who stopped young Jewish women from finishing their medical studies: in the troubled economic conditions of the 1930s, fathers like Helga Reutter's insisted she learn dressmaking instead of studying medicine, or made their daughters give up courses they had embarked on, as happened to Klary Friedl. Josephine Bruegel was the only one who resumed her medical studies in Britain and went on to a career as a doctor. Peter Gellhorn had to leave the University of Berlin in 1933, but was able to continue his musical studies at the Hochschule für Musik; not that it did him much good, since his application to join the Reichsmusikkammer, the organisation to which all musicians had to belong, was rejected and he was unable to work legally, eking out a perilous existence in illegal work until his emigration. The dismissal by the Nazi regime of university professors who were considered politically suspect, as well as those who were racially undesirable, also made itself felt. Hilde Auerbach decided that she could not complete the obligatory public defence of her doctorate, since the professor who had been her supervisor had been dismissed. Ruth Herring managed to obtain her doctorate just before leaving the country, though loyalty to her supervisor, who was under threat from the authorities, led her to leave before her dissertation was published.

A number of interviewees, some of whom never intended to study at university, took vocational courses that were broadly comparable to university studies: Lotte Berk studied modern dance at the Mary Wigman School in Cologne; Hanne Norbert-Miller, who had attended acting classes while still at school, initially without informing her parents, trained to become an actress at the prestigious Reinhardt-Seminar; and Adelheid Schweitzer studied to become an interpreter at Mannheim for a year before she had to break off her studies. Several refugees were well on the way to university when Hitler intervened, like Hilde Ainger, who emigrated at seventeen; almost all those who left before the age of eighteen suffered major disruption to their education, which, however, they mostly took impressively in their stride. Otherwise, as is clear from their accounts of their education before emigration, there is little doubt that many would have progressed through Gymnasium to university.

The manifold talents of the interviewees are evident even before emigration: Peter Gellhorn laid the foundations of a highly successful musical career; Hanne Norbert-Miller started out as an actress, and Lotte Berk as a pioneering practitioner of modern dance; and Eva Sommerfreund, whose determination to become a singer led her to spend every available minute on music, joined the Singing Babies, a light classical, all-female counterpart to the Comedian Harmonists, the hugely popular harmony singing group. Other refugees took jobs that showed literary interests: Eugen Brehm worked in a secondhand bookshop and took an interest in Jewish books, Christel Marsh sold books for the academically prestigious publishing firm Max Niemeyer, and Ilse Wolff quickly gravitated to the world of letters and journalism. Eva Pollard worked as a translator in the offices of a Berlin chemical firm; and Klary Friedl salvaged something from her unfinished academic studies by making an independent life for herself as a beautician. Nelly Kuttner started her own millinery business, a salon called Fleurette Fashion, at the age of twenty, and later carried it on with distinction in London. Alfred Dörfel displayed considerable gifts under very

2. CULTURE, EDUCATION, POLITICS BEFORE EMIGRATION

unfavourable conditions: obliged to leave school at fifteen, he insisted on training as a lithographic printer, for which he showed great aptitude, and when he decided to devote himself full-time to unpaid work for the Communist Party, he rapidly rose to an important position in the Party's youth movement.

3. Political attitudes and activities

There are considerable differences between the political activities of Jews and non-Jews, especially in the parents' generation. The attitudes of the Jewish refugees' parents reflected the limited number of political options open to prosperous middle-class Jews in Germany and Austria. The anti-semitism of the parties of the right made it impossible for Jews to support them; but the parties of the left, the Social Democrats and Communists, with their Marxist rhetoric and their strong association with the working class, were not attractive to bourgeois professionals and entrepreneurs. Many Jews therefore lapsed into political inactivity, except for the single issue of combating anti-semitism. Those who identified with a specific party tended towards the liberal parties of the democratic centre, but these were small and largely ineffectual.

The parents of German-Jewish interviewees reflect these trends; in most of the interviews the parents' politics are simply never mentioned, or it is explicitly stated that they were apolitical. Adelheid Schweitzer's parents, respected figures in the local community, supported the originally liberal DDP (German Democratic Party), but her mother was reluctant as a Jew to stand for election to the town council. Hilde Ainger's parents were of similar political inclinations, fearing the anti-semitism of the DNVP (Nationalists) even before the Nazis, but not politically active. Margarete Hinrichsen's father played a prominent role in public affairs and was a town councillor; both parents supported the Staatspartei (as the DDP was renamed in 1930), but liberalism in a Pomeranian town surrounded by swathes of Nationalist-supporting Junker estates could count only on a small urban, mainly Jewish vote. Renée Hubert's parents, supporters of progressive causes like a number of Jewish intellectuals and professionals, were unusual in being drawn to the

Socialist parties. In Austria, where political liberalism was even weaker, the appeal of Social Democracy was stronger. Ernst Flesch's father had no class barriers to cross in supporting the party, but Helga Reutter's father, a factory-owner, did. A progressive employer, he mixed with the dignitaries of Social Democracy like Karl Seitz, Mayor of Vienna, at the holiday resort of Breitenstein, and he earned his workers' loyalty as an enlightened employer by allowing them time off to attend a football match.

The one German-Jewish family in whose life politics played a central role was Elizabeth Rosenthal's, whose parents were both born into families with strong Communist convictions: her paternal grandmother, a Party member since the early years of the century, was a friend of Lenin, Karl Liebknecht's sons were family friends, and it was her father's connection with the old Bolshevik Karl Radek that led to his arrest and imprisonment during Stalin's purges. Her parents' faith in Communism has not come down to Elizabeth Rosenthal; she herself is a committed Socialist, but her experiences after 1933 have made her strongly aware of her identity as a Jew. Her family's story, which might almost have come from the pages of Arthur Koestler, is a vivid example of the destruction of the left-wing Jewish intelligentsia of Central Europe by the two great totalitarian dictatorships. Mother and daughter felt themselves fortunate to have found a safe haven in what Elizabeth Rosenthal calls 'my dear old Oldham', whose essential decency and Lancastrian common sense were worlds away from murderous ideologies.

The family backgrounds of the middle-class non-Jewish refugees are inclined towards the right, as one might expect. Ruth Herring recalls that her mother and grandmother, like many middle-class Germans, were unable to come to terms with the political bankruptcy of the Imperial regime in 1918 and were shattered by the news that the Kaiser, the figurehead of the authoritarian system, had abdicated; predictably, their reactions to the Revolution of 1918/19 were negative. She mentions anti-semitism in her parents' social circles more than once; the family became acquainted with the von Richthofens because Frau von Richthofen wanted her sons to play with German girls, thus avoiding any association with Jewish children. Ruth Herring also records certain commonplace nationalist

2. CULTURE, EDUCATION, POLITICS BEFORE EMIGRATION

prejudices of the 1920s: the 'insulting' presence of black French colonial troops in the occupying forces in the Rhineland; the unfairness of the postwar reparations imposed on Germany; and the illegitimacy of the territorial settlement on Germany's Eastern borders, where the 'German' provinces of Posen and West Prussia were now Polish.

Erika Young's parents were anti-Nazi, but they were monarchists at a time when support for the House of Habsburg was incompatible with allegiance to the egalitarian democracy of the new Austrian Republic. The right-wing views they had acquired from the family's strong military connections – her paternal grandfather had been head of the military academy where Imperial officers were trained – caused them to call a Socialist school inspector a 'Red', an indication of the right's demonisation of Social Democracy, which led it to support the anti-democratic policies of Dollfuss and Schuschnigg that eventually opened the way to Hitler. Even Christel Marsh's impeccably liberal family had grandparents on one side who were old-fashioned nationalists, supported the Kaiser and welcomed the remilitarisation of Germany under Hitler. Indeed, her sister became a fanatical Nazi and her brother a Luftwaffe pilot. Christel Marsh's fascinating account of life in the Third Reich records a wide range of nuances in the behaviour of ordinary Germans, from outright supporters of Nazism, through opportunists, victims of indoctrination and those who allowed themselves to be manipulated, to courageous opponents of the regime and those more wily who hid their opposition behind a show of conformity.

Parental background appears to have been a key factor determining the political attitudes of the small group of left-wing activists. Alec Armstrong inherited his belief in Communism from his father, a supporter of the Bolsheviks who travelled to the Soviet Union. Alfred Dörfel's family provides a case history of left-wing commitment. His father could not stomach the Social Democrat (SPD) leadership's support for the German war effort in 1914 and gravitated naturally to the more radical Independent Social Democratic Party (USPD), then to the Communist Party. His son learnt to hate the society that discriminated against his family because of their politics, and grew up with the example of his siblings' participation in various anti-war, revolutionary and pro-Soviet activities vivid before his eyes. He joined the Young Communists at sixteen, achieved considerable success as a youth organiser for the Party in Saxony and even attended a conference in Moscow. Another activist among the interviewees was Eugen Brehm, who after the 'Machtergreifung' worked underground for the Sozialistische Arbeiterpartei (SAP), one of the small left-wing groups that stood between the Social Democrats and the Communists. Josephine Bruegel also had contacts with the SAP, and with her elder brother was involved in spiriting left-wing opponents of the Nazi regime, including the SAP leader Max Seydewitz, across the border into Czechoslovakia. But like the majority of those politically active in their youth, she did not remain so in emigration after the war.

In Austria the Social Democrats had succeeded in maintaining their hold over the great majority of the working class. Young radicals like Gertrud Wengraf, who was heavily involved in the Socialist youth movement, remained within Austrian Social Democracy and were politically active in the critical period during and after the suppression of the left-wing uprising of February 1934. She was herself imprisoned for four weeks in 1934 for distributing leaflets:

> Well of course it was unpleasant, it was jail, but I met so many people there, Socialists, and we weren't in single cells, we were in groups, and also at mealtimes we met quite frequently, and conversed. And I met people I would never have had the chance to meet – interesting people – and there were a lot of things going on, and people talking through windows, very exciting, I enjoyed myself!

Ernst Flesch grew up in a politically aware environment in Vienna, and went on to be politically active in exile.

Otherwise, it seems that the remainder of the interviewees were politicised only by the advent of National Socialism, as in the case of Hilde Auerbach, an anti-Nazi political activist who joined the SPD as a student in Heidelberg. And as we shall see in Chapter Four, most of the group's political involvement stopped early, in exile.

2. CULTURE, EDUCATION, POLITICS BEFORE EMIGRATION

4. The impact of historical events before Nazi rule

That does not mean that our interviewees were unaffected by the great historical events that convulsed the world of their youth: the First World War, the brief and turbulent period of democracy that fell under the shadow of Nazism and its concomitant anti-semitism, and the shock of the accession to power of the Nazis (preceded in Austria by some five years of authoritarian rule under Dollfuss and Schuschnigg). It is hard to overestimate the difference between the world of ordered stability and prosperity in which most, though not all, of the interviewees' families had lived before 1914 and the conditions in which many of them grew up thereafter, in a defeated Germany racked by economic and political instability and an Austria that was the barely viable rump of the Habsburg Empire.

The disruption caused to a number of families by the First World War is clear. Ilse Wolff's youth was overshadowed by her father's death in the war; the loss of income it entailed prevented her from going to university. Peter Gellhorn's father never fully returned to his family after the war, and the separation left the boy to grow up with his impoverished and embittered mother. Ruth Herring's father was in the German army from 1914, returning from captivity in Russia only in 1919; when he came home on leave in 1916, she did not even recognise him. Some fathers, like Hans Brill's and Hans Seelig's, who was awarded the Iron Cross, took pride in their war service, and a number, including the fathers of Erika Young, Peter Johnson, Walter Wolff and Margarete Hinrichsen, readjusted well to postwar civilian life. But for others the disruption was enduring, as in the case of Nelly Kuttner's father, who after the ordeal of the trenches could not resume the profession that had before 1914 ensured his family a comfortable standard of living and his wife a life of leisure. The disintegration of the Habsburg Empire meant that many of those who, like Gertrud Wengraf's father, had been public employees before the war could never find similar employment in successor states like Czechoslovakia; from this stemmed the chronic instability that affected her family's economic fortunes and eventually reduced them to relative poverty in Vienna during the Depression.

There are also vivid accounts of the suffering of families left to fend for themselves while the men were away on active service. When her husband was called up in 1916, Mimi Glover's mother faced a desperate struggle to provide for herself and three children amidst the shortages of food and coal. The Allied blockade of the Central Powers, who were reliant on food imports from overseas to feed their urban population, hit cities like Vienna particularly hard, causing families like Gertrud Wengraf's to leave for the country during the breadwinner's absence. Christel Marsh states at the start of her interview that she was born in the notorious 'Kohlrübenjahr' of 1917, the 'year of root vegetables', when food shortages were at their worst. Alfred Dörfel describes vividly the suffering endured by his mother:

> Mother was alone with Lotte and with me. That was a very, very hard time for my mother. I remember the winter of 1917 when I was at school already for my first few months, it was the coldest winter and my mother had to go out very early in the morning and I was still in bed, [I] cuddled that little girl in a blanket. The word went round there that you could get margarine, potatoes, so you could see the women huddled in front of one of the shops, standing there alone, and then they got half a pound of margarine.

The family felt doubly aggrieved because they were convinced that they were being victimised on account of the father's political record, and that his conscription in his late forties was a crude device to curb his anti-war activities.

The disruption caused by the war continued after its end, when the influenza epidemic known as Spanish Flu brought about millions of deaths in a population weakened by hunger and privation; among the victims was Eva Sommerfreund's infant brother, whose death led her parents to move back to Prague from Vienna. Ruth Herring remembers the trauma the Kaiser's abdication at the end of the war represented for patriotic middle-class Germans, as well as the sporadic outbursts of revolutionary violence that disturbed even the small Silesian town of Glogau in the turbulent postwar months. The collapse of the Habsburg Empire affected some interviewees as children: we have already alluded to the wave of Czech nationalism that

2. CULTURE, EDUCATION, POLITICS BEFORE EMIGRATION

accompanied the foundation of Czechoslovakia and caused Gertrud Wengraf's German school in Moravia to be closed, obliging her to move to a school where the medium of instruction was Czech. Erika Young's mother was one of many who lost their wealth in the crisis that affected the economy of postwar Austria; but her father turned the new situation to his advantage, abandoning his now redundant military career to secure an important position in the Ministry of Finance.

In both Germany and Austria the postwar years were a time of economic crises and dislocation, causing severe problems to individuals and families among our interviewees. The factors behind a family's economic plight were often peculiar to it alone, but there are also cases where our interviewees suffered as a result of general economic developments, like the great inflation that reached its climax in Germany in 1923. Hilde Ainger remembers the hard times of the inflation years being discussed by her parents, while Hanna Singer's father, who had gone into his father-in-law's private bank – an institution hard hit in the crisis – had to resort to working as an estate agent.

By the mid-1920s, many of the interviewees' families were enjoying renewed prosperity, but this was cut short by the Great Depression at the end of the decade, which affected all strata of society. Christel Marsh's father, a teacher, experienced the school closures enforced by Chancellor Brüning's emergency decrees aimed at cutting public spending; Margarete Hinrichsen recalls suicides among the impoverished Junker estate owners in her area hit hard by the crisis in agriculture; and Helga Reutter's father's clothing factory suffered from the general economic downturn. When factory owners had to lay off workers, and also servants at home, the resultant rise in unemployment led to the radicalisation of politics that undermined parliamentary democracy in both Austria and Germany. Several of our interviewees recall the political violence that characterised the dying years of the Weimar Republic, as extremist parties gained support at the expense of the democratic centre. Christel Marsh witnessed violent left-wing street demonstrations and Hilde Auerbach remembers the clashes at her university between Nazis and left-wing students:

Before [1933] there were terrible conflicts between the Hitlerites and the others. I was in Heidelberg during this great conflict between Social Democrats and Communists and the Nazis and their parties. That was amongst young students as well, these were profound conflicts.

5. Anti-semitism

The principal beneficiaries of the crisis in Germany were the Nazis, and their rise to power brought the issue of anti-semitism sharply to the fore, most obviously for Jews. In the years before Hitler came to power, almost all the Jewish interviewees mention anti-semitism, though in Germany none suffered from it severely. Several state that they personally had little or no experience of anti-semitism before 1933, though that may in part be due to the middle-class milieu in which they moved as well as to their assimilation. Hilde Ainger remembers only rare occasions when a lout in the street or a jealous schoolmate made anti-semitic remarks:

> There were odd remarks, yes, and you suddenly had somebody shouting or something across the road, but usually, you know, lower-class. . . I mean, . . . nobody in your [social circle], but you would occasionally get an impression of anti-semitism: [you would hear] insulting things like 'alte Juden' ('old Jews') or something like that, or 'Judenhexe' ('Jewish witch'); that wasn't frequent, but we did come across [it].

Adelheid Schweitzer observed anti-semitism during her studies, but was never subjected to it herself before 1933, while Peter Johnson had enough non-Jewish friends at school to protect him from the threat of Nazi violence. Eva Pollard recalls:

> I had a very happy uneventful childhood, with my parents and brother and sister, and at school there was no trouble with being Jewish, we had mixed classes and my very best friend happened to be what afterwards you called 'Aryan', so everything seemed to be very smooth and normal.

Lotte Berk likewise remained untouched by anti-semitism before

2. CULTURE, EDUCATION, POLITICS BEFORE EMIGRATION

1933, while Hans Seelig recalls none until he had to change schools in 1935 or 1936. Although her father lost his job at the Berlin Technische Hochschule because he was both Jewish and stateless, Elizabeth Rosenthal remained oblivious to anti-Jewish sentiment, as in the early days was her mother, whose non-Jewish appearance protected her from the petty manifestations of anti-semitism that made most Jews aware of the prejudice and hostility around them.

This perception of anti-semitism in Germany as a relatively low-level phenomenon may partly account for the underestimation of the Nazi threat to the Jews, which is a recurrent theme in our interviews. Hilde Ainger states: 'At that time most people thought it was such madness, it couldn't last, including my father and many of his friends, it couldn't last, they were going to sit it out and it could not possibly last in their country, in their culture.' Adelheid Schweitzer's father also thought that it would 'blow over'. Lotte Berk recalls: 'Naturally no one believed that Hitler would come. My father thought it was too cultured, Germany, because he came from Russia, my father, so he had already experienced pogroms.' Nor could he believe that the Nazis would retain power long, a tragic miscalculation that cost him his life. As the repeated references to German culture show, the reverence felt by many Jews towards Germany as the land of progress and civilisation now came to represent a real threat to their safety.

This false sense of security was reinforced in some fathers by their patriotic and deeply-rooted image of themselves as Germans first and Jews only second. Margarete Hinrichsen's parents, amazingly, were still trying as late as June 1938 to persuade their daughter to return to Germany from Britain:

> Unbelievable now, with hindsight, to ask their seventeen-year-old daughter to come back to Germany... My father did not want to believe... 'It will blow over, I should think.' He was so absolutely convinced. He had fought in the war for the Germans. He just did not...

Within five months he was dead. Renée Hubert's father showed rare prescience when he explained to his daughters in 1932 the importance of having a passport readily available, so as to be able to leave

Germany at any time. But such awareness before 1933 of the threat posed by National Socialism was unfortunately the exception.

The interviewees from Austria, where anti-Jewish feeling had long been prevalent, report a considerably higher level of anti-semitism, and their consciousness of it was correspondingly greater. Even before 1918 Mimi Glover remembers being greeted on her first day at school by the anti-semitic ditty 'Jud, Jud, spuck in Hut,/ Sag der Mama, das ist gut', and stones being thrown at the Jewish pupils. Ernst Flesch had similar experiences in the predominantly lower middle-class sections of society in which he moved. 'It didn't need the Anschluss', he comments wryly:

> There was already an enormous amount of anti-semitism in Austria anyway among certain sections of the population... You could barely walk along the street without somebody shouting behind you in certain areas... In Austria anti-semitism is a much more virulent and long-standing thing than even in Germany, I would say. It's more like in Poland or the Ukraine, to be compared with... not quite as awful as that until Hitler came, but bad enough.

Stella Rotenberg was strongly aware of the prevalent anti-semitism:

> I've had anti-semitic experiences all my life. After all, I did live in Vienna and in Austria. That, yes, of course. It existed. From the very beginning, I believe, from the beginning I understood that I lived there not because I had the right to live there, but because it was reluctantly, not at all willingly granted to me. No, that was something the Jews, if they felt anything at all, something that they couldn't avoid feeling.

She also encountered Nazi violence at university, where the party had gained mass support among students very early on. Although her family, like most middle-class Jews, was not directly affected by the suppression of the left-wing uprising of February 1934, the abolition of democracy under the 'Ständestaat' (the authoritarian system of government instituted in Austria in 1933) left her with an uncomfortable sense of foreboding: 'The taste of dictatorship was already in the air.' Always aware 'that we were heading for the

2. CULTURE, EDUCATION, POLITICS BEFORE EMIGRATION

abyss', she was not as surprised as some by the Anschluss, but still experienced the volcanic eruption of anti-semitism in its wake as the catastrophe of her life.

It appears that those from wealthier backgrounds were more sheltered from anti-semitism. Hans Brill remembers none at all before the Anschluss, while Helga Reutter remained unscathed herself:

> I mean, at that time, I personally wasn't a victim of anti-semitism. I mean, you had to be a complete idiot not to know it was there. Of course it was... There was a very, very violent anti-semitism, you know, you could see it, 'Saujud' ('Jewish pig') being said to an old Jew with a beard and things like that.

Moving in cultured, educated circles reduced the risk of encountering anti-semites to isolated individuals, like one of Eva Sommerfreund's teachers at her Gymnasium: 'I never noticed it except for this one teacher who hated me and I hated her.'

The strength and prevalence of Austrian anti-semitism perhaps accounts for the fact that some of the Austrian refugees' families took precautions against persecution: Hans Brill's father had a business bank account in Britain, though this may not have been opened with emigration in mind, and Hanne Norbert-Miller's father, uniquely, anticipated that Hitler would invade Austria and registered his firm in Britain around 1936. But many Austrian Jews were blind to the Nazi menace, like Helga Reutter's family:

> I mean, I can remember, even a day before it happened we didn't believe it was going to happen. We were just as stupid as the Czechs and the Poles. And we always said, oh France, oh America, they wouldn't allow it... The Italians are going to march in. They wouldn't allow Hitler to swallow up Austria. Little did we know. We were really stupid.

They were also blind to the nature of the Nazi regime; Helga Reutter's father was bewildered, as late as 1936, that a German acquaintance could have been arrested simply for being a Jew – 'I cannot understand, he seemed such a decent man'. Unlike Germany, where Ilse Wolff in Berlin saw little sign of anti-semitism in the early period of Nazi rule, the annexation of Austria triggered an immediate and appalling convulsion of anti-semitic violence and cruelty. Erika Young's description of the horrors that disfigured post-Anschluss Vienna is perhaps the most telling, coming as it does from a non-Jew:

> Until the Anschluss I knew nothing about that at all. But from the first day of the Anschluss you saw those slogans and shop windows and glass being broken and people committing suicide, and you heard the shots in the night. Jewish men and women, elderly men and women [scrubbing] the pavements, being kicked and beaten. Of course you saw it. What you saw in the rest of Austria, I don't know. But what you saw in Vienna in March '38 I do know. You couldn't go into a street without seeing, or go anywhere around Vienna, without seeing all that happening everywhere. I thought it was terrible and I have never forgotten it. It influenced me for the rest of my life.

6. Conclusion

These historical experiences of prejudice and persecution and the interviewees' reactions to them do not, however, provide the integrating factor that can give some sense of social and cultural coherence and of shared values to the refugee community in exile, except in the obvious but limited sense that they are all victims of Nazism. No more do their religious beliefs. Far more important as a common factor are the refugees' origins in the educated, prosperous, cosmopolitan, professionally successful middle classes; this is true both of the Jewish majority and of the non-Jews. The Jews were able to continue the process of assimilation in their adopted country, once they had settled, especially as anti-semitism was less pronounced in Britain. Also important is their shared culture, with the German language as the vehicle for the values to which the cultured class of Central Europe, and especially its Jewish élite, owed allegiance. Other key factors from their mainly middle-class backgrounds are the commercial element of entrepreneurial talent and the grounding in professional and intellectual life, which allowed so many of the refugees, or their spouses, to build the economic basis for a new and, all things considered, successful existence in Britain.

CHAPTER THREE

Departure and Arrival

Marian Malet

1. Historical framework 1933–39

Adolf Hitler became Chancellor of Germany on 30 January 1933 in an atmosphere of high tension and random violence. His National Socialist party did not have a majority in the Reichstag, nor did it obtain one as it had hoped at the elections of 5 March 1933, but this was in fact immaterial since the party moved rapidly by means of decrees and proclamations to establish its ascendancy over the German state. The process by which it did so – 'Gleichschaltung' – consisted of a unification of the different elements of German life under the control of the Nazi party: thus, for instance, in May 1933 all trade unions were taken over and united under a single 'union', the Deutsche Arbeitsfront, and in June and July the opposition parties were abolished. Opponents of the regime were taken into what was euphemistically called 'Schutzhaft' ('protective custody', but in reality preventive detention) and placed in prisons or concentration camps, without trial, for an unspecified period.

The process of excluding Jews from both economic and public life was signalled by the boycott of Jewish businesses on 1 April and the 'Gesetz zur Wiederherstellung des Berufsbeamtentums' (Law on the Restoration of the Professional Civil Service) of 7 April, which declared that all unqualified, disloyal or Jewish staff should be dismissed. This, together with other measures, excluded Jews at a stroke from such positions as lawyers, judges, journalists, orchestral musicians and university professors, and led to wholesale dismissals in these professions. Only those Jews who had fought in the First World War – the 'Frontkämpfer' – were specifically protected whilst President Hindenburg remained alive (until 1934).

These events triggered a first wave of departures: for racial or broadly political reasons, 60,000 people are estimated to have left the country in 1933, largely between March and July.[4] Most of them did not go far, choosing to stay in the countries close to Germany, such as France, Czechoslovakia and the Netherlands, for they fully expected to be able to return home in a few months when, they thought, the upstart Hitler, the 'Eintagsfliege' (mayfly), would have spent his energy. From the beginning of 1933, the British authorities noted the appearance at ports of entry of increased numbers of Germans, some of whom admitted to being refugees. Figures were officially recorded as about 300–400 per month in 1933, falling to around 100 per month in 1934.[5] Geographical distance from Germany obviously kept numbers low in the initial stages.

Mid-1934 in Germany saw Hitler move against one of his old allies, Ernst Röhm, an ambitious man of radical views who had built up the SA into a force of over four million men, a force moreover that was far larger than and quite independent of the Army and which was now clamouring for a more important role. The implied threat to his power from within the Nazi camp was not lost on Hitler, who ordered the SA leadership to be killed on the night of 30 June in an operation later known variously as the Night of the Long Knives, the Röhm Purge and the Blood Purge. Röhm was among those murdered.

The anti-Jewish campaign became more active again in early 1935 around the time of the plebiscite in the Saar (January), which was to result in that territory being reincorporated into Germany. Victims of the campaign were once again businessmen and professionals working in Germany. In the summer of that year, Jews were increasingly barred from public places such as cinemas, theatres, swimming-pools and resorts, and several Jewish newspapers were forced to suspend publication for some months.

A symptom of the growing consolidation of the Nazi regime was the promulgation of the Nuremberg Laws in September 1935. Their purpose was to codify rules excluding the Jews completely from

---

4. A.J.Sherman, *Island Refuge. Britain and Refugees from the Third Reich 1933–1939*, 2nd ed., London, 1994, p. 23.

5. ibid., p. 47. The official statistics are notoriously unreliable. In the British case there was almost certainly deliberate underestimation in order to avoid adverse public reaction against the refugees.

3. DEPARTURE AND ARRIVAL

normal society in a uniform way throughout Germany. These laws laid down a new basic definition of who was to be considered a Jew, and established two classes of citizenship, 'Reichsbürger' (the pure-blooded citizen), and 'Staatsangehörige' (all others, including Jews), forbidding intermarriage between the two groups. As was often the case with Nazi laws, they in fact set the official seal on practices that had long been current in parts of the country. These laws did not lead to a large increase in emigration: they contained, after all, no specific provisions which might give rise to the necessity for a hurried departure and they seemed to give Jews a clear, albeit second-class, legal status in the country. Overall emigration figures from Germany at this time did not rise appreciably, estimations for 1935 being 20,000 departures, for 1936 24,000 and for 1937 23,000.[6]

On 7 March 1936 came Hitler's first real move to test the will of the signatories of the Treaty of Versailles, when on a flimsy pretext he occupied the Rhineland which had been demilitarised under the terms of the Treaty. France and its allies failed to oppose the move strongly and Hitler's daring action (he actually had no forces ready for war) carried the day. It not only spelled the demise of the Treaty of Versailles, but also that of the Treaty of Locarno of 1925 (which had established a peaceful framework of relations between Germany and her Western neighbours). Later in 1936 Hitler seized the opportunity to present a positive image to the world when Berlin hosted the Olympic Games (awarded to Germany before the Nazi seizure of power), which proved to be a publicity success for Nazism despite the presence of some athletes who did not conform to Nazi norms in various ways. Anti-Jewish propaganda was removed from Berlin for the duration of the Games. Leni Riefenstahl's acclaimed film *Olympiade* gives a flavour of the event. From 1936 Hitler joined with Mussolini in supporting the Nationalists under General Franco in the Spanish Civil War, which provided German troops and airmen with experience that would stand them in good stead in the Second World War.

It was Hitler's annexation of Austria – the Anschluss – of 12 March 1938, with its attendant violence and persecution of anti-Nazis and Jews, that caused the second great wave of emigration, a wave, moreover, that was much more disorganised than that of 1933

6. ibid., p. 60.

in Germany. Jews, members of the left-wing political parties, supporters of Schuschnigg's regime and others who had reason to fear the Nazi takeover rushed to leave the country. The appropriation of Jewish property and businesses, which had been gradually going on in Germany since 1933, was accomplished within a few months in Austria, and was generally carried out summarily and often with brutality. Jews were given to understand that they must leave, and it was now that forced emigration emerged as a clear objective of the regime. A report by the League of Nations' High Commissioner for Refugees stated that at the start of September 1938 there were more than 15,000 Austrian refugees in other European countries, in a 'most precarious' position since they had mostly been unable to take any funds with them.[7]

Whilst the Nazis were setting up their systems in Austria, Konrad Henlein, leader of the Nationalist German minority in Czechoslovakia and of the Nazi-inspired Sudeten German Party, was being financed by Berlin to foment a crisis by waging a violent separatist campaign in the Sudetenland against the Czech government. The resulting Sudeten revolt and the ensuing flurry of diplomatic activity culminated in the Munich Agreement of 29 September 1938. This provided for the immediate cession of the Sudetenland to Germany, without consultation either with the population or with the Czechoslovak government. Chamberlain returned from his third visit to Germany with his famous piece of paper guaranteeing 'peace for our time'. The appeasement policy was now looking like capitulation. Jews and anti-Nazis who lived in the Sudeten territory fled to Prague, thus adding to the large number of German refugees who had settled there after 1933. The writing was on the wall for all these people, who now joined the ever-increasing numbers trying to escape Nazism. The British Government was felt to have had a moral responsibility in abandoning the Czechs at Munich and was persuaded, largely by public opinion, to make a special effort to aid them. A four million pound fund was voted by Parliament to help resettle these groups. It was administered by the British Committee for Refugees from Czechoslovakia, created for the purpose. This committee was later renamed the Czech Refugee Trust Fund (CRTF).

7. ibid., p. 128.

3. DEPARTURE AND ARRIVAL

Whilst the repercussions of Munich were being felt, Germany and Austria experienced a burst of concerted attacks on Jewish businesses, synagogues, schools and homes between 9 and 11 November 1938: the Kristallnacht. This pogrom unleashed the next great wave of emigration, causing a tide which did not abate until war was declared ten months later. The pretext for this new bout of Nazi violence was the shooting of Ernst vom Rath, Third Secretary at the German Embassy in Paris, by a desperate young Jew of Polish origin, Herschel Grynszpan, whose parents were trapped between the German and Polish borders at Zbonszyn, unable to enter either country due to anti-semitic policies.[8] (The Jewish community was later collectively fined one billion Reichsmarks for the murder of vom Rath.) During the Kristallnacht period, some 20,000 Jews were arrested, many of whom were then placed in concentration camps and only released against their promise to leave the country as soon as they could make the necessary arrangements, in line with the new forced emigration policy. Many Austrian Jews were moved out of their flats and 'ghettoised' in other flats, one family to a room, pending their departure, and even more stringent regulations against them were now issued, especially in regard to the 'Aryanisation' of their property and the registration of their valuables. It was decided at this time to eliminate Jews entirely from the economy, which meant that the Jewish population remaining in the countries occupied by the Nazis would live a life at bare subsistence level. Kristallnacht caused the numbers departing in the face of these policies to rise steeply, and this was exacerbated when Hitler marched into 'rump' Czechoslovakia on 15 March 1939 and established the 'German Protectorate of Bohemia and Moravia'. On 17 March Neville Chamberlain finally spoke against the policy of appeasement he had followed for so long, warning Hitler that Britain would resist any further territorial ambitions Germany might demonstrate. By the end of the month the British Government was assuring Poland of its support for that country's independence following the Danzig crisis, so that when Hitler's troops invaded Poland on 1 September, the British Government declared war on Germany (3 September). A month afterwards, Sir Herbert Emerson, League of Nations' High Commissioner for Refu-

8. For more detail, see Sherman, op cit., pp. 164–65.

gees, estimated in his report to the Assembly that a total of 400,000 refugees had left Greater Germany since 1933.[9] At the same time, the Home Secretary gave the figures for entry of Germans and Austrians into Great Britain as 49,500, including 9,000 children, but excluding some 6,000 Czechs.[10] Revised statistics of 1943, however, estimated the number of refugees present in Britain at the outbreak of war (excluding children who came with their parents) at somewhat over 78,000, and these are now generally accepted as being much closer to the true figures.[11]

2. Departure from the Continent: Introduction

The range of departure dates of the interviewees in this book spans the entire period from Hitler's seizure of power in January 1933 until well into the first year of the war (July 1940). And although the group in no way represents a scientifically selected sample, the overall pattern of their departure dates does roughly reflect the overall trend towards a veritable flood of refugees making their departure from Germany, Austria and Czechoslovakia after the watershed of March 1938. Hence the division below into departures before and after that date. The range of departure dates not only reflects the outer, objective events occurring in the different countries, but also the personal circumstances of the individual refugees, although the former may often be seen to determine the latter. It will be noted that there are five instances of a person having to emigrate twice and, further, that the group includes two women, Margarete Hinrichsen and Ruth Herring, who were technically not refugees when they arrived, in that they came for educational purposes, and one, Christel Marsh, who came to get married, although she had also experienced the attentions of the Gestapo.

9. ibid., p. 270.
10. ibid., p. 271. For some contemporary refugee intake figures for other countries, see pp. 264–65.
11. Louise London, 'British Immigration Control Procedures and Jewish refugees, 1933–1939', in *Second Chance. Two Centuries of German-speaking Jews in the United Kingdom*, ed. Werner E. Mosse et al., Tübingen, 1991, p. 487, fn.7, also pp. 512–13. See also her *Whitehall and the Jews 1933–1948. British Immigration Policy and the Holocaust*, Cambridge, 2000, pp. 11–12.

3. Pre-March 1938

Twelve of the group – roughly one-third – left in the pre-Anschluss period, indeed ten of these departed between March 1933 and the end of 1935, and only two in the fifteen months prior to the Anschluss. All were German; nine were Jewish and of the remaining three, two were political refugees and one was leaving for educational purposes. Three were still at school.

Of this group, four were very early leavers, departing from Germany within weeks of Hitler seizing power, and three of them left because of clear anti-semitic persecution. Renée Hubert's parents, left-leaning doctors, had been subject to harassment for some time as she recounts (she was seventeen at the time):

> We had repeated visits from – I don't know whether they were from Nazi headquarters or city people, but they came again and again and wanted to look at our house. There were inspections. We were constantly being inspected. And they were looking at the books also. We had lots of books. But they didn't find anything, or they didn't say anything. Then they came again and my father was asleep and I had to wake him up and he immediately said, 'This time I'm going to prison'. I couldn't quite believe it, but then they took him away. It was called 'Schutzhaft'. Then they also took my mother... My mother found out that she was threatened because of her abortion activities, and that if she stayed any length of time [in Germany] she might have to go back to prison and it would be much more serious.

Some family friends happened to have an Italian visitor staying who was a personal friend of Mussolini and through his intervention her parents were quickly freed from prison. The whole family left at once for Switzerland, where they had friends, and from there moved on to France.

Adelheid Schweitzer, who left around June 1933, whilst emphasising that she was not 'involved in any violence, not even in direct anti-semitic comments' in the period prior to March 1933, relates that a young man from a well-known local family, a university friend, 'said he was very sorry, but he could not continue his friendship with me'. When she asked him to return the many books she had lent him, he did so, but would not enter her house: 'This gave me a terrible shock. It suddenly became real and I had never suspected him of having Nazi sympathies.' A second incident occurred the day before the Nazi 'Boykotttag' (1 April 1933) whilst she was engaged in a work-experience programme at her local bank. A young clerk, a boy who had been with her at school:

> ... came over to the desk and said, 'You'd better not come tomorrow. It won't be safe for you. We don't want to see you.' That was another shock. It came in a way that made me think, this is not for five minutes. There was so much vituperation because we were a very well-regarded middle-class professional family.

Hilde Auerbach, too, witnessed racial and political prejudice at work, although it was not directed at her. She was finishing her university degree in 1933, 'and then Hitler came to power and in Heidelberg all the Social Democrat lecturers and also the Jews were dismissed straightaway', so she decided to return to England to do some more research and wait and see how matters would develop in her own country.

Some parents were already sending away their children as early as 1933, which was the case with Peter Johnson, then seventeen, whose father, following the example of other fathers he knew, decided to get his son out of Germany and gave him the choice of going either to France or England. Peter Singer was also sent away in 1933, but to Italy, to a school with Jewish connections in Turin. He was ten at the time and experienced such homesickness that he succeeded in persuading his father to allow him to return to Germany. It was not until 1936 that his parents finally found a way to send him to England, along with two other boys.

Hilde Ainger left Guben an der Neisse in 1934 aged seventeen, like Peter Johnson, and had not finished school either. Like Adelheid Schweitzer, she had observed a change in attitudes (in her case, among some teachers), but she also had the example of her elder sister who announced in 1933: '"I'm not going to go on living here, I'm going to leave this country." She was seventeen then, and at the time most people thought it such madness, it couldn't last, including my father and many of his friends.' This was, alas, an all too

3. DEPARTURE AND ARRIVAL

prevalent attitude at the time, mentioned often by the interviewees, and it cost many people their lives, including Margarete Hinrichsen's father. Hilde Ainger's sister, however, obtained an au pair job in Denmark (where she did not of course know the language) and Hilde left when she in turn became seventeen, after completing the 'Obersekunda' (fifth year at academic secondary school), and began to work as an au pair in England.

Four of the interviewees left Germany because of direct political persecution in differing degrees, although one had other reasons as well. Untypically, there are no Jews among them. (The only representatives of those numerous refugees who were both Jewish and had very strong political affiliations in this group of interviewees would be the husband of Austrian refugee Gertrud Wengraf and perhaps Josephine Bruegel, who helped her brother to aid Socialist refugees from Germany.) Eugen Brehm and Alfred Dörfel were both very politically engaged, as we have seen in the last chapter, and both were imprisoned after the Nazis seized power. Brehm was in 'Schutzhaft' from March to May 1933, after which he worked underground in Germany for the SAP for 18 months (with a three-month spell abroad, largely in Britain) until he was re-arrested in Dresden at the end of 1934. After a short period under Gestapo arrest, he managed through a ruse to escape and was guided over the Czech frontier to freedom. In June 1933 Dörfel was arrested for anti-Nazi activities in his hometown of Leipzig, and detained first in police prison and then in a concentration camp. He was released before Christmas, 'in connection with the big amnesty for offenders', after which he worked underground in both Germany and Czechoslovakia for the Communist Party, as a courier, for instance, or an observer and contact person at the Czech border, and was also responsible for gleaning information about the current situation within Germany. Besides this, he undertook special missions into Germany. Alec Armstrong (formerly Hans-Ludwig Baehr), who escaped in dangerous circumstances to Denmark in 1935, was also a Communist in the early 1930s, leaving the Party, however, when he realised how nationalistic Stalin was. The fourth in this group, Christel Marsh, a member of the Bekennende Kirche (Confessional Church), will be dealt with in the next section, as she left after March 1938.

Both the musician Peter Gellhorn and the modern dancer Lotte Berk lost their livelihood owing to their Jewish connections, the former describing himself as 'jüdisch versippt' (related to Jews) in Nazi parlance, and the latter being Jewish. Peter Gellhorn's Jewish father had been a prominent architect and president of the Reichsverband bildender Künstler (National Association of Fine Artists), and had had to flee in late 1933. Gellhorn, his sister and his non-Jewish mother (divorced for years from his father) led a rather dangerous life, expecting to be arrested any time; this period he remembers as follows: 'Every evening we fell into bed like a sack of potatoes, having played a part in a play we hated. And it was always a pleasant surprise still to be alive.' Having completed his course at the Hochschule für Musik, he had meanwhile applied to the Nazi Reichsmusikkammer (the body which organised musical life in the Reich) for membership, despite his racial background, because he needed to earn money to support his mother and sister and 'you had to be a member to teach or play'. The period he is referring to was that just preceding the enactment of the Nuremberg laws (September 1935) and was a time of particularly aggressive anti-semitism. Lotte Berk, daughter of a wealthy Jewish businessman in Cologne, was working at the Mannheim Nationaltheater when she was sacked on racial grounds. Her response was to arrange a recital in Cologne with her new husband, a non-Jew and a dancer:

> We hired a theatre, we had an orchestra of twelve people and he and I were going to give this recital. Two hours before the recital the police rang . . . and said I could not go onstage. I was forbidden to appear. My husband could dance alone: he wasn't Jewish. My father was very upset for me, and I got angry. Really, I was young enough to be angry about it. So I didn't dare to dance because the SS and SA were also in the theatre, and they put posters up at the theatre: 'If you are a good Nazi, don't come here.' So a few of the people didn't dare go, but it was still pretty full, and the SA filled it up completely. And Ernest danced alone, but very movingly. He would dance, oh, there is Lotte, oh, there, come, and all this; and the people were very moved and they all screamed: 'Lotte, dance, Lotte, dance.' And I didn't know what to do. . . After the recital, the composer, who was also the con-

ductor, fetched me onto the stage. He could not bear it, so he dared to do this and I was so angry that I wanted to do it. But when they called, 'dance, dance, dance', I couldn't... And then I calmed them down and said: 'All I want to say is, thank you for not all being Nazis.' The SA was on the stage, of course, immediately: 'Out!' I was at the back, they didn't let me go to the front, and that was the end of me.

Ruth Herring and Margarete Hinrichsen both came to England to further their education, the former in 1934 after having completed her university studies, the latter in 1937 at the age of seventeen, being something of a 'mixed-up kid' in her parents' eyes, and having reached the age when as the daughter of comfortable parents she should go abroad to acquire languages. Whilst Ruth Herring had seen very little of the worsening political situation in Germany, absorbed as she had been in completing her thesis, Margarete Hinrichsen had been forced into a certain awareness of the deteriorating conditions, especially whilst still at home in the small Pomeranian town of Bad Polzin, which was very Nazi-inclined and surrounded by large estates. Thus she had seen a caricature of her father as a major landowner ('Großagrarier') in a 'Stürmerkasten' (public display case for the rabidly Nazi newspaper, *Der Stürmer*) and had witnessed the gradual withdrawal of civil rights from Jews, for example the barring from the local swimming-pool of Jewish children, which was particularly ironic in her case, as we have seen in Chapter One. Although she came to Britain as late as 1937, she detects no sign of her parents having decided to send her away for safety's sake, indeed they were, as has been explained in the previous chapter, among those who never believed Germany would turn against them.

4. *March 1938 and after*

Hitler's occupation of Austria in mid-March 1938 transformed the situation there overnight, for although Nazi influence had been steadily gaining ground, the movement had been to some degree contained, publicly at least. The Nazis at once began to put in place pell-mell the practices they had gradually been perfecting over several years in Germany, and people became ever more desperate as they tried to find countries which would issue them with an entry visa. Events were by now moving ever more quickly. The Sudeten crisis of summer 1938 was seemingly defused by the Munich Agreement of late September. Britain thus gained a few months' breathing space, but the Agreement spelled destruction for Czechoslovakia, which was occupied by Nazi troops on 15–16 March 1939. Meanwhile Jewish life in Germany continued much as before, until the Kristallnacht atrocities of 9–11 November 1938 prompted a great wave of now desperate Jews to make preparations to leave Germany as soon as they could, for even those who had not thought themselves at risk realised finally the degree of the menace. Thousands of Jewish males were taken away to prison or concentration camp, and released after a short while on the strict understanding that they leave the country; otherwise they would be taken back into custody.

There were twenty-seven emigrations in our group of interviewees between March 1938 and July 1940: seven in 1938, nineteen in 1939 and one in 1940. Of these, five in 1939 and the one in 1940 were in fact second emigrations, in which people having already left Germany or Austria and 'settled' elsewhere were forced by circumstances to move on to Britain. Of the seven who left in 1938, one was German with a Jewish father and six were from Austria, five Jews and one Catholic. Three were still at school. As to those who emigrated between January 1939 and July 1940, four were Austrian (all Jewish), three were Czechoslovaks (all Jewish), and eleven were German (of whom eight were Jewish, one of them originally Austrian; one was Lutheran and two were non-Jewish political refugees who had been in Prague for some years. Five were still at school). Seventeen actually moved between January 1939 and the outbreak of the war (3 September 1939), one moving twice.

Hanne Norbert-Miller happened to be acting the role of the Empress Elisabeth in a play in Innsbruck on 11 March 1938. It was a temporary job for her – she could never have obtained anything permanent there on account of her Jewish background. But this turned out very positively, as she could leave much more easily than from Vienna. She recounts the scene: 'After that performance where

3. DEPARTURE AND ARRIVAL

they were all shouting, "Die Panzer rollen schon herein" (The tanks are already coming), I rang my parents in Vienna. We all had the idea that I should try and leave immediately for England.' The following morning she was asked to go to the management and was told 'that "of course you can't go on working". That was 12 March. . . I was so stunned that I didn't move for a couple of days'. She was the only one of the group initially to be refused entry to England, being sent back to France (see below).

Both Gertrud Wengraf and Stella Rotenberg were students at the University of Vienna in March 1938, and both had to abandon their studies forthwith because of their ethnic origin. Whilst Stella Rosenberg does not recall actually being told to go (she simply comments that she knew at once that it was all over), Gertrud Wengraf remembers that all Jews were 'immediately thrown out'. Amidst the atmosphere of mounting tension, she married the older man she had been living with, an art-dealer who was very active politically and who had already tried to leave, but had been turned back at the border; they planned a more orderly exit together. One day whilst they were waiting for their exit papers, they went walking in the Prater:

> And on that very day the Nazis decided to mop up all the Jews in the Prater . . . and march them all into town, and make them – us – scrub the pavement. . . I mean, I didn't mind scrubbing the pavement, but one never knew what was going to happen then. And somehow I was quite a rebellious person and I found it very difficult not to lash out. . . And my stepdaughter was made to scrub a lavatory for no reason; I don't know where the lavatory was, they just took her to a lavatory to scrub the floor. Stupid, it was really stupid, and they gave us green leaves to carry – you know, these Jews going into Jerusalem with palms in their hands. On the one hand . . . we felt very superior to these fools and loonies, and on the other hand one was very frightened. You couldn't prove or show or have any dignity, obviously, because that would have meant only beatings.

Unlike Gertrud Wengraf, who was excluded from the University just before completing her degree, Mimi Glover finished her university studies comfortably in February 1938. She was in Vienna at the time of the Anschluss, but lodging in Sievering, where very few Jews lived, so there was no trouble at all. She was already in the process of arranging through family connections to go to England on a domestic permit. She managed to make all the necessary departure arrangements quite rapidly, leaving Vienna on 31 May 1938.

Hans Brill was a child of seven at the time of the Anschluss. Although his parents were Jewish, they were 'not remotely religious' (indeed, his mother may have been 'Christianised', he observes). But he particularly recalls the Anschluss because his father sent him with the family chauffeur to the Central Synagogue in Vienna: he felt, as his son sees it, 'that it was vital to show solidarity with the rest of the Jews'. Brill remembers with his child's eye seeing 'a great number of people' there who were 'very troubled'. Friends of his father in Germany telephoned on the night of the Anschluss advising him to leave, or at least to send his children away, but like so many, he failed to see the urgency of such a course: 'No, we were Austrian citizens, we had done nothing wrong and it would be wrong to "abandon ship" at this point', was his father's reasoning. When, however, he was arrested shortly after through the efforts of a disgruntled ex-employee (dismissed for wife-beating when drunk) who turned out to be a Nazi, he began from prison to organise his children's departure and they were finally able to leave later that year.

The Anschluss was also an important date for Erika Young's family, although they came from a very traditional (Catholic, Monarchist) background. Not wishing his family to live under Nazi rule, her father decided to arrange the departure of his eleven-year-old child first, then that of his wife, but it was far from easy in spite of their not being Jews: 'The Germans were very loath to let respectable people, traditionally, like my family leave. Even me.' But he managed to make the necessary plans through the French teaching order of nuns at whose Viennese convent school Erika was a pupil.

Helga Reutter looks back on the period after Hitler's troops marched into Vienna almost with astonishment, recalling how she continued to go out in public with her non-Jewish fiancé (strictly forbidden by the Nazis). Generally life continued with a certain semblance of normality, for although the family were aware of anti-semitic acts suffered by others, they were lucky enough to escape

3. DEPARTURE AND ARRIVAL

them initially themselves. They were starting, however, to make arrangements to leave. Her fiancé departed in August 1938 and was able to secure a domestic visa for her, so that she could leave in December, but not before experiencing her father being taken by the Gestapo to Dachau as part of the roundups connected with Kristallnacht.

Walter Wolff, too, recalls the 'crisis situation . . . which was near the time of Kristallnacht', remembering it as a time when he was given four weeks' English tuition, since he was on the point of departing for England to join his brother at a Quaker school. Because his father was Jewish he had been debarred from state schools in Germany around 1935 and sent to private Jewish schools.

The repercussions of the cataclysmic political events of that year continued into 1939. The Munich Agreement and subsequent German occupation of 'rump' Czechoslovakia, for example, led to the departure of all the interviewees living in Czechoslovakia by May/June 1939. Eugen Brehm summed up the political situation succinctly when asked at what point he started trying to obtain a visa for England:

> Well, I'd say immediately after Munich. You see, we knew that Hitler would occupy Prague. Although he said, 'Ich will doch gar keine Tschechen' ('I don't want any Czechs at all') of course we knew that this was untrue, he wanted and needed . . . Czechoslovakia . . . for his war, he needed the Sudeten, he needed the excellent fortifications the Czechs had built there. He needed the Skoda works for his war. We knew that it was a matter of time. I know most Czechs and Jews, local people that I knew, all knew that one day he would march in.

So for him as a political refugee in Prague, as for Alfred Dörfel, it was imperative to move on before Hitler arrived. And it was thanks to the British Committee for Refugees from Czechoslovakia that they were able to reach Britain, Dörfel in January and Brehm in February 1939. As the latter explains:

> After Munich the people in this country [Britain] were deeply shocked about what happened. The Chamberlain Government, who had promised peace in our time, and who had spoken about a

'faraway country of which we know nothing', had been forced to do something for the refugees for whom it had created a terrible problem: not only German and Austrian refugees but Czechs and Jewish Czech refugees.

The three 'non-political' refugees from Czechoslovakia all left between April and May/June 1939, travelling by train. Understandably perhaps, none expressed the same urgency to depart as did Brehm and Dörfel, although all knew they would go. Klary Friedl, a young married woman with her own perfume and cosmetics business in Bratislava, had her first taste of anti-semitism after the Nazis occupied neighbouring Austria: 'The Germans broke into my shop and broke it up and wrote: "Jew, Jew, Jew".' After this her husband, whose place of work was very close to the Austrian border, decided to move to Prague, and during their short time there Klary Friedl taught Max Factor courses for intending emigrants who needed to acquire a qualification, and also helped to hide fugitive political refugees. Her husband left for England on business in January, and she followed at her second attempt in April, after Hitler's seizure of the country on 15 March 1939.

Josephine Bruegel also has cause to remember that day, for it was the one on which she received her permit to go to England from the British Consulate. She had been hoping to be able to complete her last term of medical studies at the university through the intervention of family contacts, but when the permit arrived allowing her to enter Britain to do nursing or domestic work, she soon left. The period she had just lived through she describes thus: 'There was such confusion and chaos from September/October 1938 until March 1939 . . . it was a really shadowy period.'

Paris was the destination of Eva Sommerfreund and her new husband. (She, like many other young people who were intending to emigrate, married shortly after Hitler's occupation of the Czech capital.) She had always moved between Vienna and Prague, and her mother and sister, living in Vienna, found it relatively easy at the Anschluss to leave with their Czech passports for Paris, where they could arrange a visa for Eva and her husband. She had had a successful stage career and one of her fans – a young Nazi in fact –

3. DEPARTURE AND ARRIVAL

arranged for the exit permit. Their most difficult journey to Paris is described below.

For several of the interviewees, the process of making arrangements to leave was very long-drawn-out. Stella Rotenberg in Vienna, for example, was all too aware of the changes in atmosphere at the Anschluss: 'Now they [the Nazis] were the heroes, and crimes were committed quite openly and ... the people in general were quite terrified... That is in the nature of dictatorship. Everyone fears everyone else... There is no trust any more.' Nevertheless, it took her a full year to organise her departure from Vienna. She saw at once that the old life was over: 'It was all over by the evening [of 13 March]. I know. One of my anatomy books was open and my brother closed it, saying, "You don't need to study any more now", and he was right.' Her brother left in June without a valid passport, following an incident when three youths attacked him on the street: 'The Jews didn't wear swastikas, so they were instantly recognisable, you didn't really need a yellow star.' Stella Rotenberg herself wanted to leave legally and was uncertain as to how to go about it, which was one of the reasons why the process took a long time.

Her family, like that of her compatriot Ernst Flesch and so many other Austrian Jews, suffered the indignity of having their flat taken from them after Kristallnacht. Stella Rotenberg describes how one day a man, a civilian, appeared out of the blue to look at their flat, 'and we were so helpless, we couldn't say, "I'm sorry, you can't do this"'. He brought his wife to see if she liked it, and simply announced that he would keep some of their possessions, such as a hanging lamp to which he had taken a fancy: 'And that's how we were forced to leave. That's how we left.' Ernst Flesch was eleven at the time. His father was imprisoned for some days around 10 November, and he and his mother had to vacate their flat as an SS man wanted it. They were rehoused in one room in a larger flat nearby, along with several other families in the same position. Within two months, however, his parents succeeded in sending him to Britain on a Kindertransport.

Nelly Kuttner, too, received an unexpected visit after Kristallnacht when she was alone at home, from where she conducted her millinery business. A local man appeared who 'had a hat-shop not very far away, but he didn't sell handmade hats, he sold very cheap, factory-produced hats... He looked round and said: "You know why I've come. I want to have these mirrors and I want that lighting." He wanted everything moveable.' She had in fact already been to the authorities to ask permission to continue her business until the end of the year, in order to support her parents; as she had received the Nazis' assent to this, she was able to put off giving up her fixtures and fittings. Austrian friends in London had arranged a domestic permit for her after Kristallnacht, but she was very reluctant to leave her parents – and a boyfriend – so did not finally leave until 3 May 1939.

Three of the interviewees left Germany on what have come to be known as the Kindertransports in 1939: Elizabeth Rosenthal, Hanna Singer and Hans Seelig, the girls coming to Britain, whilst Hans Seelig travelled initially to Sweden. Elizabeth Rosenthal and her mother were in a particularly difficult position because they were stateless (having originally held Polish passports). Elizabeth Rosenthal's happy life as a pupil at the Jüdisches Landschul- und Kinderheim Caputh near Potsdam had come to an abrupt end when the Nazis arrived there at Kristallnacht to wreck the school, and she returned to Berlin to join her mother who was living illegally in someone's basement and who now moved heaven and earth to get her daughter away. This she managed in February 1939, sending Elizabeth to Oldham to a family she had contacted through the Quakers. Hans Seelig, too, has good reason to recall Kristallnacht, when – as we have seen – he was chased through the streets by the Hitler Youth at one point. The (non-Jewish) maid put him in her room in the attic whilst she went out to see what was going on. Their flat was not smashed up, and fortunately his father had just left on a business trip, and was safely outside Germany. His mother devoted all her energies to getting her son away, which she managed in March 1939, sending him on a Kindertransport to Sweden. The family was able to regroup in England just before war broke out.

Both Eric Rose and Dorothea Galewski left as children with their families, and both from Breslau. Each family received visits from the SS in November 1938; Dorothea Galewski's father was taken to Buchenwald, whilst Eric Rose's was fortunate enough to escape this

3. DEPARTURE AND ARRIVAL

as he was abroad. The Galewski family had been discussing emigration for some time and casting around for a destination – Dorothea remarks: 'I learned a lot of geography at that time' – but her father was clearly reluctant to leave 'because he was really more German than many Germans'. Experiences in November 1938 made them accelerate their plans, however, and they obtained a six-month transit visa for Britain, where they arrived in April 1939. The outbreak of war was lucky for them as they had no onward visa, but were now allowed to stay. Eric Rose's father was already in Britain arranging the family's emigration when the SS came to call. As a Zionist, his father had been trying to go to Palestine, but could not obtain a certificate, so asked the British authorities to allow his family to go to England instead.

Although both Ilse Wolff and Eva Pollard arrived in Britain in April 1939, they had each been intending to emigrate for a long time; indeed, both had taken English lessons for years with precisely that in mind. Each had also been engaged in helping other Jews to leave: Ilse Wolff since she had lost her employment in 1933 and had then joined the Reichsvertretung der Deutschen Juden, the representative body of the German Jews, working in a department concerned with emigration; and Eva Pollard from around August 1938 when, feeling that the situation had become really dangerous, she decided to resign from her job in Berlin and return to her hometown of Breslau to 'prepare for emigration', volunteering to work in a Jewish institution preparing children to leave. She must have gone there in autumn 1938, for she recounts that she soon found herself practically in charge owing to the fact that 'the Director and all the young teachers were taken off to concentration camps'. Among her duties was the preparation of the dossiers to accompany the children on the Kindertransports. Her family's attempts to arrange their departure were meanwhile accelerated by the news that, if they did not leave soon, her father would have to return to Buchenwald, where he had been taken at the time of Kristallnacht. She herself obtained a domestic permit.

When Christel Marsh's future fiancé and his family passed through Halle from Prague in September 1938, she thought she was seeing him for the last time. She vividly recalls the ups and downs of emotion in the latter part of that year, most especially the 'traumatic' period before Munich, the relief when Chamberlain waved his piece of paper, a 'particularly awful' speech by Hitler, 'and then came Kristallnacht and that was just about the end'. By January 1939 the couple had made plans to become engaged at Easter, and for her to take a job at home in Magdeburg whilst awaiting her departure. Just before leaving Halle, however, she was denounced by a colleague to the Gestapo as an anti-Nazi and grilled by them not only about herself, but about two other colleagues who had also been identified as unsympathetic to the Nazi cause. The night before her Gestapo interview, she had torn up her membership card of the Confessional Church so that she could assert she was not a member, a 'really dreadful [action] for which I have never forgiven myself'. It is probable that her impending engagement to an Englishman (she showed the officials the formal announcement for this), coupled with the opinion expressed by the Gestapo interrogator ('You are so young and so stupid and you're only a girl'), helped her to escape imprisonment. Once in Magdeburg, it took her three months to get the necessary papers to leave, an 'appalling' time during which she was extremely torn, realising she might never see her family again. She left in mid-1939.

Renée Hubert, Hanne Norbert-Miller and Eva Sommerfreund had all emigrated to France (in 1933, 1938 and 1939 respectively). Political circumstances forced the two latter to re-emigrate, whilst educational need was Renée Hubert's prime motive in moving on. Hanne Norbert-Miller reluctantly left France in August 1939 on the advice of more far-seeing friends, when film work dried up due to the general mobilisation. In sharp contrast to her earlier attempt to enter Britain little over a year earlier, she entered with ease this time, for her family was by then established there and had included her on their visa. Renée Hubert left both France and her family for a one-year teaching appointment in Norfolk on 1 September 1939, feeling 'dreadful'. Her father was convinced that Britain looked safer for his daughter, but the uncertain future must have seemed terrifying to her. As for Eva Sommerfreund, it was the fall of the Maginot Line (one could hear the noise of the battle from Paris, she comments) that caused her to leave France in May 1940, and the

3. DEPARTURE AND ARRIVAL

extraordinary story of her roundabout journey to England is recounted below. It is no coincidence that, as the sole member of the group to have emigrated during the war, her story should be exceptional.

Besides progressively barring the Jews from their trades and professions, the Nazis sought to relieve them of their assets. Thus they gradually expropriated Jewish businesses, especially after 1935, and in a more systematic way after 1938. The owners, not surprisingly, received very little, or nothing, by way of compensation. As already noted above, the Jews also had to pay a hefty payment (the 'Sühneleistung' – literally 'atonement tax') as a punishment for the assassination of the German diplomat vom Rath, and the act of emigrating itself provided another excellent opportunity for taxation, primarily in the shape of the 'Reichfluchtssteuer' (Reich Flight Tax), levied on the property and assets of everyone who emigrated from Germany. Originally conceived in 1931 as a deterrent to emigration, it was turned by the Nazis to their own advantage, and made a sizeable contribution to the receipts of the Finance Ministry. The deliberate impoverishment of the would-be emigrants compounded their difficulties in finding countries willing to accept them – this being a necessary condition for departure – for immigrants without funds have never been an attractive proposition, especially not at a time of generalised economic difficulty such as the 1930s. Various plans to solve this problem of funds were mooted at government level, in reception lands such as Britain and also in Germany, but none came to fruition.

Aside from the tremendous psychological problems confronting individuals who were contemplating emigration, the sheer material difficulties of departure, of winding up a whole existence, became ever greater as the years progressed. We can observe this in a muted form, at second hand as it were, in the accounts of the interviewees, for it was actually their parents who had to deal with the myriad bureaucratic steps involved. Several of the group have memories of the bureaucracy surrounding departure: for instance when Margarete Hinrichsen met her parents in Bremerhaven in 1938, she recalls them sitting poring over the papers – 'Judenvermögensabgabe' (Jews' Wealth Tax) and others – 'everything had to be declared'. Eric Rose's mother had to negotiate tax clearance and exit permits by herself as her husband was caught abroad at Kristallnacht. In the event she was permitted to take all her household effects but no money. Helga Reutter vividly remembers worries over tax matters and the unpleasant circumstances surrounding the 'sale' of her father's business to someone from Bielefeld, who proceeded to cheat her father out of his firm, going as far as to throw him off the premises empty-handed when he returned from Dachau after Kristallnacht. Not surprisingly, her father never received any compensation. Once again, it is useful to divide experiences at the year 1938, after which getting travel documents, obtaining visas (obligatory before one was allowed to leave), winding up one's affairs and exporting one's possessions became not only much harder but also much more pressurised, as speed now became paramount. Dorothea Galewski, who left in April 1939, recalls not only the restriction on the amount of luggage one could take out but also the effect of the tax levied on one's belongings, which gave rise to a particular scene:

> . . . in the schoolyard children standing there scraping their shoes on the gravel to make them look old, because if you had new shoes your parents were going to have to pay a very high tax to take them out. So we had instructions to wear our new shoes to school, which normally you would not have been allowed to do, to make them look worn.

There is frequent reference in the interviews to the ten Reichsmarks that each emigrant was entitled to export from Germany. The currency law in which this figures dates from 1934 and the limit of ten Reichsmarks was the result of successive reductions of the permitted amount. An obvious strategy for getting some small benefit from cash that one was not allowed to export was to invest in portable goods: Ilse Wolff mentions new clothes, for instance. Eric Rose's mother was particularly skilful in this respect:

> She went on a sort of spending spree, because we obviously had some money which she couldn't take out of Germany and she decided to buy things – she didn't know how poor or otherwise we would be in London. She bought things she thought would be saleable in England. For instance, she bought two portable manual typewriters

3. DEPARTURE AND ARRIVAL

and a big Singer sewing-machine and quite a lot of things she wouldn't normally have bought, really to get rid of the money, to invest the money in goods.

Strategies for coping with the emigration that was to come have already been mentioned, in the shape of the English lessons taken by Ilse Wolff and Eva Pollard, and cookery classes too in the case of the latter. Others speak of having taught classes for future emigrants, Klary Friedl in beauticians' skills and Nelly Kuttner in millinery. Hanna Singer skipped a year in school in order to begin more useful subjects such as English, when it became clear that the family would have to leave.

An interesting point to emerge from the interviews is that some of the interviewees did return to Germany for short periods during the years before the war. This was usually in order to see their families (Adelheid Schweitzer, Ruth Herring, Margarete Hinrichsen and Peter Singer), whilst Hilde Ainger returned home at least once to await a new job offer. None was tempted to stay; they were confirmed in their feeling that they were much better off outside Germany. For Ruth Herring, her 1936 visit was a watershed. She had already been home before, for short periods, and had been subjected first to parental pressure to stay, and then to pressure from the authorities, who made it clear that there would be a job for her should she join the Party. Whilst in Königsberg in 1936 attending to arrangements for the printing of her doctoral thesis, she was approached by a university official to sign some papers which, she learned, would cause her 'Doktorvater' (supervisor) to be removed from his professorial Chair. She checked up on the situation, then decided to leave Königsberg the same day, not wishing to be a part of such an underhand enterprise. This crystallised her feelings towards Germany, for she now realised she no longer wished to live there, and from then on she considered herself a 'voluntary refugee'.

5. Why England?

Britain was neither a close nor an easy place for the refugees to reach nor was it always very welcoming, especially on an official level, as several historians have shown.[12] Some brief general remarks about immigration into Britain in the 1930s may serve to provide a context for the experiences of the interviewees. In 1927, visa requirements had been abolished between Great Britain and both Austria and Germany. All aliens entering for employment did, however, need to be already in possession of a work-permit from the Ministry of Labour before they arrived. It was up to the Passport Control Officers at the ports of entry to decide whether to allow aliens who arrived there from abroad 'leave to land'. If they received this, aliens might have formal conditions written into their passports, the most common being a time-limit or a restriction on employment. There was no legal right of asylum for refugees, although the state could grant this at its discretion.

In April 1933, the leaders of the Jewish community in Great Britain asked the government for temporary asylum to be granted to Jewish refugees from Germany, and in return they gave the government a written guarantee that no Jewish refugee would become a charge on public funds. They also offered to meet new arrivals, give them hospitality, support them if necessary and help them to re-emigrate rapidly. Britain was thus seen right from the start as a country of temporary refuge, in other words of transit, and not a country of settlement, which suited the British authorities also.

The Home Office decided to maintain the immigration system as it was, i.e. without visas, after April 1933, but did institute the requirement that refugees should register with the police when they reached their destination. Immediately after the Anschluss, however, the greatly increasing numbers of refugees presenting themselves at ports of entry, together with the fact that the Jewish community, overwhelmed by demands for assistance, withdrew its automatic guarantee for future immigrants, led the British authorities to reintroduce visas for both Germans and Austrians (on 2 May and 21 May 1938 respectively). This meant that the onus of selection of the refugees fell on the individual consulates abroad. The new visa procedure was much more complicated, cumbersome

12. For authoritative treatments of British refugee policy see Sherman, op. cit., Bernard Wasserstein, *Britain and the Jews of Europe 1939–1945*, London/Oxford, 1979, and Louise London (2000), op.cit.

3. DEPARTURE AND ARRIVAL

and slower – and inevitably led to a chaotic situation as consular officials struggled to cope with the new regulations. But there was some relief after Kristallnacht, when immigration policies and procedures received a long overdue overhaul and the latter were simplified. The number of prospective refugees was now, however, swelling so rapidly that the authorities in London could not cope with the caseload, and the main voluntary committees that had been set up by different bodies to aid refugees now received permission to draw up lists of people for admission, which the Home Office then approved en bloc (on the understanding both that the prospective arrivals were suitable people and that they would be maintained by the sponsoring organisations), issuing block visas to cover their entry.

This arrangement was applied to certain categories of refugee, for example children being brought to Britain on a temporary basis for educational purposes under the auspices of the Children's Inter-Aid Committee, the Movement for the Care of Children from Germany and other similar groups who, by dint of very great effort, managed to bring some ten thousand children out of Germany and Austria on the Kindertransports by the time war broke out.[13] The new block visa system also provided for the entry of 'refugee domestics', one of the very few categories still available at this stage; thanks to it many women, including several of our group, were able to gain entry to Britain when the doors were all but closed. Block visas for up to 400 persons per week were issued from January 1939, and the women taking them up no longer had to have a job already arranged before they came. As many as 14,000 women entered Britain in this category in the last year before the war: indeed, Tony Kushner points out that 'over one third of all the Jewish refugees in Britain came through the domestic service option'.[14] The third main category to benefit was that of transmigrants, those in transit to other countries, because their cases did not require such careful scrutiny, as they were expected to move on soon.

---

13. This very significant humanitarian measure covered about one in ten of the Jewish children in Germany at the time.
14. Tony Kushner, 'An Alien Occupation – Jewish Refugees and Domestic Service in Britain 1933–1948' in *Second Chance*, op. cit., p. 576.

For children arriving on the Kindertransports, a guarantee system was in operation. Guarantors had to post deposits of £50 per child (for some time, at least, although this was later abolished). In the cases of adult refugees, their sponsor or guarantor was required to put down between £50 and £100 per person. Many British Jews gave personal bonds to enable refugees to enter the country, and many non-Jews, too, responded to the public appeals that were launched both to collect money and to offer hospitality to those fleeing from Nazism.

Finally, if one was fortunate enough to fall into the 'capitalist' category, i.e. to have considerable assets in Britain, or to be able to transfer a business there (almost impossible after the Anschluss), or if one had a guaranteed income from elsewhere, entry to Britain posed little problem.

6. Early Experiences

The regulations sketched out above can be seen reflected in the experiences recounted in the interviews. The reason why several early arrivals (Hilde Ainger and Adelheid Schweitzer, for instance) entered Britain as 'students of English', even though they were really taking refuge from Nazi Germany, was because they could not obtain labour permits, as these were severely limited as a matter of government policy in view of the high levels of unemployment among the established population. Further, Adelheid Schweitzer points out that since a labour permit was tied to a specific job, one was very loath to leave any position one did obtain, however unsuitable it might be. An example of someone who genuinely came to study the language is Margarete Hinrichsen, arriving in 1937, and she recalls having to declare her funds (which came from her family). After Kristallnacht, however, when her father was killed and the family had to emigrate hastily, she engaged in part-time work. Someone reported her to the Home Office and she was called in to explain why she was contravening the rules. By the time Christel Marsh arrived in summer 1939, her English lawyer fiancé was unable to obtain any type of work-permit for her.

Several interviewees recall having the phrase 'no paid work'

3. DEPARTURE AND ARRIVAL

written into their passports as a condition of entry.[15] Peter Gellhorn, who came in September 1935, alludes to this: he was in fact able to keep afloat at first thanks to help and some string-pulling on the part of his English friends. Alfred Dörfel, too, remembers that his travel document contained the stricture 'no work, paid or unpaid', but he quickly began to do jobs for the Czech Refugee Trust Fund. As for Klary Friedl, she was soon doing housework and giving face massages. Ilse Wolff's case is particularly interesting, because she met Dr Alfred Wiener of the Jewish Central Information Office shortly after she arrived in London; his secretary was ill and so he offered her the job. Ilse Wolff had no trouble in proving that she was not displacing any English applicant for the position of his assistant and could therefore be permitted to take it up: 'I drafted the application myself to the Home Office proving that there was nobody in the whole of England who could do what I had to do, who had the German and Jewish knowledge and background and so on; and I got the permit very quickly.'

Among those interviewees entering Britain under the category of 'refugee domestic', Eva Pollard's case deserves mention here, since her cousin applied for her permit, although she could not in fact employ her. So Eva Pollard soon went to an employment agency in Finchley, where she obtained a domestic job. As far as guarantors are concerned, these are mainly discussed below, but the case of Gertrud Wengraf belongs here. Her husband managed to find:

> ... somebody who guaranteed for him, and guaranteed he would keep the family for a year. That was the way we got the visa. But he [her husband] had to write to this man saying that the guarantee was invalid and that he would not really ask him to do that [i.e. pay for the family]. It was a very dicey thing, a very frightening thing.

Eric Rose's father, a wine merchant, was given a choice by the British authorities: either come in with assets, that is, as a capitalist, or as the agent or representative of a foreign firm: 'We'll let you open an office and you can take pot luck.' Since his assets in

---

15. Once the war began, the situation altered dramatically. Manpower was suddenly urgently needed for the new tasks to hand and the refugees were then not only allowed to work for the war effort, but actively encouraged to do so.

Germany had already been seized, he entered under the second option, as did other relatives of people in the group in a similar position such as Klary Friedl's husband Ernst.

In the cases of exactly half of the group (17), they had family members, friends or acquaintances, either in Britain or on the Continent, who helped them or provided the necessary impetus, although this was not the only motivation for their choice of Britain as a destination. Of these seventeen, only six had previously visited the country themselves. Family members already established in Britain naturally afforded the easiest entrée: Ilse Wolff's brother, here since 1935, was able to find a host family to receive her and her husband when they came as penniless late arrivals, having only being allowed to leave Germany with 10 Reichsmarks. Helga Reutter's Austrian, non-Jewish fiancé preceded her by some months and obtained a domestic permit for her – his business, electrical advertising, was very new then; the English had expressed an interest in it, and the new regime in Austria, eager to further commercial contacts with England, agreed to his departure. Eva Pollard had two English connections (through marriage), and one of these was able to secure her a domestic visa. This is not, however, to suggest that it was plain sailing even for those who were fortunate enough to have connections, for in some cases it patently was not: Helga Reutter, for instance, found herself initially working for a most unsympathetic lady; and the situation of Christel Marsh was by no means easy, for she soon realised that her English parents-in-law, who had been 'very nice' to her when she came for a holiday in summer 1938, were most displeased at her arrival as a fiancée and at her subsequent marriage to their son, which made her early months 'very stressful', particularly as she had to go and live with them after her new husband was called up.

Hilde Auerbach had recently spent a year in England during the preparation of her thesis, knew the ropes and people to boot, so her choice was self-evident, as was that of Adelheid Schweitzer, who had made an English friend at an international children's gathering at Bedales School some years before and with whom she had then exchanged visits. This friend invited her to 'come over ... because it seems rather unpleasant in Germany at present'. Peter Gellhorn had

3. DEPARTURE AND ARRIVAL

met some English people at the Berlin home of Lotte Reiniger, the silhouette artist and filmmaker (although she was officially not supposed to introduce him to anyone). Gellhorn visited them in 1935 and arranged:

> 'If I write to you saying I have time for another little holiday then you know it is dangerous.'. . . Soon, a few months after, I was forbidden to do any work. I wrote [to England] and I went on working because of the money. I had to risk it. . . And immediately my friend in Ascot sent me a £5 note, which was a month's salary in those days, to help me to get away.

Nelly Kuttner was sent a domestic permit by Austrian friends in England after Kristallnacht.

Others had to reach back into the past to find an English connection, for example Elizabeth Rosenthal's mother, whose own father had assisted the Manchester Quakers when they were feeding starving children in Danzig in 1918. She now asked the group to find a family willing to receive her daughter when she saw no other way to get the child out of Germany, where they were both by then living illegally. Sometimes, especially as the situation worsened, people had to revive contacts that were all but lost: when the promised Australian visas the family had applied for were extremely slow in coming, Hanna Singer's mother, for instance, had to think of another solution, which involved tracing an Englishwoman she had known years before at school in Switzerland:

> Via some other ex-student . . . [she] managed to get in touch with this English friend . . . [who] was connected with the Jewish Board of Deputies. She was a very dynamic lady and in fact organised for my sister to come out on a nursing permit, although she was only seventeen, . . . for my brother and me to come out on the Kindertransport . . . in July 1939, and then for my mother to come out in August.

Hans Brill's father, trying to get his children out of Austria after the Anschluss and having no contacts in Britain, managed to find a scientist colleague from years before, now a recluse living in Putney and rather unwell, who agreed to vouch for the children (who never actually met him).

Whilst Peter Singer, who had no contacts in Britain, was helped by friends in Germany to prepare his departure, a more unusual arrangement was struck by the father of Erika Young, who had originally planned that his daughter should go to France to continue her education with the same order of nuns as in Vienna. The French house refused to take the young girl in 1938, considering that the situation in France 'wasn't safe', and England was then agreed upon as a second choice, although the child spoke no English. Her father was to support the few nuns left in Vienna in return for the order educating his daughter in England. The way Josephine Bruegel relates how she came to secure a visa makes it all seem very casual: a friend whom she saw on the street in Prague proposed putting her on a list for emigration to England and she was interviewed by the Quakers; when the Nazis invaded Prague, the British Consul informed her she had a visa. This may well simply reflect the fact that she was very young and carefree then; what is abundantly clear, however, is that she had had a real interest in English for some time, even before spending nine months at an English boarding-school in Prague when she was fifteen or sixteen. There is also a quite casual air in the way Lotte Berk describes her choice of England as a place of refuge. She was a rather successful modern dancer, trained by a pupil of Mary Wigman, the eminent proponent of modern German dance. Her husband, although German, had a British passport, but apparently no roots or contacts in Britain:

> We also had two studios where we were teaching. So we had to close them and what could we do? Fritz Gruber said, 'Have you got an English passport?' 'Yes.' 'Well, you go to England; you don't need a permit there.' So we were lucky. But it was still very difficult. They hadn't heard of modern ballet. They were very backward in every respect... At school we had learned the English only talked about the weather and were very backward artwise.

Family business connections enabled four of the interviewees to come to Britain. Since they could not bring out enough money to qualify as 'capitalists', three managed to obtain agencies for firms abroad: Eric Rose's father is typical: he was permitted to become the representative of a Hungarian Riesling grower ('Hungarian Riesling

3. DEPARTURE AND ARRIVAL

being completely unknown in Britain, only French and German wines [then] being consumed here'). Hanne Norbert-Miller's father was particularly prescient, registering his firm in London as early as 1936, 'so I think if he had money coming from Sweden or America, he didn't have it sent to Vienna, but to his English office'. Hans Seelig's father had obtained an agency from a Swiss firm after he had been obliged to sell his own soft-furnishing business in Mannheim; his permission to stay in England was based on this agency, whilst his personal choice was also dictated by the fact that some other family members who had fled to Britain after Kristallnacht would be able to assist him and his family in settling in.

Several of the interviewees confess to having had a particular interest in England or the English language some time before the necessity of emigration imposed itself. Eugen Brehm puts it quite simply: 'I was very pro-English. I wanted to go to England.' As an example of his interest he cites the fact that he had been able to buy the *Manchester Guardian* for some time after the 'Machtergreifung': '[It] was interesting... a breath of fresh air from the free world ... and very often I had to translate it orally for my friends and colleagues.' Ilse Wolff, too, had been very drawn to Britain: 'I just loved the idea of England and the English language.' From 1933 she had taken evening classes in English, 'because somehow I said, if I have to emigrate, I would love to go to England'. Sometimes the source of the interest is easily traced: Hanne Norbert-Miller had not only had excellent English teaching at school – her head was fanatical about English – but she had also been to England three times and spoke the language well. She describes herself as having been 'sort of fond of England' and 'completely England-orientated'. For Hilde Ainger and Adelheid Schweitzer the ostensible reason given to the British authorities for coming was to learn the language, whilst their real aim was to escape from Nazi-ruled Germany.

In the cases of Margarete Hinrichsen and Ruth Herring, on the other hand, neither of whom were refugees when they originally arrived, the prime motive for travelling to Britain was to extend their knowledge of English. Margarete Hinrichsen's parents intended it as part of an educational programme for the seventeen-year-old, which was to continue with a year in Switzerland to study French, and it would also conveniently separate her from an 'unsuitable boyfriend'; whilst Ruth Herring, although she had studied English as part of her degree, had never visited Britain, and on the advice of her professor in Königsberg attended a course in Birmingham (Woodbrooke College) upon completion of her doctorate. Renée Hubert, having studied languages at the Sorbonne, also came to improve her English in order to better her job prospects. All three young women were overtaken by events: Kristallnacht in Germany signalled for Margarete Hinrichsen the death of her father and the imperative necessity for her other close relatives to emigrate, and she chose to stay in the now familiar environment of north-west London; Ruth Herring (non-Jewish) had the chance of a job in Yorkshire after her course was over and decided to stay on in England for a while, particularly as she had nothing arranged in Germany; the war started just after Renée Hubert's arrival in Britain and kept her there longer than originally intended, until her family was able to regroup in the USA during the war.

Finally, a small number of the interviewees can be considered to have come to Britain more by chance than by design. Ernst Flesch's family, for instance, had no links with Britain, and the child came because he was offered a place on a Kindertransport. Similarly, Alfred Dörfel had no special connection with Britain, but, as a political refugee, was able to obtain a seat on a Czech Refugee Trust Fund flight when it became clear that the Nazis were about to overrun the whole of Czechoslovakia. Dorothea Galewski and her family came primarily because they obtained a six-month transit visa and they were still desperately attempting to arrange an onward visa when hostilities broke out. As a humanitarian gesture the British authorities permitted refugees in transit to stay in Britain and regularise their position at this time, so it was the outbreak of war itself that was responsible for the family's establishment in that country.

7. The journey

Approximately half of the interviewees were able to recall feelings, impressions or actual incidents relating to their journeys into exile. Not surprisingly, three of the most vivid accounts came from

3. DEPARTURE AND ARRIVAL

interviewees who made the journey as children, but without their parents: Hanna Singer, Elizabeth Rosenthal and Erika Young. Three others, Renée Hubert, Eva Sommerfreund and Hanne Norbert-Miller, already young adults, were among those for whom the journey to Britain was in fact a 'second' emigration in one way or another, and they will be treated separately.

The dominant feelings expressed range from nervousness through to fear, which naturally persisted as long as they were still in German-controlled territory. Nelly Kuttner puts this most sharply: she found herself leaving the Westbahnhof in Vienna in a sealed train, feeling all the time as if there were 'a string over [my] tummy', and her fear did not abate until she saw the first bicycle in Holland: 'It was like a miracle. . . I felt at once a different person.' Even those who flew did not escape this feeling. Eugen Brehm, on one of the Czech Trust Fund flights from Prague in January 1939, recalls: 'We were a little bit afraid because one such flight had actually had to land somewhere in Germany. But nothing happened: the plane was repaired and allowed to go to London. For diplomatic reasons the Nazis didn't interfere with the passengers.' Erika Young, flying as an unaccompanied minor from Vienna in September 1938, found herself in an 'uncomfortable situation', being unexpectedly rerouted and having to change planes three times, including once in Germany itself; all this because she happened to travel at the time of the Munich crisis.

The fact that Germany was clearly visible as one flew, planes then not flying above 5,000 feet, did little to allay refugees' fears. Others had more to fear and more to endure at the border when exiting from Germany. Christel Marsh, for instance, immediately interpreted the fact that the SS man there held her passport for a long time as evidence that he had been told that she had had to submit to Gestapo questioning at home. Lotte Berk, who (with a British passport thanks to her husband) travelled back and forth several times, partly in order to get out more of their money, was once strip-searched by the SS in Aachen. Margarete Hinrichsen was subjected to the same treatment in Bremerhaven in June 1938, where she had gone to meet her parents for their silver wedding. After several very unpleasant experiences, she was searched as she was about to return to England:

It was all frightening. I was a young girl ... and they kept on threatening concentration camp. When I was body-searched, the woman looked at my address book and there was an address of some people from Hanover who were in England now, very old friends of my mother. She looked at that address and burst into tears and she said: 'Do you know them?' I said: 'Yes, yes, sure.' So she burst into tears and said: 'For years and years I was working in their store. I had a very good job, I loved the family and when [they] left, the only thing I could do to bring up my son was this – searching Jews who are leaving the country.' So that was my farewell to Germany.

The relief felt once the border was safely negotiated, was, however, tempered by concern for those still left behind in Germany; this is neatly captured on a child's level in an anecdote recalled by Elizabeth Rosenthal, travelling with a Kindertransport: 'And then we got to the frontier. And there was one boy who spat out of the window and the others said: "No." We stopped him spitting, and I don't remember if I said it, or they said it: "We still have family in Germany, you know."'

Several of those who came as children had very positive recollections of their reception in Holland, where they variously report being greeted by the Dutch with soup, hot drinks and the like, and most of all with kindness. These uniformly positive recollections surely mirror to some degree their relief at having crossed into friendly territory. Two of the group who came as young adults had a very different reception, however, for reasons which were not clear to them: Stella Rotenberg's English visa had not yet reached Holland and she had to spend some unhappy months awaiting it; and Klary Friedl's train, coming from Prague in April 1939, was not permitted to enter Holland, so for four days the Germans held the refugees, fearful and apprehensive, in a makeshift camp with precious few facilities. Klary Friedl had the extraordinary good fortune to encounter an SS man who was unusually humane. He saw she was carrying some jewellery, covered it up and said, 'I haven't seen anything', and later even gave her an apple: 'It meant a terrific lot because we started travelling early in the morning. You had very little food, they just gave you some bread and I think margarine or

3. DEPARTURE AND ARRIVAL

something.' The other bright spot was that by chance she met her husband's best friend and they continued the journey together.

Ruth Herring, from her perspective both as a 'voluntary refugee' and as someone who considered herself quite uninformed on political matters at the time, provides us with the view from the outside, as it were:

> I became aware, even in 1934 when I travelled to England, that something happened to some passengers when the train left Germany . . . but it didn't happen to me. I realised they were Jews. I saw how they were treated by the German officials on the train. They had to get out on the platform and had to show everything. . . Somehow when they [the officials] . . . saw my then Prussian passport . . . and they realised I wasn't Jewish, all wreathed in smiles, ah, you're one of us . . . fine, and then the same people completely changing in their behaviour towards the passengers who were Jewish. . . I was wondering what was happening. I just watched it all. . . I thought, ah, that's happened because you are Jewish and are emigrating and that's your goodbye to Germany and the treatment you get. It was like a kick in your bottom.

Five further vivid snapshots from the journey warrant mention as they serve to illustrate the historical context. Transport was not always as orthodox as might on the surface appear. Walter Wolff, a child alone, 'came over . . . from Hamburg to Hull . . . on a small boat carrying a load of plums. I got pretty sick of plums by the time we landed in Hull thirty-six hours later.' Erika Young 'had to wear a tiny little silver swastika, the smallest one could get, because you had to, which I took off the moment we landed in Amsterdam or Hamburg, or wherever we landed. I took it off. I threw it away, I regret throwing it away now. It would have been interesting to have kept it.' Peter Gellhorn visited friends in Saarbrücken en route (September 1935) and 'the French Occupation Army after the last war had only just left, and the Nazi intoxication was as bad as it had been two years before in Berlin. All the pubs saying "Jews not served here" – that sort of thing'. Finally, Christel Marsh has a memory of her boat crossing in summer 1939: 'It was absolutely chock-a-block full of refugees in their fur coats although it was the middle of summer.'

(She did not regard herself as being a refugee, coming as she was to marry her English fiancé.) This ties up with Ilse Wolff's memory of clothes shopping before leaving Berlin – 'we had brand new clothing, of course, and suitcases full of a supply of stockings we were not expecting to afford for quite a while' – which gave rise to a humorous incident on arrival (see below). Refugees were no longer permitted to carry jewellery with them, and clothes were one of the few items they were still able to take.

But it is the accounts of two of those who came as young girls on Kindertransports which give the most graphic insight into their state of mind. Elizabeth Rosenthal was very eager to come to England; she even describes herself as 'dying' to go – in part a tribute to the very positive preparation for exile given at the Caputh school. She particularly recalls the sea-crossing: on the boat, the bunks; the notices in three languages which, to her delight, she could read with ease and the fear that gripped her when she read about the evacuation safety measures:

> I was absolutely convinced I would have to swim in the dark. . . I knew that I could swim very well, because I had been swimming . . . since I was a baby, before I could walk. But I didn't really like swimming in the dark and it was February. It was dark and it was cold.

She also recalls her strong desire to look after a much younger child, and the great satisfaction when she was able to do so; and finally the first glimpses of England:

> And it was so exciting, you know, to see England. It was wet, it was cold, it was raining, it was misty. It wasn't particularly attractive and there were these large expanses of wet land round Harwich. And I was so thrilled all the time. I knew it rained in England. All the geography books said it was misty and it was full of rain. So I accepted that was England.

Hanna Singer also recalls her journey, especially

> . . . going through Holland and kind ladies giving us sticky buns and lemonade. [On the boat] I shared a cabin with a girl from Rostock, and I was dying to go on the top bunk, but she was younger than me so I thought well, maybe I'd better be magnanimous, so I stayed on the bottom bunk.

3. DEPARTURE AND ARRIVAL

She vividly remembers her fear that a mistake had been made on the train to London:

> The seats were upholstered, they weren't wooden seats, and I was very worried that we might be in first class by mistake. I was also worried that we were going to Liverpool Street, because I thought we were going to London and I thought Liverpool was somewhere else.

The itineraries of Hanne Norbert-Miller, Renée Hubert and Eva Sommerfreund are more complex than the rest. It will be recalled that Hanne Norbert-Miller was working in Innsbruck at the Anschluss and was at once dismissed from her theatrical engagement:

> I was so stunned that I didn't move for a couple of days... But I could actually buy a ticket to London, get on the train. At the border they took all my money away apart from ten Marks. I didn't have a clue what would happen. Funnily enough there is a veil over the actual details. I can scarcely see myself there being interviewed... I said I'm visiting friends... And they let me get back on the train and I got out.

When she reached Dover, however, she was refused entry to Britain, the only one of our group to have had this experience. She was not nonplussed, took advice from various people she met en route, and eventually got to Paris where she gained a toehold in the film industry thanks to Austrian contacts. Meanwhile her family had emigrated to England and had included her on their visa; indeed, she even visited them in London on the strength of that, returning to work in Paris afterwards. Finally, in August 1939, when she was about to start work on another film in Paris:

> The phone rang and I was told the film had been cancelled because of general mobilisation... My friends in Paris said: 'Go to your family.' I kept saying: 'No. England refused me and France took me in' and all this idealistic claptrap. But then I realised I'd be better off in the bosom of the family.

She then entered England with no difficulties.

Renée Hubert was sixteen when Hitler took power. She and her younger sister had been prepared by their parents for a possible sudden departure, and indeed this came to pass in March/April 1933, when her parents were both put in 'Schutzhaft'. They managed to get released quickly, whereupon the family left the very same day for Zurich. The girls were told during the journey that they would never return to their house, and 'my father told me when we crossed the border that we were penniless. And we had been quite well off', she comments. She recalls it as 'inconceivable that there would be nothing left of our lives except the family', going on to describe her feelings thus: 'I was just dealing with the complete separation. I didn't really care where I was going.' (Peter Gellhorn reports a similar feeling on leaving Germany: 'I went into a complete vacuum, not knowing what would happen.') The family finally settled in Lyons in France, later moving to Paris. It was from here six years later that Renée Hubert left to go to England to improve her English (she was studying languages at the Sorbonne whilst waiting to train in social work). War was clearly imminent:

> The whole thing was awful. My father said that England was going to be safer and he advised me to go there where I had a job. Family council said I should go and then they also suggested that I take what I could, and I left with four suitcases and nowhere did I find a porter to help me. I had to change trains three times.

Eva Sommerfreund had by far the most complex journey into English exile, and it occurred in two distinct stages: first from Prague to Paris via Italy (June–September 1939), and secondly from Paris to London via the south of France, Gibraltar and Liverpool (May–July 1940), when she was expecting a child. She and her new husband made for Italy originally, because no visa was required to enter that country. They were awaiting a visa for France, which was to be procured by her mother already in Paris. After waiting two months in Milan, they proceeded to the French border, where she was not allowed to contact her mother as had been arranged:

> They [the French border officials] said: 'Do you realise the war may break out any minute. We have no room for private telephone conversations', and they wanted to send us back to Italy, but we didn't have a re-entry visa for Italy, so it would have meant Germany immediately. I refused. I absolutely refused. I said: 'You can shoot me here . . . but I'm not going back.' And there we spent many hours

3. DEPARTURE AND ARRIVAL

... actually, ten men tried to get me into the train but they couldn't manage it.

The story finally ended happily, thanks to the fact that her name was recognised (her grandfather had been very eminent), and they were allowed to enter France, even obtaining redress for the bad treatment they had received. The severe treatment first meted out at the border post had in fact been caused by some people posing as Czechs trying to enter France there earlier under false pretences.

The following May, on the fall of the Maginot Line, Eva Sommerfreund, now heavily pregnant, had to walk hundreds of miles from Paris south to Montpellier with her mother and sister to meet her husband who was serving with the Czech forces. Contrary to expectations, her pregnancy turned out to smooth the way in a quite unexpected manner, for 'in France, a woman who's expecting a baby is a holy thing, so we had help from all quarters'. When they reached the south, they came upon the Czech army and were embarked with them at Sète onto an English coal ship, 'and I cannot describe to you that feeling of happiness that we had when I saw that boat moving away from the shore'. On the ship were about 2,000 soldiers, 150 women – and no water. In Gibraltar they had to await a convoy from India. The cleanness and order on the ship they were transferred to made a deep impression on her. They finally docked at Liverpool, after various detours to avoid U-boats and mines. It had been an epic journey.

8. Arrival

Peter Gellhorn puts the problem of the hopeful refugee approaching the English coast in a nutshell when he explains: 'In those days [prior to May 1938] visas weren't necessary between England and Germany... But there was also a great risk and throughout the journey you didn't know if you would get in. The Immigration Officer in Dover or Folkestone said if you could come in or not.' It was thus with feelings of trepidation that he approached 'the white chalk cliffs rising out of the sea, still not knowing if I would get in'. His next memory is of sitting in the train, his invitation letters in his pocket, unscrutinised in the event. Hanne Norbert-Miller, by contrast, vividly recalls 'a very cool, tall, blond gentleman with a moustache who said sorry and was unapproachable'. Christel Marsh, who came late, in summer 1939, remembers that to the Immigration Officer who questioned her, her reason for coming – to get married – did not warrant more than the granting of a one-month visa: 'They thought it wasn't a good reason for being in England for more than a month.'

There is only one report of a really unpleasant encounter among the interviewees, that of Hilde Ainger, not on her first arrival in 1933 but, significantly, after a later visit home when she returned to Southampton:

> The Immigration Officer said: 'I'd like to talk to you afterwards. We're going to have our dinner first.' So I had to sit in the first-class dining-room whilst they were dining on wine and I don't know what else. Everybody else had left the boat and I knew I was going to miss the boat-train and . . . there was difficulty in taking money in either direction and I had my ticket back, my return ticket, but no other money with me. . . I was going to be met at Waterloo. . . Also, I didn't know what they were going to say to me. They – or rather the Immigration Officer, who had boozed a great deal and was absolutely horrible with me – said, all right, I could go now, but they would look at me very seriously in another three months. . . And then when I walked from the boat into the customs hall, I think it was the loneliest moment of my life. I walked down there, only my luggage was left . . . everything else had gone. There was one impatient customs official and one impatient porter waiting for me and of course they just chalked off my luggage. They were dying to get off for lunch.

A kind porter then took charge of her, however, helping her contact her friends and complete her journey, 'so it was very heartwarming', concludes Hilde Ainger.

Roughly one third of the interviewees had some help from committees in their travel and arrival arrangements, and these seem to have worked very well: the Kindertransport children were well catered for by all accounts. Only one, Elizabeth Rosenthal, was not picked up, for the good reason that her family were awaiting her in Manchester, but the adults in London would not listen to her, an

3. DEPARTURE AND ARRIVAL

eleven-year-old at the time, when she explained this. Hanna Singer, also on a Kindertransport, was picked up by her guarantor:

> We arrived in this great big hall and this lady came along. I was clutching a doll . . . which I named Evelyn because I thought it was madly English and this lady came along and said: 'I'm your Aunt Mary.' She'd come to collect us. She said: 'Your Uncle Alfred is still at the office.' She drove us off and deposited us at some little Lyons' café and I think she ordered fried eggs for us and departed. We were sitting there with all this English going on around us.

Guarantors who did not know the refugees beforehand, when they are evoked, seem on the whole to have been adequate, if somewhat 'semi-detached'. The one who particularly sticks in the mind is 'this English rich old lady, ill. . .' from Oxted, Surrey, who vouched for Stella Rotenberg when she was in difficulties with her entry into Britain, and said to her quite simply when she arrived after some difficult months in Holland in a somewhat sorry state ('I was very down at heel. . . I must have looked quite wretched'): 'To you it happened today; it might happen to us tomorrow.' The only case where the situation appears to have been less than satisfactory was that of Hans Brill. His father found as guarantor a former colleague who in fact suffered from radium sickness and lived as a recluse in Putney. He guaranteed for the three Brill children to enter Britain in 1938. Hans aged eight was put 'in a sort of orphanage place backing onto Richmond Park', whilst his sisters were placed in families and were to attend local schools. There seems to have been no adult in charge in the orphanage: 'we were entirely looked after by older refugee girls', and his sisters 'were used as skivvies' by their host families.

Only one interviewee recalls a total lack of communication with the person meeting her: Erika Young, on her way to a convent school in Worthing, was met by a Quaker lady on her arrival in Croydon – and found that they had no common language. Although she was clearly a very self-possessed child, she was temporarily knocked off balance by this event, coupled with the awful impression she gained of London from the train, and she remembers having her only bout of weeping the following morning.

Another example of initial help from an organisation is provided by Nelly Kuttner. As she arrived three weeks before her job was to begin, she was given lodging at the Jews' Temporary Shelter in Mansell Street, Aldgate, which she recalls most graphically to this day:

> We arrived, all the people from Vienna, everybody arrived with a little piece of paper saying where we should go, and my friend and I, we had no idea, but we were very lucky. The Jewish Committee always had a man at the station to collect people if they hadn't got an address to go to. And not only that man, I had an uncle . . . a very young man, already here in London. . . He came to the station to pick me up, so of all those people I was the one person who had someone come to pick me up. [The man from the Committee] said: 'Don't you worry, you will have a home.' We were accepted in that office [the Jews' Temporary Shelter], and the man was nice. We were made very welcome. They were very good to us. . . He said: 'It's late, but I am sure you will get something to eat.'. . . I remember a hall with a very long table. You know, I can see the table. . . A hot meal we got, but before it started. . . I became sick at the table. I felt so awful. It was all the reaction.

Others who specifically mention being aided by the Jewish community include Peter Singer, who was placed at the Rudolf Steiner School at Kings' Langley with the support of the West London Synagogue Committee, and Mimi Glover, who appears to have spent some nights at a Jewish hostel in the Commercial Road on arrival for, like Nelly Kuttner, she came a little before her job was to start. Ernst Flesch, on a Kindertransport from Vienna, spent his first three days in England in the flat of a Miss Heineman in Swiss Cottage, which was a transit point for the children before they were sent to their ultimate destination, in his case a Jewish orphanage in Glasgow.

As far as those coming from Czechoslovakia were concerned, they were in a considerably stronger position than the German refugees – as Josephine Bruegel puts it: 'We were much luckier than the German refugees' – thanks to the existence of the Czech Refugee Trust Fund whose foundation she explains thus:

> The CRTF was founded to paper over the sins of the English for having sold Czechoslovakia out the way they did. It was a special

3. DEPARTURE AND ARRIVAL

thing. It was really first and foremost for the support of the Sudeten Germans, political émigrés, who were mostly non-Jewish. And there were thousands of them.

The main advantages she sums up thus: 'Support was assured, and we had a right to that support... I had no difficulties at all.' Eugen Brehm who, it will be recalled, also came with the CRTF, but as a political refugee, explains how they were not only lodged in a boarding-house on arrival, but also found more permanent accommodation through the good offices of the Fund: 'Many people in this country were shocked by what had happened and... offered to take a refugee for a fortnight, for a week, for a month or so.' Whilst at the boarding-house, he was given a postcard with an invitation to stay with an Englishwoman in Hampstead, who ended up becoming a lifelong friend.

For Eva Sommerfreund, also originally from Prague, who reached London in 1940 after her extraordinary itinerary from Paris, arrival at a reception point for refugees at Empress Hall, Earls Court was the straw which broke the camel's back:

> It was like a circus, you know, with the arena at the bottom, it was a refugee camp... We came in at the top at 11 o'clock at night and I was worn out, terribly hungry and thirsty, and far at the bottom in the arena I saw tables with white tablecloths and things on it and I didn't speak English. My mother did, but we didn't, not really. And I know I understood that a nurse asked me if I wanted tea and sandwiches, and she brought me a cup of tea with milk, which was a terrible thing for me because we only had that when we were ill [otherwise they drank lemon tea]... And the sandwich was of white bread with breakfast sausage in it. You know, we were very spoiled for sausages and things like that, the Czechs, and when I saw this tea and bit into this sandwich, for the first time in two months I burst into tears, and of course everyone laughed then; when you're safe, you cry.

After one night they were put in the charge of the Czech Red Cross, who found them a room, with meals provided by none other than a Hungarian refugee. The following morning, Eva Sommerfreund summed up her feelings as she gazed out of the window:

> The sun was shining... and I saw a soldier walking with obviously his wife and a pram. It was so quiet, the sun was shining and I kept on thinking, don't they know what is happening in Europe? Don't they know there is a war? You know, it was so peaceful, quiet, no noise, no air-raids... I was delighted, but of course worried because I knew where I had come from it looked totally different.

Another example of an incongruous situation experienced by the refugees newly disembarked from continental Europe, but on a lighter level this time, is Ilse Wolff's account of her arrival with her husband in London. Her brother, already in England, had arranged for a family to invite them, as they had no work permits:

> They [the family] looked very British, very casually dressed, and expected these poor refugees to arrive. And out came two elegant people, dressed from head to foot in new clothing, with new suitcases. Afterwards we laughed a lot about this first encounter, but we were not what they expected, and they were not what we expected. But they were wonderful people.

Renée Hubert's arrival in the small town of Downham Market in Norfolk turned out to be rather dramatic, as she travelled literally on the eve of the outbreak of the war:

> I had to change trains three times and finally got to Downham Market and found the Headmaster. He said: 'I don't know whether I can pay you or can do anything because all connections and everything has changed now. Nothing is like it was before.' Then I went to the place where I had rented a room by mail and she [the landlady] was convinced I wouldn't come and she had taken in refugees. But eventually things worked out, at least for a few months.

But Klary Friedl's arrival was even romantic, for her husband had travelled several weeks ahead from Prague and she found him awaiting her at the station with a flower in his hand, although the train arrived four days later than scheduled.

Until they arrived in Britain, the main energies of the interviewees and often of their families had been channelled into arranging for their emigration and dealing with the psychological pressures attendant on their daily lives in Germany, Austria and Czechoslovakia.

3. DEPARTURE AND ARRIVAL

Now that they had been safely admitted into a country they believed would be more sympathetic, a new series of challenges faced them: learning to live in a very different society, and one, moreover, that was not economically flourishing; adapting to much less comfortable circumstances than those to which they had been accustomed; learning to operate in a different language (which they mostly knew only imperfectly); and, for some, taking on new types of work, often far below their previous social status. Furthermore, they were counselled on all sides to make themselves as inconspicuous as possible; and they encountered much ignorance about the political situation in their countries.

Nevertheless, they had the advantage of youth and the stimulus that a new country of necessity provides to meet those challenges, and they were all more or less ready to forge an existence in Britain, at least temporarily. That they were most successful in this endeavour – so much so that, with one exception, they decided to remain in Britain – is amply demonstrated in the chapters that follow.

CHAPTER FOUR

Everyday Life in Prewar and Wartime Britain

Stefan Howald and Irene Wells

'I don't know how I managed it, but I did'

Everyday life is a vast and somewhat vaguely defined area. In this chapter we will concentrate on eight specific subjects selected from it. The first three sections deal with basic needs: employment and jobs; accommodation and rents; earnings and standard of living. Sections four to eight probe some aspects which helped the refugees to constitute a new symbolic framework for their lives: education and language; food and cooking; marriage and children; politics and political experience; English peculiarities and leisure. Section nine, dealing with the question of social contacts, prepares the ground for the following chapters on problems of integration.

1. Employment and jobs

'They didn't pay me enough, and I went to somebody else'

When the first refugees arrived in 1933/34, Britain was struggling out of its economic depression. In 1935 industrial production was already 10% higher than in 1929. Although wages had deteriorated by 3%, the cost of living had fallen even more, by 13%. Long-term unemployment, especially in certain heavily depressed areas, was a devastating fate for many families. Nevertheless the labour market was expanding modestly.

Those refugees who could not rely on money or assets that they had brought with them were not at first able to profit from this economic recovery. Normally, refugees were not allowed to work, except in domestic or agricultural occupations. This was in line with British immigration policies over the previous hundred years, which had tried to confine the mass of immigrants to low-paid jobs. There

4. LIFE IN PREWAR AND WARTIME BRITAIN

was scope for relaxing the rules in individual cases, but in general the situation changed only with the outbreak of war.

As we have seen in the previous chapter, many of the women refugees came to England on domestic visas; and jobs as domestic servants were often the only possibility of earning money. There existed a baffling misconception on the part of many potential employers, as Gertrud Wengraf recalls:

> A lot of people rang up this Austrian Self-Aid, they had heard about it, and they wanted a housemaid or a butler or something else, but when they heard they had to pay those people, they were very surprised. They thought, 'They ought to be glad to get out of their country. And have a house and a roof over their heads. Pay them?' So lots of people put their phone down and said, no, I don't want them.

As the refugees had to accept the first employment they could find, negative experiences were not uncommon. Hilde Ainger travelled to Bristol to meet her employer and was nervously warned by her predecessor of the difficulties of the job. Rightly so, she thought afterwards:

> There was a young mother with a baby, her husband was in the Navy, she was lonely, and her parents, who had come from Jamaica, lived there and expected me to wait on them the way their servants did in the Caribbean. Everything was left all over the place, I have never seen anything like it. I got up at six to pick up the jigsaws and the embroidery and so on, it was unbelievable . . . my employer was absolutely appalling, she treated me abominably.

Similar stories are told by Gertrud Wengraf, Helga Reutter, Klary Friedl and Mimi Glover. It was not easy to come to terms with such setbacks. Eva Pollard's narrative is typical in its way of structuring this sobering experience. Her first job was clearly very demanding: she had to get up at seven o'clock, and to perform tasks to which she was not only quite unaccustomed, but which were also completely unknown to her from Germany, for instance 'to stoke a fire or light a boiler, or cook some bread-and-butter pudding'. There were psychologically disturbing moments, too, as when the small son of her employers called her 'you Hitler' and threatened her with a knife. At first, she felt that there was no real cause to complain, because nothing else mattered but that one had saved one's life and those of one's relatives. But when her employer moved to a summer residence, the situation deteriorated further. The workload grew; most of all she was hurt by the thoughtless and uncaring attitude. She had to accompany the family to the beach with a hamper, but was not allowed to go for a swim herself and had to wait on the family for the whole day. Her second employer was more friendly, but the working conditions were even worse since they lived in a big house in the country with no amenities whatsoever, and in complete social isolation.

Walter Wolff's mother encountered similar experiences. Although a good housekeeper, she was nevertheless not used to hard domestic work. She endured it in order to be able to stay near her children. Again, what stuck most in the memory were unfeeling, uncaring episodes, as Wolff recalls:

> Her first Christmas in England with the family – the family decided that she was not to be invited to have Christmas dinner with them, and could have her turkey and sprouts in the kitchen. The gentleman of the house pushed a glass of champagne through the hatch and said, 'I wish you a Happy Christmas', and that was that.

Nelly Kuttner also suffered very bad treatment from her first employer. Once again, a seemingly minute detail is recalled most vividly: every morning she had to bring out cushions for her employer's garden swing from a shed and put them away again in the evening. After the Blitz, when the family was evacuated to the countryside, her employer made her stay behind in the empty house. When she left it for two days, fearful of bombs, he refused to write her the reference she desperately needed for a new job. On her return to collect her belongings, she experienced a severe humiliation:

> The message was, I was allowed to pack my luggage, but if I did not scrub the floor in my room, I was not allowed to take my luggage away. The cook handed me the bucket, the brush and the soap, and Mrs Myers said I had to kneel down. At that moment, I was

4. LIFE IN PREWAR AND WARTIME BRITAIN

thinking, under the Nazis I escaped from kneeling down to wash the pavement, and here I have to wash the floor.

Common exploitation of servants was intensified by the particularly vulnerable status of the refugees. Disturbingly, some of the most stinging remarks where employers are concerned are applied to members of the Anglo-Jewish community. Eva Pollard refers to this fact several times: 'My sister, she was in an English family, unfortunately a Jewish family, and they starved her.' Helga Reutter mentions the cold attitude of English Jews towards the new refugees from Central Europe and relates it to the former's different social and cultural background. Nelly Kuttner's employers, mentioned above, were also Jewish.

For quite a few, domestic jobs were only the starting-point. Helga Reutter started as a cleaner, then moved into tailoring and worked in precarious circumstances in her father's small firm; she kept working to augment the family income until 1960, when her husband was promoted to the position of managing director in his firm and they at last felt comfortable. Hilde Auerbach, after some initial au pair jobs, managed to move into teaching. Dorothea Galewski recounts with some irony the job at the Girl Guide Headquarters which she was able to obtain in 1942 after persistent efforts:

> I got a job as a filing-clerk, junior filing-clerk, at the princely salary of one pound a week... I stayed there for about three years and I made vast progress in that time, because I became the junior secretary of the secretary of the general secretary, and by the time I left I was earning the even more princely sum of three pounds a week, and I was extremely proud of this.

Even refugees with a special skill did not find many better opportunities. Eva Sommerfreund began in a small firm, run by fellow refugees from Vienna, to whom she was recommended as a handweaver of considerable experience. But 'they didn't pay me enough and I went then to somebody else'. Refugees with professional qualifications or experience sometimes fared even worse. Stella Rotenberg, who had studied medicine, started work in England as a nurse, although the work was extremely hard. On the other hand, her later job as a pharmaceutical assistant was very boring. In this case, exploitation was experienced more psychologically than materially: the wife of her employer thought she should wear a cap and a uniform. Lotte Berk, in Germany a talented modern dancer, underwent some embarrassing experiences when looking for a job as a model:

> The professor, or the director, or whoever it was, said, 'Yes, are you a professional model?' 'Oh yes, yes', I said. So he said, 'Do you do nude?' And I hate nude, but I said, 'Oh yes'. Because I had to feed a child. And he said, 'You can start tomorrow'. So I started, two shillings an hour, one could do four hours, that was eight shillings, you could feed a family a day with that. But I was so nervous to be in the nude, hating it, that cold sweat broke out, and the director came up again and said, 'You're not a professional model'. 'No, I'm not, I need the job, I'm a refugee.' And he said, 'Put your clothes on, you're interesting enough, and sit for the wealthy', and that's what I did.

One of the few career paths open to the refugees was in teaching. Ruth Herring, already established in England as a German teacher before her conscious decision to leave Germany for good, was able to obtain a secure position. At the outbreak of war, however, she lost her job and was interned (alone among the women we interviewed). Whilst in internment, she was given the opportunity to start classes and, after her release, she returned to teaching through a network of professional and personal acquaintances. Renée Hubert was able to continue working as a French teacher without interruption even during the war. Others followed her into the teaching profession, principally after the war, among them Ernst Flesch, Hanna Singer and Hans Seelig.

For most of the men who were already planning to build new careers, war and internment meant a sharp rupture. Peter Gellhorn was in the process of becoming integrated into English musical culture, and in 1939 was able to conduct his first opera. Shortly afterwards, he was interned and later did war work in a factory. It was only after the war that he was able to resume his musical career. Peter Singer was unable to begin his studies because of the war and was instead sent to a farm. Soon, however, he managed to take up an apprenticeship in a mechanical engineering firm. Alfred Dörfel, who worked

4. LIFE IN PREWAR AND WARTIME BRITAIN

for the Czech Refugee Trust Fund, was deported to Canada; and Peter Johnson's work as a furrier and fur trader was cut short by his deportation to Australia.

Somewhat ironically, the war actually improved the professional situation of others, not only because of the chance to do war work in factories and the general shortage of labour when so many men were in the forces, but also because it created new opportunities and demands. Towards the end of 1939 Eugen Brehm applied for a post at the newly created BBC Monitoring Service and was appointed as a German Monitor. There was a short break because of his internment; but the BBC succeeded in having him released from internment quite quickly, and gave him his job back and he remained in the Service for the next forty years, rising to become Assistant Head of the Reception Department. Hanne Norbert-Miller, who had scraped a living from some poorly paid acting parts within refugee theatre, was hired by the BBC as well:

> All the actors did quite a lot of freelance work at the BBC from 1940... Politically aware people were interested in us. Richard Crossman, I think, told whatever part of the Foreign Office it was about us and we all went for an audition. There were all these dramatised features. They needed a lot of voices, a lot of actors. From 1940 onwards we were really quite busy at the BBC.

Ilse Wolff was able to argue successfully that, because of her previous work in Germany, she was uniquely qualified for the position she was being offered at the Wiener Library. The library soon became an important source of material for the BBC and for government propaganda output in general. These early successes contrast sharply with the experiences of other refugees. Whereas Hanne Norbert-Miller found work with the BBC as an announcer, this was not possible for Lotte Berk as a dancer. She lived very precariously for several years, due both to lack of opportunities and, as she concedes, out of choice.

An analysis of the professions in which the refugees worked for the greater part of their working lives or in which they worked last (in the case of women who stopped working for family reasons) shows that they were concentrated in a limited number of areas:

eight were in teaching and education, seven in domestic and similar jobs, five in publishing, journalism and the media, six in clothing, textiles and leather goods, four in the medical, pharmaceutical and nursing professions, three in the arts and architecture, and one in the travel business. We have already referred to the high proportion of domestic and teaching jobs undertaken by our interviewees (the former exclusively by women). In the industrial sphere, textiles and clothing are strongly represented, to which can be added some jobs in the chemical and leather goods sectors. This reflects the origins of a number of the refugees. Further important areas are publishing, medical care and the arts. In the industrial sector we find manual workers as well as entrepreneurs who owned their own businesses, itself a more or less direct reflection of the different social and economic backgrounds of the refugees.

It is suggested from our sample of interviewees that men could, after some initial difficulties, find jobs for life. Eight had jobs in the same industry or profession for some thirty years: Alec Armstrong, Eugen Brehm, Alfred Dörfel, Peter Gellhorn, Peter Johnson, Eric Rose, Peter Singer and Walter Wolff. The only exceptions are Ernst Flesch, who left photography for teaching, and Hans Brill, who made the radical transition from naval officer to librarian and lecturer in art.

The situation for women was different; their path was frequently more chequered. There are some who had come to England well before the war or had previous connections, for instance Ruth Herring, who had been a teacher and could resume her career after internment, or Erika Young, who obtained her first job as a teacher through her school. There are some who worked part-time in their chosen occupation for many years, for instance Nelly Kuttner. There are also those who secured a long-term job, for instance Ilse Wolff. There are others who started in a job to which they could return after their children had grown up, for instance Hanna Singer. There are some who qualified for new jobs, for instance Dorothea Galewski. And there are a considerable number who started work in odd jobs and ended by supporting the businesses and professional success of their husbands (Klary Friedl, Mimi Glover, Christel Marsh, Eva Pollard, Helga Reutter, Stella Rotenberg and Gertrud Wengraf).

4. LIFE IN PREWAR AND WARTIME BRITAIN

On the whole, women appear to have been more ingenious than men in adapting to new situations and in changing their choice of professional career. Hilde Ainger discovered her abilities as a cook and a manager, administering the small budget of a school and developing cooking 'into a fine art'. Klary Friedl started making cheese when her husband lost his business at the outbreak of war. For a while this provided them with their main source of income, supplying customers as distinguished as Marks & Spencer and Fortnum & Mason; the business only collapsed with the introduction of food rationing. At one stage Josephine Bruegel earned some money by cooking for other refugees in a boarding-house. There is nothing comparable in the life stories of the male interviewees. Hilde Ainger describes the feeling of inventing new careers and new identities: 'Occasionally, when I think back, I feel I've lived about ten different lives.'

However, several of our interviewees are ambivalent concerning the flexibility demanded of them. On the one hand, it was traditionally expected of women to cope better in such circumstances, and they sometimes had to fall back on traditional women's work. The harsh fate of Erika Young's mother is the best example:

> She was never good at languages, so her English was never terribly good, but she had gone to classes to learn to type and to do bookkeeping; she was good at figures. But before she did that she got a job in one of the sweat factories in Soho making artificial flowers, making buttonholes, finishing. She knew nothing whatever about sewing because... she was very, very short-sighted... But she was also very practical, so she managed. She said she had to ask people to tell her how to hold scissors and then she held them up to her eyes, like that, [to see] what she had to sew.

On the other hand, there were opportunities and challenging changes as well. Adelheid Schweitzer managed to adapt to freelance journalistic work in a news agency in Red Lion Square, not far from Fleet Street. Her account provides a glimpse into a world of journalism which is long gone:

> My job was to go and interview people, all sorts of people, write it up, get them to sign it, and it was then sold as an original article by that

person. It makes you laugh, really. I don't know how I managed this, but I did.

A fairly typical experience is that of Josephine Bruegel. She had studied medicine in Prague, but had been prevented from finishing her studies. After arriving in London in 1939, she worked as an au pair, and later in a hospital in a poor area in the Docklands. After this demanding job, she spent a short period earning pocket money by cooking meals in a boarding-house and selling them for sixpence. When she married, she started studying again and was awarded her medical degree in 1942. She worked for six months until her son was born. Returning to Prague after the war, she and her husband encountered difficulties with the newly-installed Communist regime; but in 1948 she began a successful new medical career back in Britain. This interrupted, delayed career, with its twists and turns, was caused by a combination of her situation as a refugee and as a woman.

Some of our interviewees remember discrimination because of anti-semitism. Hilde Ainger's employer declined to engage a cook through Bloomsbury House (where the refugee aid organisations were located), and told her: 'I couldn't really employ more than one Jew.' Adelheid Schweitzer asked the father of her friend, who had acted as guarantor for her and was head of the famous tea firm Brooke Bond, for a job: 'And he said: "Why don't you go to your own people?". . . I think he meant his competitors, the Lyons.' Anti-semitism recurred when she worked in an engineering firm in Leeds and had a fearful row with her superior. But she was able to keep her job and even to get her father-in-law a job in the same firm because the owner prided himself on being an eccentric. A similar account from the period after the war is given by Eric Rose, who insists that his early career in the textile industry in Lancashire was affected by anti-semitism. Other incidents of discrimination had different causes: Mimi Glover, for instance, once quit a domestic job when her employer made advances to her; Alec Armstrong was not allowed to join the Royal Institute of British Architects because his German qualification was not accepted; and Hans Seelig encountered difficulties in getting into Oxford because he did not come from a public school – a handicap obviously not unique to refugees. In most

4. LIFE IN PREWAR AND WARTIME BRITAIN

cases, however, these setbacks were short-lived. After the war, the refugees began to build up successful careers, as will be seen below in Chapter Eight.

2. Accommodation and rents

'We called it the Black Hole of Calcutta, but it was wonderful'

The types of accommodation secured immediately after arrival in England have been mentioned in Chapter Three. After the first few days, or even weeks, the picture becomes more differentiated. In some cases the refugee was put up by the person or family who had supported his or her application for entry to Great Britain; in others, the refugee had to find a boarding-house, mostly with the aid of charities; a few of the refugees with greater financial resources were able to rent a room or a flat. Alfred Dörfel offers a vivid description of the boarding-houses in which those supported by the Czech Refugee Trust Fund were housed:

> They were usually run by elderly spinsters and Irish families, and they were very primitive and very simple. All along the street, and this street doesn't exist any more, it's all rebuilt, there were all little boarding-house signs out, 'Bed & Breakfast 1/9d, 2/3d' . . . we had bed and breakfast for one night, and most of them were boarded there for two shillings and five pence for some nights before they were dispersed.

Eugen Brehm, an independent Socialist fervently opposed to the Communists, declined to go into Communist-controlled accommodation and sought private hospitality:

> A few days after our arrival [in February 1939] Heinz Schmidt [leader of the German Communist group within the Czech Refugee Trust Fund] threw a postcard at me, I'll never forget that, it nearly fell into my cornflakes or whatever it was we had for our breakfast: 'There's your hospitality.' And that was an invitation from a Mrs Kirstin Mary Goodman in Hampstead, prepared to take a married couple for four weeks, which was a very decisive and again incredibly lucky turning in our life. . . Kirstin kept us till the outbreak of war.

But hospitality could create its own problems. Space was sometimes quite cramped and this occasionally led to emotional difficulties. Although, as Ilse Wolff recalls, their host had vacated their best bedroom for her and her husband, it was a relief for them when they finally found their own accommodation. On the whole, mobility was high, especially in the first years after arrival, and then again, inevitably, after the outbreak of war, when some of the refugees were bombed out of their homes. Christel Marsh moved four times between June and December 1939; Klary Friedl moved from Camden Town to Golders Green and then to Kilburn in the first few months. Peter Johnson lived in four different boarding-houses in the first few years. The same is true of Stella Rotenberg, who moved four times in the first three years, and of Helga Reutter, who at first moved when she changed domestic jobs and then followed her husband, who had joined the Pioneer Corps. The most important criteria determining the search for accommodation were money and/or a job.

For women on a domestic visa, the situation was quite clear-cut. They were dependent on their employers. Hilde Ainger started in 'a box room'. Eva Pollard recalls her first job in a house with a 'nice room which overlooked the garden', but she could not use it during the day; she had to get up at seven o'clock in the morning and was not allowed to return to her room till ten o'clock in the evening. Helga Reutter's first employer, who lived in a big house in Golders Green, made her sleep outside the house in a 'cold cubicle'. Others had better experiences, and after some time the network of friends and colleagues began to function, so that both Helga Reutter and Hilde Ainger could move on to better employers and accommodation.

Some women who did not arrive on domestic visas had to survive on benefits. Erika Young recalls that her mother received sixteen shillings a week to live on, out of which she had to pay ten shillings for a room in Brixton. She was one of the few who lived in south London, and her rent, although barely affordable for her, seems to have been cheaper than most of the rents in north London. Adelheid Schweitzer recalls: 'So I lived in numerous digs. . . If you had partial board, breakfast and dinner, you paid something like twenty-seven shillings and sixpence a week.' Peter Johnson started in a Contin-

4. LIFE IN PREWAR AND WARTIME BRITAIN

ental boarding-house at two guineas a week; later he paid only thirty shillings in an English one. Lotte Berk remembers that her first flat in Sussex Gardens, although consisting of only one room, cost two pounds and ten shillings, without any meals.

Occasionally it was not the money that posed the biggest problem. Stella Rotenberg, who could rely on the wages her husband earned in the British Army, nevertheless felt alienated: 'Living as a subtenant was terrible, it made me ill... I was fifty before I got my own roof over my head, no, before I even got my own flat.' A room of one's own did indeed have its own rewards, as Hanna Singer explains. She lived with her mother in a room at the top of a house:

> Well, you shared the bathroom on the floor below... There was a sink which was also a sort of washbasin, and there was a little cooker that you could do boiled cake in, and this was tremendous. It was just one room, a tiny window looking onto a wall, and we called it the Black Hole of Calcutta, but it was wonderful.

Others were rather more comfortable. Ruth Herring (not a refugee at the time, it will be recalled) came originally as a student to a Quaker college where she could board; Peter Gellhorn was able to live and study at Toynbee Hall, the original Universities Settlement in Commercial Road in the East End of London. As soon as one found a reasonable job, other possibilities opened up. Ilse Wolff and her husband were quickly able to rent a flat, and after a year, even during the war, they could move to a bigger flat. When Hanne Norbert-Miller was taken on as a member of staff by the BBC, she took a flat in East Molesey, near Hampton Court. This two-roomed furnished flat cost nearly sixteen pounds a month, the most expensive of all the rents we have been able to establish and quite exceptional for the wartime period. In due course, the situation improved for most of the refugees, although accommodation sometimes remained cramped.

The rent they paid and the size of the accommodation it bought them divided the refugees somewhat along social lines. But there was a uniting bond. The geographical location they chose to live in was predetermined by social and family connections. London was obviously the main place to stay, although some of our interviewees lived in other parts of the country, and there was a sprinkling in the countryside during the war. In London, only one, Mimi Glover, first stayed very briefly in the East End. The majority of the refugees moved directly to the traditional areas of Jewish settlement in north-west London: Golders Green, Maida Vale, West Hampstead. A notable exception was Hans Seelig whose parents deliberately chose to live in other London areas, as he did himself. The few who lived in south London, for instance Erika Young's mother, were often non-Jews.

Simply acquiring a roof over one's head sometimes exhausted all one's financial resources. Eva Pollard gives a lively description of the shortage of furniture she had to cope with:

> We had a tiny little flat . . . a room, and we had no furniture at all. A cousin of mine gave us a divan which was the only thing, and for a wedding present we got from an aunt of Walter's a bridge table, which we still have and which we still use. That was our only table, because we could fold it, because there wasn't room for a table. Walter slept on a deck-chair, but then we had a camping chair, which was a little bit more comfortable. . . Cutlery – we didn't have one piece – we bought at Woolworths, for sixpence, that was the highest amount you could spend. But I remember that Walter was disgusted, because the coconut mat to wipe your feet on, outside the flat, was already eight pence, which was the first inflationary mat.

Adelheid Schweitzer characterises the different phases of accommodation and the concomitant changes of mood. At first she had lived with her husband in a room in St John's Wood:

> . . . in the very respectable house where the landlady let several rooms. It was inhabited by three or four different tenants, and herself and her husband on the ground floor. It was also inhabited by various flourishing families of mice who came out of the gas fire connection and ran round the room. I suppose that cost about two pounds; there was no food with it. It had a little gas cooker in a cupboard. It had running cold water in the basin, and a shared bathroom with a geyser across the landing.

Nevertheless, she did not feel that she and her husband were living an impoverished life: 'We had enough to eat, we had a bed.' There again, every improvement was welcome and took on a psychological significance:

4. LIFE IN PREWAR AND WARTIME BRITAIN

By that time we were married. We had a little flat in Wembley Park. My parents had sent furniture, enough to furnish a two-and-a-half room flat, which was such luxury after years in digs, and that was on the exhibition ground in Wembley. We had, believe it or not, central heating and the rent was twenty-seven shillings and sixpence a week... It was paradise, absolute paradise.

3. Earnings and standard of living

'So you really looked after each penny'

Many of the recollections are supported by figures. Wages and rents in particular are recalled exactly after some fifty or sixty years. Wages of one pound per week were not uncommon, compared with an average weekly wage of some two pounds thirteen shillings in 1938, rising to some four pounds sixteen shillings in 1945. Josephine Bruegel suggests, though somewhat uncertainly, that for her very demanding job as a nurse in the East End she earned only one pound a month and had only one free day per month. Hilde Ainger had to be content in her first job 'with a little pocket money' of about five shillings a week, and only when she received her labour permit did she get a wage of fifteen shillings a week. Christel Marsh started as an au pair at fifteen shillings plus board and lodging. Mimi Glover's first employer also paid her fifteen shillings a week plus board and lodging; the next family paid one pound, and in 1940 she got another job at thirty shillings. Erika Young's mother, who had started on benefit at sixteen shillings a week, worked in a sweat-shop in 1940, earning thirty shillings. Margarete Hinrichsen earned one shilling an hour as a charwoman; from this one has to deduct her fares to the different locations. Taking into account the small number of hours worked, her weekly earnings came to approximately one pound. Sometimes even that amount of money was not forthcoming, as in the case of Mimi Glover:

> I was homeless, and I went to this aunt who let me sleep in an attic... There was only wood on the floor and I had only one blanket, but you know, in those days, you could buy a pound of jam for sixpence,

and then I bought some bread which was even cheaper, and that is how I lived.

It is generally agreed that a couple needed some three pounds per week to survive in the late 1930s, and a single person nearly two. Nelly Kuttner received one pound from the Jewish Refugees Committee and thought it quite a lot; but this obviously reflects the fact that it was a gratefully accepted benefit and does not mean that she found the amount sufficient for all her expenses. Adelheid Schweitzer explains:

> You couldn't manage on thirty shillings. When I was first starting to work and I had earned my first thirty shillings, I thought, 'Wonderful, what shall I do with it? Buy a new bathing-costume'. And then I suddenly realised it was only two shillings and sixpence more than what it cost me to live a week, without fares. I didn't buy a bathing-costume.

Walter Wolff earned even less during the war. A strict financial regime was necessary:

> My salary in 1942 was one pound a week, which even in those days was not very much money. And I seem to remember that I gave ten shillings to my mother towards my keep and had to live on the other ten shillings for everything else. I can assure you, it was very little money, some of which I spent on going to concerts and theatres, to my great amazement. I don't even know how I managed to do it.

Elizabeth Rosenthal mirrors this experience in similar words. Still at school, she lived with her mother in a small room: 'My mother went to work and she had one pound a week. The rent was nine shillings and sixpence and the rest was to live on. And we managed. I don't know how my mother managed, but we managed.' Helga Reutter began making clothes and earned thirty-five shillings as a dressmaker. As her husband was in the army, she got another ten shillings army allowance. But even then, she recalls, she could only survive because she saved money by making her own clothes. The difficulty of meeting special expenses also dogged Renée Hubert:

> I had enough to eat and I could occasionally buy whatever my personal needs were. At the beginning, I remember, at Downham

4. LIFE IN PREWAR AND WARTIME BRITAIN

Market, I was really very, very poor, and my only coat fell to pieces in the middle of the winter. It was very difficult. I walked all over London to find a coat for which I had enough money. It was just incredible.

Margarete Hinrichsen, who did not feel that she was badly off, remembers nevertheless that buying a pair of shoes for twenty-five shillings was the 'height of extravagance'. One had to save money whenever possible. Some anecdotal evidence also illustrates the everyday struggle, for example from Eva Pollard:

We had for instance friends in Golders Green, beyond there, near Hoop Lane, and we lived beyond Swiss Cottage, so when we went to visit them – of course, you brought your own sandwiches and everything – we took the bus up to Childs Hill; that I think was the fare stage . . . and then we walked the next fare stage, because you saved a penny each. . . On the way back, of course, we did the same. So you really looked after each penny, but that was normal. Everybody had to do it.

A similar story is told by Nelly Kuttner, who did not even have the money for the bus from Charing Cross to Hammersmith. At the end of the week Elizabeth Rosenthal's mother could not afford to take the tram to the factory where she worked, and had to ask for credit in the workers' canteen for a roll and a cup of tea or coffee.

Most of the refugees had to rely on other sources of income. The musician Peter Gellhorn was able to live as a resident in a college, due to the generosity of English colleagues. Some friends paid the comparatively modest amount for board and lodging for him: 'They clubbed together and I think they gave me ten shillings pocket money every month. I managed and I was also working.' Refugee organisations played an important role, especially the Czech Refugee Trust Fund, which provided work for Alfred Dörfel and Josephine Bruegel. Lotte Berk, who had to pay a rent of two pounds and ten shillings, received one pound and ten shillings from the Jewish Refugees Committee, so she had to rely for the rest on money she had brought over from Germany. Later, the Committee gave her money to fetch her daughter from Germany.

If Dorothea Galewski and her family had not been supported by an uncle in South Africa, they would barely have been able to survive the war. Margarete Hinrichsen had to rely on money her father sent to England before he was killed in 1938. To start with, Adelheid Schweitzer's parents and even her grandmother were able to send her some money. Later, although on a tight budget, she did not feel as if she and her husband were living an impoverished life. Her situation soon improved; as a bilingual shorthand typist she earned four pounds a week, which rose annually by ten shillings. In 1938 she was already earning £250, and her husband £175, so they were comparatively well off. The same is true of Ilse Wolff, who in 1940 earned three pounds and ten shillings a week in a secure position, and her husband was able to work as well. Jobs at the BBC guaranteed a reasonable standard of living for Hanne Norbert-Miller and Eugen Brehm. During the war Nelly Kuttner's husband got a job at a bank for six pounds a week, 'quite a lot at that time', as she recalls.

4. Education and language

'When you have to, it's surprising what you can do'

Several of our younger interviewees faced daunting problems in adapting to a strange system, the first of which was being taught in a foreign language. Peter Johnson had become a pupil at an English boarding-school where he thought that he was making good progress with his English. This proved not to be the case:

> I improved my English. I prepared myself for the Matric. Then I promptly failed all subjects – except German. I only passed German because I wrote in German script. I did not finish any education. In any case, I was fed up with school.

Perhaps it is not surprising that Peter Johnson failed: he was attempting to take the Matriculation examination (the school-leaving and university entrance exam), within a few months of arriving in England. Instead, he became an apprentice to a furrier, attending a furriers' training school part-time for several years.

Eric Rose was sent to Holloway Grammar School, where he experienced a considerable culture shock. It was a single-sex school, with Latin as the first foreign language:

> The thing that shook me most, apart from the fact that there were all boys and no girls, was that they were doing Latin, which I had never even touched on . . . because the Reformrealgymnasium didn't do any Classics. And they were reading Caesar's *De Bello Gallico*, and I had no Latin and no English, and it was a little bit . . . difficult. But when you have to, it's surprising what you can do.

Walter Wolff did have difficulty in adapting to his boarding-school, although his brother was at the same school and there were three other German boys there. They, however, were three years older, a great difference for a twelve-year-old:

> I was very much on my own and felt desperately unhappy . . . at the beginning. Initially, because of my lack of English, I was put in a lower form than I would normally have been for my age, and I found all the lessons, apart from French and Mathematics, very difficult.

The other young children in the school had homes to go to, but his mother, working as a domestic servant, could not offer him a place to stay. The problem of holidays was only solved for Walter Wolff when his brother made friends with another pupil at the school, whose parents were 'very generous in inviting me to stay with them in Darlington whenever I needed to stay somewhere'.

A similar situation occurred for Hanna Singer. On arrival in England, separated from her twin brother, she was sent to a boarding-school in Folkestone. This school had a number of children of army and overseas civil service staff, so it was used to coping with children having to remain at the school in the holidays; Hanna's mother, who was in domestic service, had no home of her own to which the children could come. As Folkestone was in a protected area, forbidden to aliens without a special permit, she only saw her mother occasionally. The school was later evacuated to Shropshire, where her mother was for a time school matron, somewhat to her daughter's embarrassment.

But on the whole, refugee children who were sent to boarding-schools seem to have settled down quite quickly. It may have been easier to establish a relatively peaceful, orderly atmosphere in such schools, particularly as most were located in country areas or were evacuated there later; and teachers were also likely to be under less strain than their colleagues in city schools. Boarding-schools provided at least the semblance of a home to many children whose mothers had entered the UK on domestic servants' visas and had to live in their employers' homes.

Ernst Flesch, who was sent to a primary school in Glasgow when he first arrived in the UK, was initially placed in a class with children two years younger than he was, because of the language problem. He had had only a little English tuition in his short time at Gymnasium, but his native ability soon showed through:

> My first year was at a primary school and . . . I skipped through one class after the other. It was very easy . . . being good at languages anyway, I became a language specialist later on. Some of my friends didn't rise that fast, but I skipped through, no problem.

However, this early success in a primary school was the prelude to a disjointed school career. He was shifted from one school to another, from one set of foster parents to another, and then from hostel to hostel.

Dorothea Galewski provides another example: she was unlucky in being too old to take the scholarship examination to enter a grammar school, and her parents sent her to what turned out to be a rather inferior private secondary school and later to an even less effective commercial college. No guidance seems to have been given regarding a transfer to a more academically suitable school after she had learnt the new language.

Erika Young had to learn English from scratch when she arrived in Britain: her difficult journey to her English convent school with a Quaker helper has already been mentioned in Chapter Three. Nevertheless, after only one term there, she was first in her class in all subjects except English. It will be recalled that her father was supporting the remaining nuns at the Viennese sister convent by way of payment for her education. Hans Brill was also still of primary school age when he arrived in Britain; though a bright child, he had a more chequered school career. He was first sent to an orphanage, which seemed to him to be staffed entirely by older refugee girls. He was not sent to school, but was allowed to play in the adjacent Richmond Park all day. When his parents arrived later in 1938, they

4. LIFE IN PREWAR AND WARTIME BRITAIN

were horrified. He was then sent to a boarding-school in Swanage under a charitable scheme. He enjoyed his time there, but the school was evacuated to Canada in the summer of 1939, so when his father set up a handbag factory in a suburb of Cardiff, he went to a preparatory school in Penarth, passed the scholarship examination and continued at Penarth County School. Thereafter, as he wanted to go to sea, he joined the training ship, the *Conway*, where the regime proved a shock:

> Then I went to the *Conway*, and there one was called a cadet and one was in uniform, and the discipline was very strict... I'd been a nice, sensitive little boy until then, swimming and cycling, doing all these things by myself, and walking, but at this point the iron entered my soul with a vengeance, and I was never so lonely as there... The first term on that ship was extremely tough... but I stuck it out... The staff... were all people who'd been torpedoed about ten times and were totally shell-shocked, and all they wanted was to go home in the evenings to their wives.

Elizabeth Rosenthal, who had arrived in England on a Kindertransport, was first placed in a family in Oldham and sent to a junior school; later she went to Oldham Girls' Grammar School on a scholarship and flourished academically under a sympathetic headmistress. Despite her excellent results in 1945 in the Higher School Certificate – the best results in the school – she could not go on to university, because she did not have British nationality and was not eligible for a grant. Hans Seelig, somewhat younger, did not have this handicap when he came to university entrance. He had had language difficulties at his first primary school, so he was soon moved to a private Jewish school in Brighton, where there were other children like himself and teachers who were also refugees; there he did well. When the family had to leave Brighton, he was placed in a small, friendly primary school in Headington, Oxford, where he was given the support he needed. In 1941 he was successful in the scholarship examination for entry to grammar school, passing English with flying colours; he was to go on to study at Oxford University, the ultimate accolade for a refugee child.

5. Food and cooking

'That was too much, the food'

Sometimes the initial shock of reaching a safe but foreign country was connected with a familiar image of England. We have already quoted, in the 'Arrival' section of the last chapter, Eva Sommerfreund's recollection of her first night in England at the Earls Court refugee reception centre, when a nurse gave her a cup of tea with milk (which she had been brought up to associate with illness) and a sandwich with white bread and breakfast sausage. Hans Brill, on the other hand, coming as a child to a boarding-school, thought his first breakfast in England a real treat: 'There was this strange liquid, brown in colour, and a large cardboard box bearing the royal coat of arms – it was Kellogg's Cornflakes, "By appointment" of course – and I thought, well, this is good, I'm going to like this.'

Elizabeth Rosenthal was similarly 'deeply impressed' by her first experience of sandwiches made of white bread and cut into triangles. Walter Wolff has mixed memories:

> The first year, of course, was still before the war, and I had to get used to eating things like porridge and other foods that were very strange to me... I think what must head the list [of dreadful food] is tripe and onions. But I did very much like steamed suet puddings, not only because they were very tasty, but they were also very filling.

His experience seems to be more typical of a boarding-school than anything else. This is confirmed by Elizabeth Rosenthal, who is scathing about the food at her teachers' training college after the war, even after taking into account that rationing was still in force:

> Now, nobody had good food after the war, we still had rations in England, but what we were fed on was not describable. We had something called pastry which was like cardboard and tasteless, and we had some brown gravy which was also flour, and we had prunes. I could never eat prunes again. And we were starving.

Not only did she have to rely on occasional food parcels from her mother; she also recalls that she was driven to beg a loaf of bread

4. LIFE IN PREWAR AND WARTIME BRITAIN

from a lady out shopping and even, 'once in my life', to steal some buns.

It was Hans Brill again who developed a healthy appetite for English lunches, 'custard and – lovely soggy things!' But such anecdotes about liking or disliking English food and cuisine are, perhaps surprisingly, rare. Most interviewees paint a broader picture of their nutritional situation. Not all had problems with food; several mention explicitly that they were well fed, for example Josephine Bruegel. But some of the women in domestic jobs found it difficult to cope with the food they were given. Eva Pollard remembers how her sister was treated:

> They starved her, I mean she got so little to eat as a domestic. . . So when she came on her day off, in the afternoon, the very first thing we did was to go to a bakery and buy her a bun, because she was crying because she was so hungry.

Nelly Kuttner describes the midday meal she shared with the Irish cook shortly before the war: 'We had half a pound of butter in a dish (maybe cheese, but I don't think so), we had bread, and we had tea, that was our lunch. . . [And the employer said] you are not allowed to have this lump of butter here on the table.' For Walter Wolff as well, one of the overriding impressions of school during the war was 'that one was always hungry and never had enough to eat'. Erika Young recalls bitter moments for her mother:

> There are certain things she told me, in those early days when she lived in Brixton, for example like passing a baker's and smelling the newly-baked bread and cakes and longing to have one, but she couldn't afford it. She loved cherries, and not being able to afford cherries, which at that time were one shilling and sixpence a pound.

Stella Rotenberg was severely malnourished for several months. She worked in an office where she became so weak between two and four in the afternoon that she nearly fainted, and she felt better only after having afternoon tea. In her case it was not so much the lack of food as the impossibility of cooking hot meals that affected her health. Several other refugees were severely affected by their inability to cook properly. Gertrud Wengraf lived at first in a boarding-house in Kensington, where she was forbidden to use the gas-ring in her room. Others tried to cope with one solitary ring. When Gertrud Wengraf moved to a larger room, she was at least able to start cooking, but 'potatoes, corned-beef and noodles, that was my cooking knowledge'. Nelly Kuttner, who only possessed a single saucepan, had to make do with one meal a day. Stella Rotenberg's case demonstrates the development of a paralysing psychological situation. She freely admits that she had not been used to cooking in her youth, but the burden of living as a subtenant intensified this into a crippling problem:

> My use of the kitchen was never . . . the best I could manage was to boil water to make a cup of tea or. . . But I never cooked, nowhere. . . For that I would have had to put up more of a fight. The kitchen belonged to my landlady, and so I couldn't just use it.

Instead, she managed on bread and margarine and marmalade. Lacking all social contacts, she was not able to circumvent the rationing, to keep an allotment or obtain supplies direct from farmers. This was, by contrast, how Margarete Hinrichsen coped: 'We had rations, but I had a very good greengrocer who came every Saturday, and he looked after me. I had eggs and he brought me poultry and I had established contacts. We certainly never starved, never.' Nelly Kuttner in turn prided herself on becoming adept at cooking with dried eggs and dried milk.

Cooking was sometimes more than just a necessity. It could become an important activity in itself and a means of settling into a particular social environment. Josephine Bruegel, after a most depressing time working in a hospital with no social contact, returned to London and started cooking meals with a friend for other emigrants in her boarding-house. Peter Johnson structures the narrative of his first years around different types of cuisine:

> At first [in mid-1933], I was in a boarding-house. There I had a bed, breakfast and dinner, and on Saturdays and Sundays full board. It cost forty-two shillings. There were two ladies. One from Riga, the other from Odessa. So I got reasonably good Continental cuisine. And I made friends in that house. I stayed there for one and a half years, I think. My second boarding-house was English. It cost only

4. LIFE IN PREWAR AND WARTIME BRITAIN

thirty shillings and was in Hampstead. The house still exists, Belsize Park. Then for six months I had to look after the house of my boss, who was away. I got meals and had nothing to pay. After that, I rented a room in Maida Vale where I cooked on a gas-ring – I mean, I was always interested in cooking, originally I wanted to become a chef. I cooked as often as possible. I was also a member of a Jewish club, founded by the West London Synagogue, where we got good, cheap meals.

For Helga Reutter, cooking became a means of social integration, when she learned it together with her second employer, a fellow refugee. Ruth Herring emphasises the importance of getting her first kitchen at the age of forty-seven. For Stella Rotenberg, it was, alas, too late: 'At first, in England, I didn't cook, and when I got my own kitchen, at the age of fifty, I didn't want to any more.'

6. Marriage and children

'. . .when the German armies stuck in
Stalingrad . . . we would risk having a family'

Half of the refugees were already married when they came to England, most of them to compatriots. Lotte Berk and Christel Marsh were married and engaged to Englishmen respectively; this greatly facilitated their departure from Germany and their entry into England. For Christel Marsh, legalising her status took on a special meaning:

> When the war broke out we were in Bath for the weekend, and when we heard Chamberlain announcing it we took the next train back to London and went to the vicar of Christ Church, Woburn Square . . . and said, would he give us a service of blessing, because we never considered ourselves as married until that moment.

A number of the refugees married other refugees in England, a natural consequence of their special social situation. Nelly Kuttner remembers the touchingly humble circumstances under which she met her future husband: he had to borrow money to buy her a coffee and, after asking her to visit his room for their first real rendezvous, 'couldn't offer me more than a tin of sardines'. Peter Gellhorn recalls his wedding in 1943: 'It was limited, what you could have, but still we were about fifteen people, you know, I remember the whole meal cost twelve pounds.' That was approximately a month's wages.

The marriages lasted with strikingly few exceptions until the death of one partner. It seems that only Nelly Kuttner found herself confronted with a moral dilemma, when her future husband, then still a married man (though parted from his wife who lived in Portugal), proposed that they should live together. An uncle she asked gave her appropriate advice: 'Look, I find him very decent, it can't be helped. Look, it's the war, we don't know if we'll be alive tomorrow with the bombing and all that, you should agree to stay with him.' Ilse Wolff's decision to separate from her husband shortly after the end of the war illustrates a kind of integration into English life on her part: she was able to find work in England, whereas the chances for her husband as a German-speaking journalist seemed to be better in Germany. She did not want to go back to Germany; at the Wiener Library she had found inspiring and very satisfying work, and she was appointed Chief Librarian in 1947.

There was clearly some family planning. Even – or especially – in internment, starting a family was a conscious act, as Ruth Herring makes clear:

> Helmut said it would be taking a very great risk, starting a family as enemy aliens behind barbed wire in a foreign country. I said, 'Look, we both applied for British nationality before the war. Maybe they still have our papers and they can be revived or something. But I am game and I think we should start now. It's getting quite late when you're thirty-one. I don't know whether you feel that way. I for one shall take no precautions from now on.' And he said, 'It's all right by me.' So John was born on 4 March 1942 and he was the first baby to be born in a married camp.

For Adelheid Schweitzer conception itself was an act of defiance and a token of hope for a future which had only a few years ago seemed impossible: 'Then we decided, when the German armies stuck in Stalingrad, that if they didn't get beyond Stalingrad, we would risk having a family. And we did. We had my daughter who was born in 1943.' But normally children were conceived when the overall

4. LIFE IN PREWAR AND WARTIME BRITAIN

material situation had stabilised. Children played a crucial part in the process of integration, via their schools and, later in life, their own marriages. As Margarete Hinrichsen puts it: 'I made a lot of friends through the children.' (This aspect of assimilation is dealt with in Chapter Eight.)

7. Politics and political experience
'I indulged in a number of activities'

As one might expect, only a minority of the future refugees were involved in politics before their exile, as we have seen in Chapter Two. Several declare explicitly, like Ruth Herring: 'I wasn't a political animal.' Nine people mention politics, with various gradations of involvement. Christel Marsh was a member of the Confessional Church. Klary Friedl was a supporter of the Czech Socialist Party. Hilde Auerbach was a member of the SPD in Heidelberg and came to England to study the measures taken by the Labour Government against unemployment. Josephine Bruegel assisted her brother, a member of the Sozialistische Arbeiterpartei (SAP), in his anti-Nazi activities in Prague. Lotte Berk was left-leaning, toyed with Communism, and worked in a left-wing cabaret. Gertrud Wengraf was active in the Socialist youth movement in Vienna. Alec Armstrong was a member of the Communist party, but says little about his political activity. Only two people were heavily engaged in party politics: Eugen Brehm had been a member of the SAP and of the pacifist GRP, and Alfred Dörfel was a Communist youth organiser in Leipzig. Both were involved in dangerous illegal resistance.

The picture in exile changed. Overall, this political involvement receded. Hilde Auerbach was too busy to be engaged in any further political activities. Gertrud Wengraf became a member of the Labour Party and Klary Friedl made the acquaintance of some leading members of the Labour Party, although neither was actively involved. Josephine Bruegel had connections with political exile groups, but was not involved herself. Later on, during the 1960s, she came into contact with Czech dissidents opposed to the Communist regime. Eugen Brehm remained politically active in England, with the Volkssozialisten (People's Socialists), with Kurt Hiller's Gruppe

Unabhängiger Deutscher Autoren (the Group of Independent German Authors, opposed to the Communist-led Free German League of Culture), and with an organisation promoting European cooperation, the European Committee of the Federal Union. However, shortly after the war he became disenchanted with party politics and his job assumed greater importance; he judges in hindsight that 'it wasn't an important part of my life'. Alfred Dörfel was active during the early years for the Czech Refugee Trust Fund and during internment, but was then expelled from the Communist party (see Chapter Seven).

On the other hand, exile politicised some refugees. Peter Singer became a shop steward and a member of the Free German Youth. Hanne Norbert-Miller kept contact with the Austrian Centre, where she acted in the Laterndl theatre, and to a lesser extent with the Free German League of Culture. Margarete Hinrichsen, whose parents had been members of the Democratic Party in Germany, joined the Liberal party in England. Ernst Flesch, who entered Britain as a child, became very left-wing and was active in Young Austria and the Free Austrian Movement (FAM).

Ernst Flesch's account of the FAM is very interesting in its ambivalence. He was aware that most of its leading members were Communists. However, he is at pains to distance its activities and those of the youth movement Young Austria from a too narrowly perceived Communist stereotype:

> Young Austria was, you could say it was a front organisation, but not really in the sense that it did the work of the Communist Party. It wasn't like that. Definitely not. It was the idea of the whole Free Austrian Movement, which the Social Democrats called a front organisation... Anyway, in the Austrian Centre they tried to bring everybody in, even Monarchists or whatever. The idea was to work for a free, independent, democratic Austria. Don't forget this was the time of the Popular Front anyway and the Party people weren't pushing the revolutionary line at all. In fact Stalinism had long ceased to be revolutionary in England by then. No, we considered we were working for Austria, and not specifically Communist-orientated necessarily. But of course a lot of people were, because one

4. LIFE IN PREWAR AND WARTIME BRITAIN

gravitated naturally to the main enemy of the Nazis, who were the Communists. It was only natural. The people of course who were in charge, the people who were the organisers and leaders, a good many of them were Communists. Not all, but a good many. Well, we had left-wing Socialists... So we had different strands in there. It wasn't by any means only Communist. It was a meeting-place, a social club for many hundreds and even thousands of Austrian refugees. We were completely non-political in many ways. So we had various purposes, but I would say that the leading spirits tended to be, not always, but tended to be Communist Party. Young Austria of course was what one would call a mass organisation, i.e. a front organisation, but again, as I said, these were not specifically orientated in that way. No, it would be wrong to say that.

Three elements combine in Ernst Flesch's narrative. Firstly, he stresses the difference between the leadership and the grass roots, where opinion was more in favour of a Popular Front. Secondly, there is the realistic assessment that for many members the Free Austrian Movement and the Austrian Centre fulfilled a social rather than a political function. Thirdly, one detects that, with hindsight, he is correcting his own political position.

For Klary Friedl, politics actually became a means of social integration into British society. Through the publisher Eugene Prager, she got to know leading members of the Labour Party, such as Barbara Ayrton Gould, MP, and even its leader Clement Attlee himself. There were also activities that can be termed political in a broader sense. These are best exemplified by Ilse Wolff's work in anti-Nazi scholarship and research. However, most of the exiles did not consider party politics important. That is in part caused by the largely non-political background of the refugees. In addition, any involvement in British politics was impeded by the fact that they felt themselves caught in a double-bind situation: they were grateful to England for saving their lives, which made them reluctant to become politically active here. This is true even of an instinctive political activist like Ernst Flesch: 'I didn't think it was my position, being a foreigner in this country. No. I was still sympathetic to the left – still am for that matter. But no, not active in anything.'

The other side of the coin was the refugees' experience of the political situation in England and of the political awareness of their English hosts. Most of the refugees judged that knowledge of Continental affairs in England was poor. This lack of information was often first observed at a harmless, everyday level, in a tendency to disregard other cultures, as encountered by Eva Sommerfreund: 'Well, I remember in Leamington I stayed with a family, and there was a football match on, and as I came down the stairs ... I said, "Who won?" The father looked at me and said, "Do they play football in Czechoslovakia?"' Christel Marsh found the people in general 'nice but not very well informed'. Even well-educated people were, according to Hilde Ainger, 'very ignorant, they really knew very little'. Basic facts of religious and/or ethnic affiliation were confused. She found it hard to explain her secularised Jewishness to her host: 'Because I hadn't got the Jewish religion. She could not understand. She couldn't understand. "Hilde says she's Jewish." It was obviously one of my little peculiarities.'

Renée Hubert confirms this experience; for a short while she was the only Jewish girl in a small town and her situation was greeted with total incomprehension. Hilde Ainger recalls that during the Munich crisis she was the only person to listen to the radio, 'nobody else was even interested'. Margarete Hinrichsen judges even more trenchantly: 'The ignorance was incredible. Absolutely. Quite incredible.'

On the other hand, there were some encouraging personal experiences with left-wing activists, as Adelheid Schweitzer remembers:

> I was very fortunate because the foreman in this engineering firm ... was, well, very left. I don't think he was a member of the Communist Party, but he was very left. He was a very well educated Socialist who had been involved with producing the *Brown Book* [*of the Hitler Terror and the Burning of the Reichstag*, London, 1933] and trying to sell it in City Square in Leeds and been stopped by the police. Jim Hugill. I wish you would use his name because he died when he was very young. He was quite a wonderful man. He made my life in that firm manageable. His wife told me that he came home after I had started work there that evening and said the boss had got

himself a foreign Jewish girl for a secretary and he felt really sorry for her, because he knew what the rest of the people were like.

Renée Hubert recalls her pacifist colleagues at a progressive school with a mixture of irony and fondness. Elizabeth Rosenthal admits being heavily influenced by a pacifist headmistress at her grammar school who had to resign when she refused to let her pupils collect money for the war effort. It is interesting to note that Elizabeth Rosenthal mentions her subsequent involvement in Third World politics as a consequence of her exile experience:

> We are members of Amnesty International, I'm a member of peace movements. I mean, I try to improve the state of the world, but having been a refugee and having had difficulties in our lives, it makes you aware and understanding of other people's handicaps and suffering.

8. English peculiarities and leisure

'I don't know why I felt so cold'

In the encounter with a new country and its culture, there are some defining moments. It can start with small things, national peculiarities; it can also start with basic physical sensations. Hilde Ainger, who worked as a domestic servant, gives a very graphic description of her first year in her adopted country:

> Incidentally, that first English winter in a cold English country house! I had never felt so cold in my life, I got chilblains – I didn't know what they were. I described what I'd got on my feet – 'chilblains, chilblains', they said, and they offered me a hot-water bottle. In Germany, invalid old ladies had those, nobody else had hot-water bottles, and I would start dressing to go to bed, and you had a jug of warm water to wash yourself with – that size – and deciding which bits am I going to wash. You had a bath once a fortnight if you had the energy to pump the water, and then it could be fairly rusty. These were perfectly well-to-do . . . people who were perfectly well off. But it was as primitive as that and it was freezing cold.

Coldness is, of course, not only a physical experience but also a social and psychological one. The English attitude to the climate is an eternal mystery for foreigners. The refugees felt it even more symbolically. This is confirmed by Margarete Hinrichsen, who describes her first winter in very similar words:

> Then I went into the school and it was so cold, it was bitterly cold. Or it was me. I don't know why I felt so cold. The first winter in England I almost froze to death. I had to stay in bed with hot-water bottles because I felt so cold. It was all so strange for me.

Nelly Kuttner had the same experience in a 'bitterly cold' house, which led to chilblains; for Ernst Flesch as well, one of the lasting impressions of his first school was the cold. In their narratives, both Hilde Ainger and Nelly Kuttner continue by contrasting the cold climate and the cold houses with the warmth of their hosts. This ambivalence encompasses alienation as well as affirmation.

As we have seen in Chapter Two, most of the refugees had enjoyed a good education, and therefore took a lively interest in music, theatre, opera, literature, art. Several of them tried to take some books into exile. But there was sometimes a misconception of what could be useful in England. Hans Seelig recounts the near-comical results of his parents' choice: 'They brought over – because we were coming to England, of course – Shakespeare, in German. And they brought over their Dickens in German, and their John Galsworthy in German – all the stuff that was really useless.'

At first, the changed situation in exile imposed other priorities, to which culture had to be subordinated. For a start, participation in cultural activities depended on real opportunities for access. For Stella Rotenberg and Gertrud Wengraf, culture was inaccessible for a long time because of their imprisonment in domestic duties; others, notably men, concentrated heavily on their careers, so that in Eric Rose's interview, for instance, we find a significant absence of leisure and cultural activities. On the other hand, for Lotte Berk, Peter Gellhorn, Hanne Norbert-Miller, Ruth Herring and Ilse Wolff, culture was part and parcel of their professional life. Furthermore, Ilse Wolff recalls indulging in a wide range of cultural activities: 'Going to the theatre. Going to the cinema. Listening to the radio, and reading. Reading.' The same is true of Margarete Hinrichsen, for whom culture appears to have been an integral part of her life, even in spite of

4. LIFE IN PREWAR AND WARTIME BRITAIN

all the wartime difficulties. She recalls the re-opening of cinemas, 'musical evenings' in the boarding-house in which she lived, and theatre performances, especially those at the Austrian Centre's Laterndl and those staged by the Free German League of Culture. Erika Young mentions reading and going to the theatre; Helga Reutter recalls the importance of cheap prices at the cinema. Walter Wolff valued concerts and cheap seats in the theatre highly, since a visit involved sacrificing other purchases: 'I don't even know how I managed to do it. Of course, the gods were very cheap!'

Other more active forms of involvement helped to establish relationships and forge friendships. Ilse Wolff started singing in a university choir, as did Ernst Flesch, who was involved in numerous other activities, mostly connected with the Free Austrian Movement. Sports activities are mentioned by Erika Young, Eva Sommerfreund and Ernst Flesch, whereas Nelly Kuttner, who had been a keen swimmer and skier back in Vienna, no longer pursued these activities. The Central European passion for the game of bridge was transplanted to Britain, where the Acol Club was founded in the refugee quarter of West Hampstead in London. Helga Reutter, whose mother had played bridge in Vienna, continued this tradition in England, as did Erika Young, whose mother had been an excellent player, potentially of international standard; Klary Friedl learnt the game during the war and Ruth Herring also played, but only during internment. Eva Pollard and her husband thus showed a proper sense of priorities when, unable to afford a dining table, they made do with the essential bridge table.

Some humorous anecdotes poke fun at the inscrutable habits of English people as well as at the naïveté of exiles. Alfred Dörfel recounts how three refugees went to a gambling shop and watched the people operating strange machines:

> There was a machine for changing money, you put a penny in and a little ball came down... And after they had watched for a little while they said, 'We'll indulge like you and have a little game.' So they put a shilling in the machine, and out came twelve coins. So they looked at each other and said, 'Twelve? Count it again.' So they put another in, and twelve came out again. So they decided the machine was

wrong, and they put all the money in. And they didn't play, they just went out and came back to this boarding-house and emptied their pockets out on the table. There were a lot of pennies, all coppers – all their five shillings they had changed.

On the other hand, humour was itself a problem. Eva Sommerfreund explains that she never laughed for the first years because she did not find English jokes and comedians in the least funny.

Other scenes were of longer-lasting importance. Ilse Wolff encountered one during her first visit in 1935:

> My brother was working, so I spent most of my time in Hyde Park, at Speaker's Corner, also to improve my English. And then I was lying on a deck-chair – at the time it was two old pennies. And I got my ticket and fell asleep and was woken up by an attendant who asked, 'Have you got a ticket?' And when I said yes, he said thank you and went away without asking to see it. And this, after Germany, was an impression that will never leave me. That people can trust one another... And another thing which I experienced in Hyde Park, in Kensington Gardens, was when I wanted to see the lovely statue of Peter Pan and asked someone for directions. And when he gave me them, I started going along the footpath, but he said, 'No, you can go straight over there', and that was the first time I knew one was allowed to walk on the grass.

Peter Gellhorn finds similar significance in an incident which seems to be concerned with matters of more serious import, but which again harks back to an age of trust:

> A lovely story happened when the King went through Hyde Park in an open carriage and people stood right and left. A Swiss person said to the policeman: 'How can they go so near? What if I were suddenly to scream "Down with the King!"?' The policeman replied: 'I would have to arrest you for being drunk and disorderly in public, sir.' That was all.

The policeman and the deck-chair attendant as twin pillars of free English society are joined by a third: the newspaper vendor. In the words of Nelly Kuttner: 'That impressed me, at Charing Cross, there were evening papers and people put their money in, there was

4. LIFE IN PREWAR AND WARTIME BRITAIN

nobody there. I thought, "That couldn't happen in Austria, they would take the money away".' This same image has, in Ilse Wolff's words, transcended personal experience and become an act of faith: 'And another small thing is that newspaper vendors left their stand unattended for hours on end, and I'm sure when they came back they would find exactly as many coins as newspapers had been taken.'

Such mythologies created an image of England which in itself sometimes structured perceptions, experiences and, indeed, attitudes. Hans Brill's father, for instance, 'grew roses and smoked a pipe, to be truly English'. Did it help to become assimilated in this way? This will be a recurring theme in the closing chapters.

9. Social contacts

'It was many years before we really met English people'

At first, the refugees appeared to have more social contacts amongst themselves than with English families. Obviously, this depended on their professional situation. Women refugees sometimes emphasise their connections with other refugees or their isolation. Margarete Hinrichsen states: 'I don't think I mixed much with English people at that time.' Eva Sommerfreund describes how she established a circle of friends, most of whom were refugees, 'not because I didn't want to move in other circles, but it happened like that'. Dorothea Galewski states in similar vein: 'The only friends they [her parents] had, for a very, very long time, were other refugees. It was many years before we really met any English people.'

Domestic jobs could sometimes lead to isolation. Eva Pollard recalls her first years, when her employer tried to spoil her one free afternoon with new demands, so that she was not even able to visit her fiancé. Hanna Singer came to hold conflicting feelings about the woman who had guaranteed her entry into Britain:

> I felt, gosh, yes, you know, without her, we wouldn't have got out, but we hadn't been that sort of close. As I said, there were, sort of, odd difficulties, I think. The relationship between her and my mother later on, when my mother, I think, was always made to feel,

always felt she was socially inferior and that sort of thing. There was still that slightly odd sort of feeling, but she was a wonderful woman.

The tension between gratitude and a feeling of unwelcome obligation is openly discussed and, in a nice twist of cultural perceptions, it is indicated by the very English word 'odd'. For Elizabeth Rosenthal, the relationship with the family that had taken her in turned sour when her newly arrived mother wanted her to live with her, and consequently they fell out with the hosts.

On the other hand, men such as Eric Rose and Eugen Brehm emphasise the factor of social integration through their jobs. Hans Seelig even states clearly his family's aim of keeping a certain distance from other refugees:

> My parents considered themselves, significantly I think, as immigrants, with no intention of ever going anywhere else; adapting, without necessarily forgetting the past, but adapting themselves to their surroundings. We never lived, for example, in the areas where refugees lived. My parents never wanted to. We had contact, of course, with refugees, the Refugee Club in Oxford – they were cultural matters rather than social matters. Our best friends in this country were on the whole not refugees, except one or two that remained from Germany.

Peter Johnson founded an organisation called The Hyphen in 1948, specifically to allow refugees to widen their social contacts (see below in Chapter Nine).

However, there is a wide range of different attitudes towards social relationships, which can best be illustrated by some detailed examples. Ernst Flesch came to Britain in 1939 with a Kindertransport, at the age of eleven. At first, he stayed in an orphanage. This communal experience seems to have set a pattern for him. He moved to London in 1942, where he was constantly involved in collective activities. He was involved at the Austrian Centre in different groups until its dissolution after the war. He describes subsequent developments:

> There were many disagreements then, of course, among the refugees, because many of them would have liked the Austrian

4. LIFE IN PREWAR AND WARTIME BRITAIN

Centre to have continued, obviously... It left a gap in my life. I then went gradually, through other friends... to a Jewish Youth Club in Belsize Square, two minutes from here. Oddly enough, it was rather interesting. It was a club in one of the private houses in Belsize Square for quite a long time, and then later on they had another house in Finchley Road.

Until 1947 he had mainly refugee friends, although, through his involvement in Young Austria, he was called on to deliver a number of public talks to British groups about the situation in Austria. Many years later he got involved with Club 1943.

The path taken by Peter Gellhorn was quite different. His first years in Britain revolved around existing personal connections or those he could establish in the fields of culture and the arts. The difference in experience is apparent in the contrasting style of the two narratives: Ernst Flesch is mostly concerned with groups and their activities, Peter Gellhorn is preoccupied with personal acquaintances and their successes. Although their early exile experiences were equally pressured – both had to look desperately for jobs and seek to earn money – their approaches and attitudes were different. Peter Gellhorn met refugee artists who lived in Hampstead, but he worked in a very English setting – Toynbee Hall – and he feels with hindsight that this helped him to become more integrated into English life: 'It was perhaps better to be a little outside that [Hampstead refugee] circle. But [that circle] was always there and it led to occasional engagements and other things.' Such acquaintances were useful. On the other hand, Ernst Flesch concludes that most of his friends are still other refugees. Thus, these different experiences of exile have to be compared not as more or less difficult, but rather in the way in which the differences between them influenced the two men's perspectives on exile in Britain and their potential for assimilation.

It is instructive to compare the recollections of some of the women. It was precisely because Christel Marsh was married to an Englishman that she felt completely isolated: her parents-in-law rejected her and she was unable to get to know her husband's friends:

There was no time to really sort of get settled. Everybody was on the move at that time... Apart from this fellow, you know, who didn't live in London but in Bath, miles away, I knew nobody. Absolutely nobody. That was one of the worst aspects.

One of her few acquaintances was the German wife of a colleague of her husband, but 'she and I had nothing in common except our German extraction, you know, and it became a sort of "Notgemeinschaft" (companionship born of necessity)'. Stella Rotenberg found herself in a similar situation. During the war, although she felt accepted as the wife of an Army officer, she had to move around with her husband and was unable ever to settle down properly. After the war, she supported her husband in his medical career, but did not feel very happy in her role as housewife and mother, and she especially missed social and cultural contacts. Hilde Ainger's experiences were very different. She came to London as an au pair in 1934, at the age of seventeen. She was completely on her own and her first experiences were thoroughly unpleasant. Later she moved to a job in a students' hostel:

> I cooked this three-course meal for eighteen people every night, including carving the meat, waiting at table, doing the dishes, everything, and I finally would sit down, but then I would start having intelligent conversations. I found it very exciting and people took me out – I had no money, you see – but I was taken out and everything was within walking distance. I was working unbelievably hard, but it was worth it.

Subsequently, she married an Englishman and her interest in Germany subsided. In fact, she is the only one of our interviewees who has never revisited her former home country.

The differences between the experiences of men and those of women, as suggested by our interviews, demonstrate the importance of gender as a determining factor. The traditional role of housewife sometimes proved to be even more of a handicap in life, though one shared by British and refugee women alike, than the precarious status of exile. But we must now turn to a closer examination of the group's lives in the Second World War, which altered their position in Britain radically.

CHAPTER FIVE

Internment

Jennifer Taylor

At the outbreak of war the 1920 Aliens Act was invoked and German nationals were regarded as 'enemy aliens'. Home Office tribunals began interviewing in October 1939, assigning aliens to one of three categories: A (for those deemed likely to hinder the British war effort), C (for those considered reliable), while the intermediate Category B with bureaucratic precision tidied away those who, while clearly not Category A material, could not convince the British authorities of their loyalty. Those in Category A were interned immediately (in some cases to be released during the phoney war), those in Category B were made subject to restrictions on travel (including a ban on owning cars), while those in Category C remained temporarily unaffected. Since the last named category was intended for those who had fled Germany because they had suffered racial, religious or political persecution, this system would, at first sight, seem to have favoured most refugees. And so it did, until in the panic after the fall of France the newly appointed Prime Minister, Winston Churchill, encouraged the internment of all categories, and hapless refugees, many of whom had survived concentration camps, were incarcerated in inadequately prepared quarters.

Several of the thirty-four people interviewed did not fall into the category of 'enemy aliens' and so were in no danger of internment. For despite the annexation of Austria to the Reich, which automatically conferred German nationality on all Austrians, there were still some German-speaking refugees who did not hold German passports: those from Czechoslovakia, for instance, like Josephine Bruegel, Klary Friedl, Eva Sommerfreund, and Stella Rotenberg, who was married to a Czech doctor serving in the British Army. Renée Hubert had French nationality, Elizabeth Rosenthal was stateless, and Christel Marsh was British by marriage. She did not need to go before a tribunal, but had to 'register with the police as a former enemy alien. Norman [her husband] in uniform came with me. They thought it was touching.' Six of our sample were exempt from internment because they were, happily, too young. Of those born after 1924 only Walter Wolff (b. 1926) was required to appear before a tribunal.

Even among those who were 'enemy aliens', no very clear-cut pattern emerges. For instance, Peter Singer, who had his sixteenth birthday in 1939, was not required to appear before a tribunal, though his father was interned. On the other hand Eric Rose was interned shortly after his sixteenth birthday, while his parents, who had been classed as Category C, were never interned. Another paradox is the case of Hans Brill, whose father had moved to Penarth in South Wales, where he opened a factory with a Government grant. During the internment period, when refugees were moved from the 'protected areas' on the coast, 'we were allowed to stay – not only free, but in an area which was absolutely on the coast'.

Furthermore, women interviewees were much less likely to have been interned, since the process was halted before Category C women were reached. In fact, the only female interviewee to have suffered in this way was Ruth Herring. Her case, though, is in itself dramatically exceptional. Newly married, she spent three years in detention on the Isle of Man, where she gave birth to her first child. Nevertheless, many women were able to recount the experiences of their male relatives. Adelheid Schweitzer reported the detention of no less than three members of her immediate family, her husband, her father and her father-in-law, while Helga Reutter (whose husband escaped internment because he had enlisted in the Pioneer Corps) felt keenly the injustice of her father's position when, not long released from Dachau, he was nevertheless interned.

1. The tribunals

In almost all cases, the interviewees' recollections of internment itself are more vivid than their memories of appearing before the tribunals. One exception is Alfred Dörfel. Politically active since his youth, he criticised the composition of the tribunal and took exception to the questions he was asked:

5. INTERNMENT

In October I had to report to the tribunal. They were all very nice. At that moment we weren't allowed to have a bicycle, a radio, a photograph, a pass with which we could travel. We were stuck, and we had to go to the tribunal. This tribunal was somewhere in Knightsbridge, in a police station, and there was an old judge... They had no judges, and they called out the old judges from retirement. And there was the police officer who handled it, the secretary... Well, you were interrogated. It wasn't like Nazi interrogation of course, but... it was still interrogation... with 'Your name?', 'Why are you here?' – and I told the story that I had been arrested by the Nazis and put in a concentration camp. And they asked me, 'Why were you arrested?' I said, 'Because I opposed the Nazi regime'. And they said, 'But it was a legitimate regime. Why did you fight against a legitimate regime? They were elected.' So I was guilty, not the Nazis!

It was, he felt, particularly insensitive of the superannuated lawyers who interviewed him to ask why he would not fight for his own country. Ruth Herring, who had been working in English schools since the mid-thirties, received similarly unsympathetic treatment at her tribunal in January 1940. Her excellent English did not help her, she recalls. Instead, it aroused suspicion: 'Your English is very good', she was told, 'You would make an excellent spy for the Nazis.'

2. Implementing the detention orders: the police

The implementation of the detention order was in the hands of the local police who, it appears, could be avoided. For example, in the summer of 1940 Hanne Norbert-Miller's future husband Martin managed to evade internment by the simple expedient of absenting himself from his registered address:

Anyway, the police came to intern him, they came for him in Putney, but he wasn't there. This is a thing I just can't understand. Instead of thinking this very suspicious, they just never bothered to find him... And another thing... So many people left home at five or six in the morning, and I used to meet him at Marble Arch, courting at six o'clock in the morning, and then, you see, everybody went to Marble Arch Corner House. So if the police had gone to

Marble Arch Corner House, they could have had them all. Then we went to eat... Then about midday one could go home.

A similar technique was successfully employed by Adelheid Schweitzer's uncle Sigmund. Taking advantage of the summer weather,

> He would go to Hyde Park every morning at six o'clock to avoid the knock on the door. The knock on the door came, his wife was there and said, 'My husband isn't here' in broken English, and they went away again. That went on for a whole week, by which time the first [anti-internment] article had appeared in the *Standard*.

Eva Pollard's husband was initially less successful in evading arrest in this way:

> We played tennis behind Belsize Park Tube station. There was a sort of a court which was hidden behind buildings, and we went there [at] seven o'clock in the morning, to be out of the house. And my poor father, who couldn't play tennis of course, but he was in danger, we called on the way. He lived in Belsize Park... He was dressed in his winter coat. I can still see him freezing. And he walked round the court whilst we played. We had two friends who were also in this way keeping away from home. But one day the police got hold of us. They realised that we had left at seven o'clock or early in the morning. They came early enough to catch Walter, and he had to go to the police station. I was very sad.

But those with business experience could avoid the summons by creative procrastination. This was a tactic employed by Gertrud Wengraf's husband Paul:

> He said he had to settle things, he had people to whom he owed money and he had to settle his business first. And, luckily, when they came to him, there was already a movement to stop things, so he never did... he really got out by the [skin of his teeth].

Fortunately for him, Walter Pollard 'had convinced the authorities that he was essential for currency payments of refugees who were still in funds and could emigrate to America... and they had, of course, to be insured. That was part of my husband's line'. Having

5. INTERNMENT

evaded arrest for so long, 'we had escaped the very first fury, it was already not quite so strict any more'.

Such remarkable lack of rigour was not evident in all cases. Once the bureaucratic machine had been set in motion, the unwary were caught in its grip. The most disturbing instances of its inexorable process were the cases of boys and girls who reached their sixteenth birthday in the spring and early summer of 1940, when the fear of invasion was at its height. No consideration was given to the circumstances of these young people, nor was there any consultation with their parents or those *in loco parentis*.

In May 1940, Eric Rose, while on holiday from Holloway Boys' School (which had been evacuated to Towcester), was summarily arrested at West Hampstead Police Station and interned without a hearing, even though his parents were in Category C:

> I had an appointment to go before one of these tribunals, I think it was in July 1940, as soon as they could arrange it after my sixteenth birthday. But in the meantime I was an enemy alien, and my registered address, which everybody had to have, was in Towcester, Northamptonshire. In May 1940 I came on Whitsun holiday to London, home to my parents in West Hampstead. And I had to report once a week to the West Hampstead Police Station, because I was away from my registered address, and they wanted to keep tabs on anyone who was away, even temporarily, from their registered address. And then one day I reported as usual at West Hampstead Police Station and they said: 'Oh, glad you're here, you're under arrest, you're being interned.'. . . They had instructions that when I reported I was to be arrested and interned, and that's all they could do. . . I said: 'Well, what about my dad? I want to see my dad.' And they said: 'All right, give us his number in the City and we'll ring him up and tell him you're being arrested, and he can come to the police station and talk to us. Not that we'll be able to help him, but we're not standing in his way.' And they phoned my father and he came and said: 'Well, this is ridiculous. I'm Category C. Do you want me as well?' 'No, we don't want you. You're Group C and you've been passed by the tribunal. But your son hasn't been before a tribunal, and the instructions are that anyone who hasn't been

before a tribunal, for any reason, is to be interned immediately.' So my father said: 'Well, he's got an appointment.' 'Ah well, our instructions are to act immediately.' So my father said: 'Well, I'm going straight to the Home Office from here to complain and protest and apply for his release.' And the policemen said: 'Well, of course. We would. You go, and we wish you luck, but in the meantime the boy must get his pyjamas and toiletries and stay. He's under arrest, you see.'

Two months later, in July 1940, Eva Goodman, a former pupil of Ruth Herring, was arrested at Wycombe Abbey School. The headmistress informed Ruth Herring:

> This morning a Black Maria drove up to [the house] and they interned... they fetched Eva Goodman because it was her sixteenth birthday. She was grown up. I had no warning about this. She's already gone. I had no chance to see the girl. Her house-mistress has just been in to report this incident to me.

In later years, after release procedures had been established, young people were treated more sympathetically. For example, Walter Wolff, on reaching the age of sixteen in February 1942, was summoned before a tribunal in Newcastle. As he had been in an English boarding-school since the age of twelve, he had no difficulty in persuading the magistrates that he posed no threat to his adoptive country. So he and another German pupil of the same age were allowed to return to school and complete their education at the Friends' School in Great Ayton near Darlington, much to the relief of their teachers and fellow-pupils. Wolff's brother Peter, six years older, had not been so fortunate. He was interned in 1941, and robbed of his earning capacity just when his family most needed his financial support.

The local police were the first link in the chain and effected the arrests. Several interviewees remarked on their kind treatment by these officers. Among these is Alfred Dörfel:

> In June [1940], when the crisis started in France, with the German push forward, then most of us, Germans, Austrians, Romanians, Italians, all participants on the German side, they were all promptly

5. INTERNMENT

arrested. So I was taken to the police station in Hampstead for the afternoon... They came in the morning to where I lived. I already had a little suitcase with a few things – you expected it. And they came and knocked on the door and said, 'Mr Dörfel?' I think I was in the middle of my breakfast. And down in the road was a little van. There were already two or three in it, because in this district, a lot of refugees lived there... It was the local police in Hampstead. Anyway, they were all very kind. They came round with trays of sandwiches. And in the afternoon a bus came and took us to a big Army hut near Kempton Down [in Surrey].

In areas outside London the refugees were likely to know the arresting officer personally, since, as resident aliens, they had to report regularly to their local police station. This was so in Ruth Herring's case. In June 1940 she was arrested in High Wycombe by an officer she had known since 1935:

The man looked so at a loss. He said: 'We've come to take you away.' I said: 'You can't do that. It's three weeks before the exams. My pupils are expecting me now. I can't let them down. I can't just walk out on them.'. . . 'All foreigners have to be interned at once.' I said: 'This is really awful. My schools need to be notified. How long have I got?' 'Half an hour.'

Nevertheless, orders were orders and the refugees had to be detained. The most dramatic example of police sympathy is given by Eugen Brehm (who in his interview referred us to an account of his internment he had written for publication).[16] When he was arrested at his home near Evesham in June 1940 by the CID and taken to Evesham Police Station, the custody officer, who knew him personally, was very embarrassed, and assumed that some mistake had been made. He apologised for accommodating Eugen Brehm in a cell, and left the door open so that the detainee could control the light himself (the switch was outside the door). Later, the officer brought tea and cooked Eugen Brehm a supper of bacon and eggs taken from his personal stores. In the matter of telephone calls, however, regulations were strictly observed. Eugen Brehm, who at that time was

16. Eugen Brehm, 'Meine Internierung', *Exil*, 2, Frankfurt/Main, 1986, pp. 41–62 (only in German).

working for the BBC Monitoring Service, was not allowed to contact his employers to explain his situation: 'The curtain had come down.' The next day he was taken to the county town, Worcester, where the Chief Constable himself dealt with his case. Learning that Eugen Brehm was a political opponent of Hitler, the officer considered that a mistake had been made and did all in his power to have his prisoner released, commenting: 'We need people like you.' Unfortunately, though, in the face of official intransigence (probably caused by the power struggle between the Home Office and the War Office over control of the detainees), even this high-ranking policeman was unable to prevent Eugen Brehm's internment. He was detained first at the army camp in Blandford in Dorset and subsequently at Huyton near Liverpool. Alfred Dörfel had no hesitation in attributing responsibility for such hard-line tactics:

> Before the internment started . . . when the crisis started, we came under the Home Office, but once the war started we became property of the War Office. The two parties actually haggled: 'What shall we do? Are they still Home Office property, or are they Army property?' Since they couldn't decide, they asked Churchill. . . So we were now not any more Home Office subjects, we were Army subjects, and under Army rule we had no say at all.

3. Detention: the initial stages

In May and June 1940 internees were held in the same temporary camps that had been used for the detention of Category A internees at the outbreak of war. 'It was all improvised . . . a bit of a rush job. There was never any malice in it at all. . . Everybody was very friendly and polite and helpful and sorry,' remarks Eric Rose. The summer of 1940 seems to have been an exceptionally good one, and many interviewees remarked that this helped to alleviate the discomforts of their situation. But conditions in Warth Mill, a derelict cotton-mill near Bury in Lancashire, which for some constituted the next place of confinement, were unacceptable. Peter Gellhorn, incarcerated there for four weeks, remarks: 'We gradually deteriorated. It was so dirty and wet.' Eric Rose, who was briefly confined there

5. INTERNMENT

before being transferred to the Isle of Man, offers a more detailed condemnation:

> This was dreadful. This was an old disused cotton-mill, which – all they'd done was put barbed-wire around the actual building, and there was nowhere to exercise, and the floors were full of holes, and there were rats running about. I remember they offered us breakfast consisting of salt-herrings and things like that, and the men were really angry, the internees were really angry at that stage.

But, for once, the Army was on their side. Fearing a mutiny, the Commandant – 'he was a Major, I think: he was helpless' – kept telephoning the War Office, insisting: 'This can't go on. This is not suitable. You've got to move them out of here.'

4. Huyton and the Isle of Man

The Isle of Man (which had fulfilled a similar function during the First World War) was eventually to provide the most satisfactory conditions for detention in the British Isles. The requisitioning of suitable premises began in May 1940. At about the same time, possession of a newly-constructed council estate in Huyton near Liverpool was obtained. The first internees were received in May 1940. The first arrivals were accommodated in the barely-finished houses, as Eugen Brehm explains:

> Coat-hooks on the door, blackout curtains over the window, apart from that empty. We each had to fetch a straw mattress, two blankets, a plate, cutlery, and an enamel mug; that was the sum total of our furniture. Our cases served as chairs.

Those who, like Peter Johnson, came at the end of July had to sleep in tents.

Yet it was less the primitive physical conditions that worried the interviewees than the poor organisation. Peter Johnson's comment on this point is succinct: 'The stupid thing was that the English side of things was really poorly organised. They didn't know how many people were there, or who they were.' Eugen Brehm is more explicit about the disorganisation that he encountered in Huyton. The back doors of many of the houses had been ripped out by the internees, transformed into furniture and offered for sale, while the skilled craftsmen among them had obtained additional wood by cutting out portions of the rafters, taking care not to cause any structural damage. Since the British soldiers themselves profited financially from the deals, a blind eye was turned to this abuse of government property:

> We welcomed this vandalism... If the camp authorities, or their immediate superiors, were not capable of providing the most basic furniture, the kind that would be taken for granted in police cells, then we had to rely on our own initiative.

Few interviewees were detained for longer than six months in the British Isles. One exception was Ruth Herring and her husband Helmut, who spent nearly three years on the Isle of Man. In November 1940 Helmut Herring had refused to participate in the deportation programme (described in greater detail below), rejecting a passage to Australia because the couple had wanted to remain together. Ruth Herring was initially confined to the women's camp at Port St Mary, while her husband was detained in Onchan camp at Douglas. When a camp for married internees was established in Port St Mary in May 1941, they were among the first couples to be accommodated there. Ruth Herring participated fully in the cultural life of the camp, and her contribution to that sphere will be considered below, including her work in running a school for the children of the internees. Soon after they were reunited they decided to start a family of their own, and in March 1942 their son John was born at the camp hospital at Port Erin:

> He was born on the Isle of Man because by that time we couldn't foresee the end of the war... I was thirty-one, Helmut was thirty-seven, and we decided, we are in a married camp. We have been married and not together really for about a year and a half. We're going to be together as husband and wife.

The couple faced the material difficulties of wartime. Clothing was scarce, and so was equipment for the new baby. But the most keenly felt privations were those resulting from their status as

5. INTERNMENT

imprisoned exiles: lack of family support and the restrictions on her husband's mobility:

> Dr Colls was the woman doctor's name, and I said: 'Dr Colls, please can I have a book on childbirth? I have no idea.' And of course I hadn't got my mother or anybody to consult. 'Oh', she said, 'I'll get you a book.' I looked at it. It was from the 1880s. Mind you, it was wartime and I thought, 'Oh dear, is that the best she can do?'. . . John was duly delivered about 4 p.m. on 4 March, just getting on for the evening. . . I wanted to see my husband. 'She can't see her husband at this time of night.' He was behind barbed-wire in Port St Mary. I just kept saying: 'I want my husband.'. . . One after another the nurses came: 'Can we have a look at the baby?' I said: 'My husband hasn't seen him yet.'. . . But of course they all went and had their look and I was really furious inside. I thought: 'This ought not to be, but I'm an enemy alien. There's a war on. I haven't been left in the street. I am in hospital. I have got a doctor. I must just count my blessings.'

5. Deportation

In June 1940 plans to deport internees to the Dominions were finalised. Canada and Australia agreed to accept quotas. As in all such political decisions, the motives were complex. Foremost among them was the fear that, in the event of a German invasion, internees would aid their compatriots in the occupation of Great Britain. This thinking failed to distinguish between prisoners of war, who might well act in this way, and refugees, who had fled Germany because of racial, religious or political persecution. As we shall see, the refugees were to suffer greatly from stereotyping and bigotry, particularly on the outward voyage.

Some internees were afforded an element of choice. This is how Peter Johnson describes his experience:

> We were asked to fill in a form to say whether we would be prepared to go overseas. A few said no – either married men with children or Nazis who thought they would become Gauleiters if they stayed in England. There were also a few suicides – people who were afraid to go overseas. But the majority had nothing against the idea.

But in Alfred Dörfel's case there was no question of choice:

> You were under Army law... And one day a transport was organised. I was informed by a friend who walked into the so-called office and said: 'Dörfel, you are on a transport.' And nobody actually knew what it meant, but we feared it was a transport for overseas.

Eugen Brehm, interned in Huyton, turned down the opportunity to go to Australia on 13 July 1940. He describes the parameters within which the Army was attempting to implement this 'voluntary' programme:

> As the number of volunteers declined, an element of compulsion crept in and the journey became a deportation... As far as I know, it was never the married men who were forced to leave Huyton in this way, only young men with no family responsibilities.

Eric Rose, interned in the Isle of Man just after his sixteenth birthday, feared compulsory deportation. But his extreme youth saved him from this fate, and he was soon released to rejoin his family.

One of those who did volunteer was Peter Johnson, motivated by youthful high spirits and a desire to travel. But he must often have had occasion to regret his decision. For he was part of the notorious *Dunera* transport to Australia in July 1940. On this voyage the internees (who comprised young people from the Kindertransports as well as First World War veterans) were subjected to concerted harassment and theft by the British Army officers and men who escorted them. These events are well documented, for the Australian authorities were so aghast at the condition of the detainees that the Commanding Officer, Lieutenant-Colonel W. P. Scott, was required to write a report. For their part the refugees recorded their experiences in the Dunera Statement,[17] and this evidence was, Johnson claims, corroborated by British Intelligence Officers who had been interviewing the internees on board.

Scott's report, in which he described the German prisoners of war as 'of a fine type, honest and straightforward, and extremely well-disciplined', and referred to the refugees, 'German and Austrian

---

17. See Peter and Leni Gillman, *'Collar the Lot!' How Britain Interned and Expelled Its Wartime Refugees*, London/Melbourne/New York, 1980, p. 253–55.

5. INTERNMENT

Jews', as 'subversive liars, demanding and arrogant',[18] explains, while it does not excuse, the treatment meted out by the officers and men under his command. This is Peter Johnson's eye-witness account of the voyage:

> As far as we knew, the soldiers guarding us were commanded by a certain Major O'Neill, an Irishman who had won the Victoria Cross in the First World War. But we did not know that Lieutenant-Colonel Scott was the superior officer. The discussions between this character (I can't call him a human being, we found him so repugnant) and our spokesmen were not very friendly. This officer, the NCOs and some of the soldiers had our luggage brought on deck. (Our cases had been taken away from us as we came on board and put in storage.) We only had the clothes we were wearing, which was very unpleasant. As we were sailing along the African coast, we were able to see what was happening on deck from the latrines. Mr O'Neill and his soldiers were busy ripping our luggage open with bayonets. They stole anything useful, and threw everything else into the sea – including PhD theses belonging to academics, doctors and so on. . . We were hardly ever allowed to go on deck, and when we did, there were machine-guns fore and aft, which had been used in the First World War. And one of the soldiers amused himself by throwing bottles down, so that the people who were on deck would cut their feet – but we jumped over [the broken glass] so that this would not happen. And while we were on deck, some soldiers tried to grab the rings from our fingers – one man almost had his finger pulled off – and we saw that our few remaining belongings were being stolen. . .
>
> We landed first at Fremantle, and then Perth, where medical officers came on board and complained that we looked too pale – we needed more fresh air. And I think we were given – just before Fremantle we were given razors so that we could shave. . .
>
> Then we arrived in Melbourne, where the Nazis and Italians were taken off. And after that we arrived in Sydney – I don't know what day it was – the beginning of September[19] – [we sailed] under Sydney Harbour Bridge. Before we disembarked Lieutenant O'Neill

---

18. ibid., p. 254; the original is in the Australian Archive, Canberra, D. 20/1/3.
19. The *Dunera* arrived in Sydney on 6 September 1940.

(he was actually a Lieutenant, although he called himself Major), wearing insignia to which he was not entitled, made a little speech from the quay, saying that later, when we were in the camp, we would often recall how well we had been treated... We thought otherwise.

It is clear from Scott's report that he regarded the refugees not as victims of racial persecution, nor as exponents of political dissent, but as cowards who had evaded military service, traitors who had fled their country to consort with the enemy. Alfred Dörfel, who was deported to Canada at about the same time, did not experience the sadism permitted on the *Dunera*, but was subject to discrimination which offended his political sensibilities and permanently tainted his perception of Great Britain as a country of refuge.

Alfred Dörfel was deported to Canada on the *Ettrick*, which left Liverpool in early July, a day or so after the ill-fated *Arandora Star* which was torpedoed and sunk in the Irish Sea with heavy loss of life, including some 450 Italian internees, in the early morning of 2 July 1940. Compared with the *Dunera*, conditions on board the *Ettrick* for the internees were reasonable and their treatment perfectly correct. The detainees were not exposed to the gratuitous violence experienced by the *Dunera* passengers. But Alfred Dörfel was offended by the institutionalised discrimination on board. In an attempt to ensure reciprocal treatment for their British counterparts in Germany, prisoners of war were accorded superior facilities. This discrepancy was particularly evident in the catering arrangements: 'We got a very nice breakfast, a real cooked one, in the morning, but nothing during the day. In the evening we got a meal, but it was a long time to go from, say, in the morning about eight o'clock till about six o'clock in the evening.' During a period of exercise on deck, Alfred Dörfel happened to pass by a porthole which gave him a view of the German Officers' Mess, shortly after lunch: 'It was empty, but you could see that they'd been there. There were beer-bottles, wine-bottles ... that was the difference. Here the Nazis and there the refugees. The enemy were well treated and we were the "scum of the earth".'

5. INTERNMENT

6. Cultural and intellectual life in the camps.

'A cultural life: that was the foremost thing'

This remark of Peter Johnson's points to the fact that the internees were determined to maintain some sort of cultural and intellectual life. For creative activities functioned as a positive counterpoint to the harsh realities of camp life, providing otherwise inactive prisoners with a purpose and so serving to raise morale.[20] The sheer range of cultural activities on offer has led to comparisons with a university, for one of the characteristics of this migration was the high proportion of refugees who had benefited from higher education. Among the internees were eminent scholars and artists. For example, it was estimated that one camp held three Nobel Prize winners and twenty Oxford professors as well as specialists with international reputations in various fields. The lecture programme at Hutchinson Camp on the Isle of Man was so varied and the contributions of such a high standard that Fred Uhlman, the German lawyer who became a writer and painter in exile, remarked that he and his companions were often forced to choose between rival attractions – for example, Chinese Theatre, Byzantine Music, Greek Literature and Etruscan Language.

The activities developed by the internees themselves ranged from those requiring very few resources, such as lectures, poetry or play readings, through recitals, cabaret and concerts to ambitious productions of plays from the classical German repertoire, as well as modern plays. Artists often sketched these activities. Additionally, more complex artistic endeavours were undertaken. For example, in Hutchinson Camp the Dada artist Kurt Schwitters regularly produced portraits of fellow inmates. There was a tariff for this – hands were extra. However, Schwitters was also able to continue with his

20. The following general remarks are based on these sources: Michael Seyfert, *Im Niemandsland: Deutsche Exilliteratur in britischer Internierung. Ein unbekanntes Kapitel der Kulturgeschichte des 2. Weltkriegs*, Berlin, 1984; Alan Clarke, 'Theatre behind Barbed Wire: German Refugee Theatre in British Internment', in *Theatre and Film in Exile*, ed. Günter Berghaus, Oxford, 1989, pp. 189–222; Klaus Hinrichsen, 'Visual Art behind the Wire', in *The Internment of Aliens in Twentieth Century Britain*, London, 1993, pp. 188–209; and Richard Dove, '"KZ auf Englisch": Robert Neumann's Internment Diary' in *'England? Aber wo liegt es?'*, ed. Charmian Brinson et al., Munich, 1996, pp. 157–67.

avant-garde work, making collages out of the ephemera discarded by others – cigarette-boxes, stamps and confectionery wrappers. And although he had to share a house with twenty-three others, the attic room where he worked and slept alone provided Schwitters with adequate conditions to continue this work. Finally, attention must be drawn to the camp newspapers. Although the internees were eventually permitted access to the exile press – in care parcels sent by their community groups – there was an urge to produce their own newspapers. This was done on roneo equipment donated by well-wishers. The *Onchan Pioneer*, *Stacheldraht* ('Barbed-Wire') and *Camp News* are examples of newspapers produced in this way on the Isle of Man, in Canada and Australia respectively.

Resources were obtained in a variety of ways, while lack of them was overcome by ingenuity. Correspondence was permitted, and friends and acquaintances were asked to provide material for readings and scripts for plays. For example, Thomas Mann in New York was asked by the German Communist Wilhelm Koenen to send a copy of Brecht's *Fear and Misery of the Third Reich* to Canada. The artists made use of material nearer home – beetroot-juice and crushed pencil leads mixed with margarine provided ink, olive oil from sardine tins was mixed with food extracts to make oil paint, drawings were made on wallpaper or newspaper and the plentiful supply of lino in the boarding houses was used for linocuts. On the whole the attitude of the camp authorities was positive, for such activities kept the prisoners occupied. In particular, the Commander of Hutchinson Camp, Captain O.H. Daniel, was very generous with his provision of resources. But not all his colleagues showed such enthusiasm. For example, the Commandant of Mooragh Camp in Ramsey was angry at the tone of the first (and, as it transpired, the only) issue of the *Mooragh Times*. The newspaper was not jolly enough – he wanted something to make people laugh, not the criticism of the internment policy it contained.

Eugen Brehm's published account of his internment describes the performance of two modern plays in Huyton Camp, *Septembertage* ('September Days') by the Communist poet Kurt Barthel (KuBa) and *Böhmische Passion* ('Bohemian passion') by the German-speaking Czech dramatist Louis Fürnberg. Eugen Brehm dismisses the former,

5. INTERNMENT

which deals with the occupation of the Sudetenland, as hastily assembled agit-prop of little relevance to the audience, most of whom were German Jews. He was a little more appreciative of Fürnberg's poetic depiction of Bohemian history, but puzzled at the satirical depiction of modern Czech leaders. Despite these predominantly negative reactions, the productions – masterminded by KuBa – were important in that they attempted to interpret modern history for an audience which had immediate experience of its consequences. Other productions of modern works included Robert Ardrey's *Thunder Rock* on the Isle of Man, and Shaw's *Androcles and the Lion* in Canada.

Cabaret was, however, a more direct method of expressing the experiences of the refugees. In Australia, the German Communist journalist Max Zimmering wrote texts for a group of actors who had previously performed in the Free German League of Culture in London and who, under the direction of Josef Almas, performed in Hay Camp. Such was the demand that a second programme, entitled *Hay Days*, had to be written. In Canada, a cabaret was staged in Camp N to celebrate the New Year in 1941, while a few months earlier the performers of a similar show in Camp L had been requested by the Commandant to stage a special performance to entertain the soldiers who were guarding them.

There were art exhibitions both inside and outside the camps. The second exhibition held at Hutchinson Camp, in November 1940, for example, contained contributions from four artists – Hermann Fechenbach, Peter Fleischmann, Paul Hamann and Georg Heller. The predominant medium was linocuts, although there were also portraits and oil paintings. Georg Heller's contribution consisted of seven linocuts, most of which were views of the camp. But camp art also reached a wider audience. For example, thirty-six pictures were exhibited at the Redfern Gallery in London in April 1941, while in the same year the Free German League of Culture held an exhibition of camp art from Canada. The standard of the works produced under such unpromising circumstances astounded the audience – in particular, the German graphic artist John Heartfield, who pointed out that the majority of the works exhibited had nothing to fear from critical appraisal. After the war Fred Uhlman published a selection of linocuts produced in Hutchinson Camp, while Schwitters's portrait of Uhlman is to be found in the Newcastle Art Gallery in the room dedicated to Schwitters.

The importance of music in the camps can perhaps be measured by referring to the post-war fame of the Amadeus String Quartet, three of whose members met in internment. The Viennese pianist Rawicz (with his partner, Landauer, a popular performer of light classical music) was also incarcerated in Hutchinson Camp. In Huyton, the Austrian composer Hans Gál composed music for the camp review 'What a Life'; a more formal composition was his Suite for Flute and two Violins (Opus 92). The choice of instruments was dictated by those his companions happened to have brought with them. Popularly known as the Huyton Suite, it was performed there and on the Isle of Man several times during the internment period, and broadcast by the BBC after the war.

One point which emerges clearly from descriptions of camp life is that many internees were very young, well below the age of majority, which at that time was twenty-one. 'There were many young men who had come with the Kindertransports. Some were . . . under sixteen. . . They should not have been interned,' remarks Peter Johnson. These young people had been deported to Australia where they were offered the opportunity to continue their education by following a matriculation programme supervised by a local university. Similar opportunities were offered to young internees in Canada: 'They could sit for external exams. . . The University of Toronto, I think. And most of them got a degree,' remembers Alfred Dörfel.

On the Isle of Man, Ruth Herring saw a similar need and approached the task with single-minded determination, teaching the children of the couples interned in the Married Camp in Port St Mary. After finding a building, 'a kind of hut', she devised a timetable, and lessons proceeded on the following principle:

> We tried to speak either German or English, because most children couldn't speak or write either language properly. They'd come over from Germany with their parents at some point to this country, so some of them had already been for a little while to an English school. All of them had German parents . . . who'd probably kept on speaking German to them. The main thing was to get these children

5. INTERNMENT

to be able to speak, read and write in either or both languages without making a muddle and producing sentences that were made of mixed vocabulary and no kind of sentence construction.

Minna Specht, the progressive Socialist educationalist who had been interned with several of her colleagues and who had earlier founded a school in the women's camp, is also referred to briefly by Ruth Herring. Previously the latter had also worked with older people, in the women's camp, using texts donated by her former school to plough her way through *Hamlet* with a group who spoke very little English; she herself learned New Testament Greek with a 'professor from Vienna'.

Other interviewees stress the sheer enjoyment of the various cultural activities, which served as an antidote to the uncertainty of their situation and the privations of camp life. Speaking of her father's experiences on the Isle of Man, Hilde Auerbach recalls:

> Well . . . he said they quite enjoyed it in a way. But he didn't know when it would end and that worried him. But what they did there was quite enjoyable because . . . they had these lectures for all kinds of people. He also gave German poetry recitals there.

'In fact, I never made more music than on the Isle of Man,' remembers Peter Gellhorn. 'We had a little orchestra. I taught harmony and I gave piano recitals.' He points out that this was done with few resources other than his memory: 'We weren't allowed printed music, but I gradually remembered my piano repertoire. Piece by piece, bar by bar. And I had enough then to give recitals without ever repeating a piece.'

The Rushen women's camp on the Isle of Man offered internees a similar range of cultural activities to the men's camps, though to date they have not been so well documented.[21] In addition to the schools for internees' children in Port St Mary, Port Erin and later in the Married Camp, there was a wealth of adult education provision, organised by the internees themselves, on offer in three centres, as

---

21. These general remarks on Rushen Women's Internment Camp are based on Charmian Brinson, '"In the Exile of Internment" or "Von Versuchen, aus einer Not eine Tugend zu machen"': German-speaking Women Interned by the British during the Second World War', in William Niven and James Jordan, eds., *Culture and Politics in 20th Century Germany*, Rochester, N.Y., 2002.

well as other educational possibilities through the Service Exchange Scheme (an ingenious economic system, operating only in the women's camp, which provided for an exchange of goods and services, paid for by a currency of service tokens). In addition, women of a scientific bent could benefit from the facilities at the nearby Marine Biological Research Station, where there were research opportunities, a lecture programme and a good science library.

Admittedly the women had to suffer a greater degree of control over their educational activities than the men did because of the autocratic style of command practised by the Rushen Commandant, Dame Joanna Cruickshank: she decreed, for example, that only women holding academic qualifications were permitted to give lectures. This tight degree of control extended to the production of camp newspapers of which one, *Der Frauenruf*, was reportedly never approved despite repeated applications and revisions, while another, *Rushen Outlook*, was so delayed by Cruickshank's censorship procedures that its editors – who included Ruth Herring's room-mate Margot Strauss-Pottlitzer – became too discouraged to attempt a second issue.

As in the men's camps, the presence in Rushen of a number of former actresses and drama teachers ensured that dramatic productions of a high standard were put on. These included a Christmas play combining the Christian and Jewish traditions, a much-praised production of the medieval mystery play *Everyman* and an adaptation of *Turandot* that set out to make a plea for the establishment of a mixed camp. Artistic production flourished as well, with Collinson's Café – a favourite internee meeting-place – being turned into an arts and crafts centre. Internees founded a camp choir and put on numerous variety shows and concerts, such as a Viennese evening organised by the resourceful Margot Strauss-Pottlitzer. In addition, music and musical events were promoted by the Methodist Church in Port Erin under its sympathetic minister, Rev. J. Benson Harrison.

After the Married Camp was set up in May 1941 in Port St Mary (later moving to Port Erin), this initially had a somewhat disruptive effect on the educational and cultural provision in Rushen, as did the growing number of releases throughout 1941. In the Married Camp, the school where Ruth Herring and her husband were to teach was

5. INTERNMENT

soon opened, and a cultural life was established that included adult education, a library, a reading circle, amateur dramatics – a production of Shaw's *Candida*, for instance – Sunday concerts and even a small dance band and periodic dances.

Compared with the relatively favourable conditions on the Isle of Man, camp life in the Dominions was characterised by physical privations. Peter Johnson eloquently describes the unpleasant desert conditions of Hay in New South Wales: 'The worst thing in Hay was the sandstorms. The sand came through the metal grids above into our rooms, onto our bedding. And when we shaved, the dust got into the shaved parts of our faces and caused impetigo.' But this did not deter the internees from cultural endeavour. Johnson mentions the various educational opportunities available to adults: 'All sorts of courses. Japanese, Greek, Latin. We had courses in medicine', and Alec Armstrong was himself one of the teachers: 'I taught whatever I could. It was mainly history – political history – and also art and architecture. Because I had . . . qualified as an architect in Germany.' Additionally, Johnson mentions that cultural activities included music and painting, and remarks that Hein Heckroth, the stage designer for the Jooss Ballet who, with other members of the ensemble, had been arrested in Dartington, was interned in Hay (while Jooss himself languished on the Isle of Man, where he formed a male *corps de ballet*).

Conditions in Camp N in the province of Quebec were not ideal when Alfred Dörfel first arrived there in the autumn of 1940:

> It was an old repair shop for locomotives, it was very dirty when we came there. . . It was not organised. The beds weren't there and the toilets weren't there, and it was more or less our job to [set it up]. And within a month it was one of the nicest places you could live in – as a camp.

Once these initial organisational tasks had been accomplished, there were 'film shows, concerts, lectures'. Alfred Dörfel, who was a Group Leader in the camp, still possesses some poems written by Alfred Becker, a fellow internee, beautifully transcribed and illustrated. 'It was a life organised wherever intelligent people come together, and it was very interesting to know,' he concludes.

7. Release

The movement of public opinion against internment was fuelled by adverse publicity about deportations. For, even in wartime, a disaster like that of the *Arandora Star* could not be concealed. Opinion turned against internment, and release procedures were established. On the Isle of Man, for instance, release tribunals began their work in October 1940.

Peter Gellhorn, detained there for just over five months, commented on the political background:

> The people who had money were released first, I am afraid to say. We had to wait. At first, it was a Conservative Government. Anderson was Home Secretary. They said: 'It is no use trying to apply for release now, because you would only be suspected of being a Socialist.' And then Morrison became Home Secretary [October 1940] and the bush telegraph said: 'Now you might try.'

Hans Seelig's father was released from Onchan after nine months' detention thanks to the intervention of an eminent Spanish historian, a refugee from Franco, living in Oxford:

> As in most cases, my father was interned as an enemy alien. He went to Onchan camp on the Isle of Man. . . My mother started doing the only job that was allowed to her. That was cleaning floors, housework. And eventually she got a job with Salvador de Madariaga, looking after one of his grandchildren. . . He pulled the strings that got my father out of the Onchan Camp. With his usual Prussian efficiency, my father got himself a job there as Welfare Officer, and they didn't want to release him, because he was so efficient.

There were, however, more expeditious methods available. Adelheid Schweitzer's husband was camp doctor in Ramsey (Isle of Man):

> My husband was privileged because he became camp doctor and wrote all of the certificates for everybody who supposedly had stomach ulcers and so on. My husband, who was a very upright, honest man, would have none of that for himself. People came out and rang me up and said: 'We bring you greetings from your husband. He was so helpful in getting us out.' He didn't get himself

5. INTERNMENT

out, because he was going to come out under the provision for scientific workers, which of course took longer. But eventually he did come out, in October, in the middle of the Blitz.

A similar technique was employed, more dramatically, by Hilde Ainger's father to gain his release from his camp,

> [from Huyton] which had an appalling reputation. . . He deliberately ate the wrong thing and made his diabetes very much worse. He got into hospital and they agreed . . . we had an English cousin who was a distant relative, and we were quite friendly with a solicitor and he did it for us, and so I collected him.

Her account of this mission contains a moving vignette of her impression of those left behind:

> It was a very peculiar experience, because there were suddenly lots of German young men, who called me 'Gnädige Frau' . . . it was very, very odd. And then . . . lots of them asked me to take letters out for them to post, because . . . all correspondence was looked at, it was all censored. So they asked me if I could post them. My father said, 'You can't do that', but I jolly well did.

But Adelheid Schweitzer's sixty-nine-year-old father, who also suffered from diabetes, was not lucky enough to have his return journey from Ramsey alleviated by the intervention of his relatives, and had to resort to a stratagem:

> My father had a most extraordinary return journey. He was put on a train, he was an old man, quite frail because of the diabetes. He was put on a train under armed guard, with a young soldier with a rifle across his lap. On a boat to the mainland, and then on the train, to be escorted to London and taken to Chelsea Barracks, under escort. . . When he got to the end of the journey, he was frail. He said to the soldier: 'Please take case.' (My father didn't speak English.) That wasn't allowed. The soldier couldn't carry anybody's case. So my father said: 'You take case or I sit, make scene.' Whereupon the poor boy picked up the case and hustled my father post-haste into a taxi, which wasn't allowed either. He should have taken him by public transport. . . So there was Father stuck in the Blitz in Chelsea Barracks.

Her father was detained until Lady Reading, a prominent patient of Adelheid Schweitzer's husband, managed to obtain his release.

Despite the manifold inefficiencies of the system, distance was no bar to release. Peter Johnson was released into the Pioneer Corps, received his preliminary training in Australia, and embarked in September 1941, approximately one year after the disastrous outward voyage. His return to Britain on a passenger ship of the Blue Star Line was marred by discomforts no more serious than the disconcerting bread-throwing habits of the Australian lumberjacks who were his fellow-passengers: 'If you have lived through the First World War and the Depression, you do not throw bread around.' Alfred Dörfel, a qualified lithographic printer, was interviewed in Sherbrooke Camp (Quebec) by a Home Office official in the summer of 1941:

> They'd realised the Board had got rid of quite able-bodied men who could replace English men who were in the Army... So we, from amongst ourselves, and with Canadian help – and I think American too – but mostly the liberal Canadian organisations stirred up a lot of trouble, and the man from the Home Office... arrived. He was very friendly actually, friendly to refugees, and he organised the ones who wanted to return and the ones who were eligible.

Dörfel's application was successful, and he was released to join the war effort. In the autumn of 1941 he returned to a war-ravaged Glasgow from the relative safety of North America: 'It was a dirty, rainy night as we were taken off the ship and then we realised that we were coming back in the shadow of war.'

Conclusion: A necessary measure?

Not surprisingly, few of our interviewees accorded the process itself their approval. One who did was Peter Gellhorn, even though he himself suffered the rigours of internment: 'Actually, the internment was in a way a good thing, because you were cleared and everybody knew you were all right. Otherwise people might have suspected you throughout the war.' Stella Rotenberg, whose marriage to a Czech national preserved her from the danger of intern-

5. INTERNMENT

ment, emphatically defends the official British point of view: 'There was a very real danger of invasion. And I can, everybody must understand that ... the English were right to fear the presence of German spies in their country.' Adelheid Schweitzer's family experienced such suspicion when a CID officer from Wembley came to arrest her husband:

> [He] was an extremely unpleasant man. He had no idea what this was all about. He asked me where we kept our Hitler picture. I said, 'We are German-Jewish refugees. We are as much anti-Hitler as you are'. He looked at the well-furnished sitting-room and said: 'Well, you haven't done so badly, have you?'

For those who had recently been released from concentration camps, like Helga Reutter's father, the trauma was all the greater:

> He felt the injustice, especially at the beginning. Afterwards, you know, he thought the same as I did. It was a case of panic stations. But in the beginning, he was absolutely... He said: 'Where is the justice? There I am considered a Jew, here I am considered a Nazi spy.'

For the sixteen-year-old Eric Rose, internment meant an abrupt end to youth, and a rude transition to adulthood. Newly arrived in England, he had been at school for little more than a year, but could not face returning: 'Mentally, I wasn't in a state to see the boys again.' In general, however, the interviewees, like the majority of the German-speaking refugees in Britain, were inclined to put the internment experience behind them as an ill-conceived panic measure, certainly, but of short duration, and one that was before long recognised for what it was and rectified by the British themselves.

CHAPTER SIX

Life as an 'Enemy Alien'

Stefan Howald

'It was such a give and take'

Inevitably, the outbreak of war changed the life of all the refugees dramatically. Internment was only the most graphic expression of this. There were other consequences. This short section deals with the direct impact of war on the lives of the refugees. Classified as 'enemy aliens', they were in September 1939 subjected to certain restrictions, at this stage often no more than irksome. This is wryly remembered by Margarete Hinrichsen, although she was categorized as C (reliable): 'Obviously we had to hand in cameras. We weren't allowed to use bicycles... My first camera probably is now an antique in the police station. But it wasn't... you know, you took it as it came.' Elizabeth Rosenthal makes the following comment: 'We didn't have a wireless because we couldn't afford such a thing, so the police were kind and pleasant and no trouble.' However, they took away her mother's camera, a present from her husband, but gave it back after the war and the family still possesses it to this day.

The outbreak of war seriously affected the lives and education of children throughout Great Britain. Fathers went into the forces, mothers went to work in factories, children from the cities were evacuated. The onset of air raids, especially at night, proved particularly disruptive, exhausting both pupils and their teachers, who were often elderly replacements for those called up. Although the many privations of wartime affected the British as well as the refugees, young refugees newly arrived at unfamiliar schools suffered under the additional disadvantage that they had scarcely had time to settle in before a fresh wave of difficulties beset them. Some children were the victims of unpleasant bullying, though, as in the case of

6. LIFE AS AN ENEMY ALIEN

Walter Wolff, who was at a Quaker school in Great Ayton, Yorkshire, it disappeared when the refugee child became more integrated:

> I was of course terribly teased, for two reasons. First of all, my lack of English, and the second thing... schoolchildren... called you names like 'Nazi' and 'Jerry', that sort of thing. So it took quite a while for me to be accepted.

One example of wartime disruption – as we have seen – is presented by Eric Rose. Scarcely had he settled at his school in Holloway when his education was interrupted, first by the school's evacuation to Northamptonshire, then even more drastically by his own internment. When he returned to London after some two months, he found he could not stomach the idea of going back to school:

> Oh, I couldn't face it, I couldn't face it. Although nothing terrible had happened, mentally I wasn't in a state to see the boys again, you know, to go back to school, and... I went to what they call a crammer, it was called University Tutorial College... to be coached for the London Matriculation examination, externally, as an external candidate... This was then possible.

However, when he took the examination in January 1941, he did very well, and this launched him on a very successful path towards graduation at the London School of Economics.

For some male refugees, as seen in Chapter Four, internment stopped burgeoning careers in their tracks. Women were affected as well. Ruth Herring lost the teaching job she had filled to universal approval for more than four years because her head teacher 'couldn't defend having an enemy alien on my staff'. Subsequently, she was interned herself. Adelheid Schweitzer also lost her job because it was deemed too sensitive for war production to be carried out by a German refugee. But she was lucky. Not only was she able to get another job with the Jewish Refugees Committee, earning two pounds and ten shillings a week, but her former employer topped her wages up by a similar amount, so that her earnings were the same as in her old job.

War production sharply increased the demand for labour. In the first eighteen months war work was largely unregulated; factories poached skilled workers. Elizabeth Rosenthal's mother, who was stateless, was classified as a friendly alien. She gave up her domestic post immediately and started to do war work in a factory:

> [She] worked in a foundry with metal and spoilt her fingertips and had quite a tough time. But she also did night work and that was very hard. She was up one night, and the next week it was days, and the next week it was nights again, changing too often so that sleep patterns were disturbed.

Hans Brill's father was allowed to keep his factory running, although it was in a 'protected area'. But on 22 May 1940, the Emergency Powers (Defence) Act was passed by Parliament, giving the government the power to direct any person to take on any suitable job the Minister of Labour deemed necessary. However, this Act was widely enforced only from March 1941 onwards. Several refugees consequently did war work. Following the successful completion of his course of studies, Eric Rose was employed in a factory for two years. After his release from internment, Peter Singer's father secured a job in a factory in Warrington. Peter Gellhorn also worked in a factory after internment, where he detected that suitability was something of a flexible concept:

> It was in Hodgkinson Motors, first in Acton and then in Lewisham, the machine-shop. First I was in the winding-shop and my hands almost went to pieces, and they put me on inspection. That was more ... you needed fine finger feeling, working with micrometers, and that apparently I did successfully, and so they wouldn't let me go, and I was there until the release came and the war was already finished.

For a time Margarete Hinrichsen avoided leaving London for war work by convincing her fiancé to legalise their relationship. Later, she was directed to work in a hospital as part of the war effort. Josephine Bruegel, as a Czech citizen, was under no threat of impending internment, but she did do war work and was sent as a nurse to a children's home in Bognor Regis:

> And that was very – that was the first time that I really had a bad time. What I mean is that I lost all contact with my friends, with other refugees. I was completely isolated there, the children were no company at all, and I had to work very hard, ten hours a day.

6. LIFE AS AN ENEMY ALIEN

Especially depressing for her was not to be able to discuss the political situation on the Continent with other people.

On the other hand, because of the shortage of men in civilian work, Stella Rotenberg found a job as a bookkeeper, although she was not qualified for it; she managed to improve her skills considerably. As mentioned previously, there were even some refugees for whom new job opportunities opened up through the war effort: for example, Eugen Brehm and Hanne Norbert-Miller found work with the BBC, an institution which expanded its staff dramatically in wartime, from 4,900 at the beginning of the war to 11,500 at its end. One must add to them Ruth Herring who, by a somewhat ironic twist of fate, did occasional work deciphering letters in German script for the censors after her release from internment. War had its positive consequences in other respects as well, as Ilse Wolff recalls: 'London was full of "To Let" signs, everywhere, and it was very, very cheap, because many people had moved out of London for fear of bombs. So this was the best time to rent a flat.' Eva Pollard could afford her first flat only because its owners had left for Oxford and rented it out very cheaply. Sometimes there were even grounds for celebration, as when Klary Friedl's husband, a Czech citizen fluent in several languages, was called up. They celebrated his admission to the British Army by going to the cinema and feasting on a piece of roast pork for dinner.

Several of the refugees had close encounters with the British police. Margarete Hinrichsen was once accused of giving signals to the enemy, but predictably the police enquiries came to nothing. Lotte Berk lived for a while in Ashford in Kent, on the path of the Luftwaffe from France towards London:

> Someone told the police I was a spy. So one day a detective comes, Detective England was his name, funny, and he said, 'I'm sorry, but I hear you are going to flash lights to the German airplanes.' I said, 'If anyone . . . flashes lights, it's to the English, because I ran away from them [the Germans], I wouldn't do that, I hate the Germans more than you do.' He was terribly apologetic and he became a kind of friend. And he said, 'If anyone says something against you, just ring me.' But it didn't happen again.

Josephine Bruegel was suspected of being a spy by the matron of the hospital she worked in, when she received money from a prewar bank account. Here again, the police took no action, accepting the assurances of the Czech Refugee Trust Fund. Later, she covered up for a Communist acquaintance during police enquiries, but felt uneasy about doing so because of rumours that during the Hitler-Stalin Pact some of the refugee Communists, who at that time opposed the 'imperialist war' between Germany and Britain, had secretly passed on information that had reached Germany.

The start of the Blitz in September 1940 affected everyday life directly. Mimi Glover travelled daily from Hampstead to Croydon, 'with the Northern Line to Balham, with the train to Norbury and with a tram to Croydon and back again. I used to lie under the seat in the train when there was an air-raid warning, but it didn't upset me'. Eva Pollard recalls the bombing, a fearful experience which the refugees shared with native Londoners, many of whom found safety in the Underground, as she did:

> We had taken a room in a flat, just one room near Finchley Road here, and we also spent all the nights in the tube station when it was very, very noisy and very dangerous, because we had a flat roof, no protection, we were on the top floor.

In contrast, Helga Reutter recalls that she, foolishly as she now thinks, never went to an air-raid shelter. Once, with friends, she even watched bombs falling on the East End from a rooftop.

From 1941 onwards, many refugees volunteered to do fire-watching. Margarete Hinrichsen recalls the procedure: 'There were air-raid wardens and there were fire-watchers, and you had to watch out and [if] there was an air raid you had to learn . . . it was called a stirrup-pump. . . On duty all through the night.' Peter Singer also belonged to the Auxiliary Fire Service and had 'to deal with the odd incendiary bomb on the roof of Earls Court, but by luck nothing serious actually happened'. He slept at his workplace while on duty. These night duties could seriously affect daily life, as in the case of Walter Wolff:

> I was working five-and-a-half days a week from nine o'clock till five, then went to College from six till nine, for both lectures and pract-

6. LIFE AS AN ENEMY ALIEN

icals... I used to stay with her [his mother, also on fire-watching duties], so in fact for two nights a week I had no sleep at all. And of course there was a lot of homework to be done.

There were better opportunities available, if one had the means, as Eric Rose tells us, slightly apologetically:

I went to this crammer and the bombs were coming down and I went on regardless, going to study, and I did the five subjects that were required for the London Matriculation. And we were living in this flat in West Hampstead, Cavendish Mansions in West Hampstead, and we didn't have a shelter, we had to go to a public shelter every night, and this was awful, because we couldn't sleep, and my father again had one of his brainwaves and he said: 'Well, we'll have to sleep outside London', and he rented a house in Henley-on-Thames. We went to sleep in Henley-on-Thames – we still had the flat in West Hampstead, and we commuted every day, he to business and I to college, every day from Henley-on-Thames to Paddington. And the Great Western Railways... laid on special trains for the people who had evacuated themselves to Henley-on-Thames or thereabouts, and we went right through from Henley to Paddington, whereas normally we would have had to change at Twyford. But they laid on these special trains for commuters, which was really pandering to people who had had the initiative to evacuate themselves. So at least we had a good night's sleep.

Nelly Kuttner's poor health prevented her from fire-watching, but her husband was recruited, and she spent the night with him on night-shifts. One day, her husband discovered a fully equipped but unused public shelter near his workplace in the City of London, and persuaded the police to open it. For many weeks the couple travelled every evening from their flat in Maida Vale to this shelter in the City, and she travelled back to Maida Vale every morning at seven o'clock. One day, when she arrived home, one of the nearby buildings had suffered a direct hit, but her own windows were only slightly cracked. The shelter in the City was also hit, luckily in their absence.

Klary Friedl suffered the worst experiences. Her flat in Belsize Park received a direct hit in October 1940. She and her husband were severely injured and had to stay in hospital for over six weeks. Doctors feared that her husband's arm would be permanently affected; and Klary Friedl herself could not conceive a child for several years as a result of her internal injuries. Eva Pollard recounts a direct hit and the consequences for her parents:

> Unfortunately my parents got completely bombed out in Belsize Park. It was a bomb which razed the whole front of the building and you could look into the room, and my parents spent the alert, when the siren went, in the basement, because they were on the first or second floor . . . and my father just happened to be outside the room when this bomb came and the door couldn't be opened any more, so my parents didn't know what happened – whether my father was alive . . . and my father didn't know whether my mother and these people were all right. . . Only in the morning somebody, some air-raid warden, could establish that they were both all right.

They lost most of their few possessions and, since her father was still somewhat traumatised by his experiences in Buchenwald in 1938, her parents relocated to Gloucestershire, where they had to live on welfare.

Mimi Glover recalls the disruption she encountered during her English lessons. Her school had been transferred to the fifth floor of a building in Russell Square, and whenever there was an alert they had to descend from the fifth floor to the basement, where classes continued. At Christmas 1944, a bomb fell in the middle of Russell Square, right on the bandstand, and blew all the windows out. Since there was no coal available for heating, teaching had to continue under atrocious conditions, affecting her health.

Earlier in 1944, Nelly Kuttner and her husband had the opportunity of renting a room in Cambridge, just to get some sleep at the weekend. So they lived in Cambridge for some months, and her husband commuted to London to work. They returned to London after the liberation of France in August 1944, only to get caught by the V2 rockets from September onwards: 'They came very, very quietly, you couldn't hear them, and when one came down, it was awful, dreadful, five times more than the flying-bombs and, of course, they did a lot of damage and you couldn't find the shelter.' Apart from

6. LIFE AS AN ENEMY ALIEN

such dramatic, life-threatening dangers, there were psychological consequences which were sometimes almost as serious. Margarete Hinrichsen recalls the very first consequence of the war: 'Once the war broke out I didn't speak German. Hardly at all. People couldn't understand why there were people walking around speaking German, even in Hampstead.' She also took to calling herself Margarete instead of Gretl, because Gretl sounded too German. Hans Seelig too urged his parents not to speak German in public any more, as did Elizabeth Rosenthal.

On the other hand, wartime also afforded positive experiences. Klary Friedl encountered numerous friendly gestures after she was released from hospital. Even the policeman who had to check her blackout became a friend. She remembers vividly the concerts given by Dame Myra Hess at the National Gallery. Margarete Hinrichsen states that she started becoming more familiar with English people during fire-watching duties. 'Through Klaus [her husband] in the Home Guard and I in the Fire Service, we mixed with quite a lot of people.' Stella Rotenberg also felt more accepted as the wife of a soldier in the British army than before the outbreak of war. Helga Reutter, who emphasises the honesty and helpfulness of the people, pays moving tribute to the qualities that the British revealed under wartime conditions. For Klary Friedl, wartime was to remain a positive experience, in direct contrast to the postwar years:

> You see, the people were wonderful, you knew that every door was open to you, but the very minute the war was over, they closed their doors, so every door closed. You see, we had been sleeping or staying hours and hours on the corridor when there were doodlebugs and the bombs came. We talked together, we ate together, drank tea together, and, you see, I never drank my ration of tea because I'd never drunk such strong tea, and I could give them my tea ration and things, it was such a give and take. Before the war was over, the friendship, well not friendship but acquaintance, maybe you didn't know their name or anything, but you said, 'Hello, how are you, when is the bombing coming?', and we had always something to talk about.

Eva Pollard delivers a more sober assessment, trying to balance the positive against the negative:

That was, what shall I say, not an unhappy time. We were young and all our friends were in the same boat, we all didn't have any money and we all were saved, luckily, so I must say that it was hard, it was surely not easy, but it was not a depressing time as such.

CHAPTER SEVEN

Religion

Anthony Grenville

As might be expected, the great majority of the refugees interviewed are Jewish, since Jews were the principal targets, among German citizens, of systematic, state-sponsored persecution under the Nazi regime. Of our thirty-four interviewees, twenty-five are fully Jewish and three more, Walter Wolff, Peter Gellhorn and Hilde Auerbach, half- Jewish. Only six are not Jewish. However, it is clear that what draws the Jewish interviewees together is more their common fate as victims of Nazi persecution than any deep and active involvement in Judaism or any shared commitment to Jewish religious values and observance. This again is what might be expected of a group taken from the largely assimilated and secularised Jewish communities in the German-speaking lands. This is not to deny that profound commitment to Jewish causes and values is to be found among some refugees, but it remains the exception, not the rule. What all the Jewish refugees have in common is that they find themselves in Britain as racial victims of Nazi persecution and as the inheritors of the rich traditions of German-Jewish culture, once treasured and now largely lost. That it is effectively impossible to distinguish between the fates of the full Jews and the three half Jews, all of whom had non-Jewish mothers and therefore counted as Jewish for the Nazis but not for the Jewish community, indicates that racial provenance outweighs religious faith and observance as determining factors in the lives of this group.

The six non-Jews, who will be discussed separately, cannot be viewed as a single coherent group in terms of their religion. It is, for a start, inaccurate to call them 'Christians', since three of their number, Alfred Dörfel, Eugen Brehm and Alec Armstrong, were committed left-wing activists, members of the Communist Party or other radical left-wing groups which rejected religion on principle and espoused militant atheism. Religion did play a considerable part in the lives of the other three non-Jewish refugees, Ruth Herring and Christel Marsh, both Protestants, and the Catholic Erika Young. However, they profess allegiance to very different sectors of the wide spectrum of Christian denominations and have too little in common in terms of religious attitudes and beliefs to be grouped together by religion alone. Rather, one might argue that the decision to reject National Socialism and leave Germany was in each case the result of a deeply rooted ethical outlook which, though Christian in inspiration, drew crucially on a private moral conviction of what was right and what was wrong.

1. The assimilated Jews before emigration

The assimilated Jews who had migrated to the German-speaking cities in the decades before 1914 rapidly became secularised and in very many cases ceased to see their Jewishness as primarily, or even significantly, bound up with religious faith. Many such Jews limited their devotion to largely symbolic visits to the synagogue on special occasions, discarding a life centred around religious ritual along with the distinctive garb of the ghetto. This is very much the pattern that emerges from the refugees' memories of their parents; indeed, the picture of thoroughly assimilated and generally non-observant middle-class families is by far the most commonly described aspect of the Jewish interviewees' lives. Hanne Norbert-Miller's household was 'very typical Viennese middle-class assimilated Jewish, if that is a good way of expressing it. We did not keep any religion really'. Renée Hubert remembers her parents similarly: 'Yes, they were both Jewish. But practising? I don't think I ever was in a synagogue in Frankfurt.'

Hans Brill calls his family 'not remotely religious':

> The only feast we ever celebrated was Chanukah, which was celebrated just before Christmas, so one got both. But no one actually knew very much about it. In fact my father . . . he could be very funny and very caustic, and certainly he was always very amused by the Jews of Vienna, he really had nothing in common with them.

7. RELIGION

These were Jews who retained a clear sense of their Jewish identity, but were no longer anchored in religious affiliation and observance; they remained conscious Jews, in Eva Sommerfreund's words, but non-practising ones. Whereas her observant maternal grandmother 'did sit in the synagogue on the High Holidays for the whole day and the whole night', her mother definitely did not. Although her parents were married in a synagogue by the Chief Rabbi of Prague, no less, this reflected the family's wealth and standing rather than their devoutness, since 'they didn't have much to do with the actual religion'.

Helga Reutter's father, also thoroughly assimilated, at least went to synagogue once a year, but not out of true religious devotion or a regard for religious ritual:

> Well, we were Jewish. But nothing was kept actually. I remember when I was young and I wanted to fast on the fast day, my father said, you be decent the whole year, then you won't have to fast. . . He just went to synagogue once a year, that was for the death prayer, not because he believed in it, but I think it was a sort of moral feeling that he had, that it was the right thing to do. Tradition. But not a religious feeling.

Klary Friedl's father too preserved the old Jewish values, like the dispensing of generous hospitality on holidays, but also stripped of any specifically religious significance: he even broke the Jewish taboo on celebrating on the birth of Christ by having a Christmas tree, allegedly for their nanny – but the family joined in the present-giving. Helga Reutter's parents did likewise; she was also enchanted by midnight mass in the mountain village of Mariazell.

Both of these last-mentioned families display similar changes over the generations: Klary Friedl's paternal grandfather, a famous rabbi from an important religious family in Poland, was a deeply religious man, while his son maintained a façade of observance, and his granddaughter scarcely even that; Helga Reutter's maternal grandfather was also a devout Jew, but none of this passed to his granddaughter, who had her daughter brought up as a Christian in England. Hanna Singer gives what is almost a paradigm account of a Jewish family from devout Orthodox stock who by the 1930s were attending synagogue only on religious festivals:

> My parents were what they would consider assimilated Jews, while their respective grandparents, certainly on my mother's side, were Orthodox, but they considered themselves liberal. So we'd go to synagogue occasionally and we'd go to Hebrew classes. . . No, no, they weren't [religious]. As I said, you know, we went to synagogue occasionally, I suppose, sort of on the main holidays, perhaps the odd Saturday service.

She learnt Hebrew only for the most practical of reasons, in case of emigration to Palestine. In much the same way, Renée Hubert's school arranged religious instruction for its Jewish pupils mainly as a way of 'helping us to cope with the situation of being a minority and one which would be made more uncomfortable perhaps in the future'.

Mimi Glover remembers the Jewish festival celebrations fondly:

> Well, father was observant, not mother, but she did know what to do and we had a lovely, you know, Pesach Seder dish and we had a lovely table when it was Pesach Seder, and father always went to pray on Yom Kippur and he didn't belong to a synagogue, so on the Hohe Warte [a smart residential district in Vienna], also on the Ring [major thoroughfare in Vienna] where we lived later, there was a Blindeninstitut, a place for the blind, and they opened it on Yom Kippur and many people went there to pray.

But her Jewishness seems otherwise to have had little influence on her life in Austria; her close circle of much-loved friends was exclusively and avowedly Catholic. Gertrud Wengraf's parents made a token show of observance: 'I mean, when we were small and when we lived in Lundenburg, in this small place, it was the thing to do, at the Jewish festivals, to go to the temple, but that was the only thing in the year that we went to.' Not surprisingly, her sense of identity later, in Vienna, developed around her Social Democratic political convictions, not her religious origins. Her parents did, however, mix mainly in a circle of Jewish families, as one might expect of a close Jewish community in a small Moravian town. Jewish families in larger towns were sometimes more open to mixing with Gentiles, and some, like Klary Friedl's, had numbers of non-Jewish friends. But often such families mixed mainly with other Jews, simply

7. RELIGION

because patterns of social intercourse tended not to cut across the racial/religious divide. This was the case with Helga Reutter's parents, who conducted much of their social life in that most Jewish of environments, the Viennese coffee house.

Peter Johnson's father was a very assimilated Jew, who celebrated Christmas and only started closing his business on the higher Jewish festivals when his son, who had learnt about them in school, reminded him to observe them. The father, like many assimilated Jews, expressed his sense of belonging to the German nation by joining the Centralverein deutscher Staatsbürger jüdischen Glaubens (Central Union of German Citizens of the Jewish Faith), founded in 1893 to combat anti-semitism, but from a position of loyal German patriotism. The patriotism of Jews is beyond question: at least five Jewish fathers of interviewees fought for Germany in the First World War, of whom one died, and at least three more fought for Austria-Hungary, while one, despite poor health, guarded Russian prisoners. Peter Johnson's father's service to his country did not save him from deportation and death under the Nazis; nor did it save Margarete Hinrichsen's father who, despite a warning, returned to Bad Polzin from Berlin to save the Torah scrolls on 9/10 November 1938 (Kristallnacht) and was killed. A member of the Centralverein, he thought of himself as a German, but also as a devout Jew. Dorothea Galewski's father hardly even considered himself Jewish and resisted the very idea of emigration, until he was arrested in November 1938 and sent to Buchenwald: '[He] was really more German than many Germans; he was a real Prussian, I would say, and didn't really think consciously as a Jew.' In a similar instance of defiant self-identification with his native country, Hans Brill's father refused to leave Austria until he too was arrested.

Margarete Hinrichsen's father, who had once worked as an assistant to Chaim Weizmann in Manchester, was one of the few observant Jewish parents. He was head of a kosher household and kept the Jewish festivals, but his wife kept the observances only for his sake, and all four daughters gave them up:

> Contrary to all the others in my family, my father was the only one who observed Judaism as such... No one kept anything except my

father, and we were a kosher household, and we were brought up [like that] – didn't do the house much good – because all of us gave it up, absolutely!

They did, however, grow up knowing that they were a Jewish family and with a clear sense of their Jewish identity. Margarete Hinrichsen's emigration was partly due to her strictly Jewish forebears: she was sent to England in 1937 to learn the language, but also to prevent her marrying a half-Jewish boyfriend, which would have caused her to be disinherited under the terms of her grandfather's will. The rest of the family fled in 1939 to Palestine, which would have been the father's natural choice of refuge.

The majority of the Jewish interviewees were more like Adelheid Schweitzer's family, who were so sure of their position as well-regarded, well-integrated members of society that the experience of the anti-Jewish boycott on 1 April 1933 and the accompanying vituperation came as a terrible shock. Lotte Berk, like several of the German refugees, only became properly conscious of her Jewishness as a result of Nazi persecution, while Elizabeth Rosenthal states: 'I didn't know I was Jewish until I was told by the Nazis.' In Austria, Stella Rotenberg dryly remarks, it was the anti-semites rather than any Jewish upbringing that taught her that she was Jewish. Hilde Ainger was another who grew up in a 'very comfortable, middle-class, professional Jewish family. We were not, my parents were not Jewish by religion, we didn't have a religion, but we knew we were Jewish, but it wasn't important, because we mixed with everyone.' At the extreme, Eva Pollard never even mentions the matter of religion. Hans Brill describes his mother as a 'Christianised Jewess' and his father as 'not at all interested in Jewish things, not remotely'. Although his family was totally unreligious, celebrating both Chanukah and Christmas with fine ecumenical indifference, the Anschluss reawakened a sense of loyalty to the Jewish community to which they after all belonged: his father sent his small son to the synagogue, as a gesture of solidarity at that critical time, though this rediscovered awareness of Jewish identity was political, not religious.

However, Margarete Hinrichsen's father was not the only

7. RELIGION

religious Jew. Lotte Berk's father, who had originally intended to become a cantor, had been a devout believer until he lost his faith on his wife's sudden death. Ernst Flesch's father was active as secretary of the local synagogue; this stood him in good stead after Kristallnacht, when he was released from arrest through the good offices of an employee of the Israelitische Kultusgemeinde, the Jewish communal organisation. Nelly Kuttner relates how her parents fell away from their previously very strict observance during the First World War, when hunger forced them to eat pork, until finally they paid little more than lip service to Jewish ritual, and even that for social convention rather than from heartfelt devotion:

> I mean, she was still lighting the candle on a Friday, but in the end the minor holidays were never kept, only the New Year was kept and the day when you fast, because my parents had a seat in the synagogue. At Easter [Passover], only one day, the second day, was kept, because all of my mother's family came, there were more than twenty people with us and mother made soup with the dumplings and all of the national things, so they all came for a good meal, and my father, he was the eldest one, said the prayer, sometimes he stopped, he could not carry on and somebody had to help him. It was a family affair, but the next day we already started eating bread, it was only ... the First World War taught my parents to give up all the religious things.

One group who broke away from the assimilationist mould, though not by returning to Orthodoxy, were the Zionists, who reacted to anti-semitism by seeking to rediscover their Jewish roots and to sever all ties with Gentile society, a project that would be realised through the establishment of a Jewish state in Palestine. Zionists were always a small minority in German Jewry, and only two appear here. Eric Rose's father was a strong Zionist, but not a practising Jew; nevertheless, he chose to have his son's bar mitzvah in the Orthodox synagogue in Breslau, because of the hostility of the rival Reform Jewish community to Zionism and its negative attitude towards Palestine. Peter Singer's father was also a Zionist who, like Eric Rose's, was only prevented from emigrating to Palestine by the strict entry requirements.

Peter Singer recalls his family as more religious than some, but they were still very far from strictly observant:

> I was barmitzvah'd when I was thirteen. We used to keep some of the [rituals], you know . . . and we had candles on Friday nights, not always, but they were trying to bring us up – me and my sister, who was three years older – with a Jewish background, but we weren't regular synagogue attenders.

He joined a Zionist youth organisation, the Habonim, in contrast to the larger number of the refugees who became members of German-Jewish youth groups that sought to emphasise both aspects of their heritage. The division between Zionists and liberal assimilationists, expressed in Ernst Flesch's outspoken rejection of Zionist nationalism, was deep and sometimes bitter. In the generation of the interviewees themselves, the process of assimilation was to continue apace, especially in exile, away from their native Jewish community and from any routine of religious practice.

2. Jewishness in exile

The experience of exile in Britain tended to accelerate the abandonment by most of the Jews among the refugees of their religion and their sense of a traditional Jewish identity. The process of assimilation, already well advanced in their native countries, resumed briskly once they became settled. The clearest evidence of this is that a fair proportion of them barely mention religion in their life stories after emigration, and some, like Eva Pollard, not at all. Dorothea Galewski does not speak about her Jewishness, except in the negative context of having had it imposed on her by the Nazis; it does not even arise when she describes the time she spent working for the American occupation authorities at a war crimes trial. Hans Seelig only mentions his Jewishness in his early decades in Britain by reference to its virtual absence, when he refused to change his religion just to improve his job prospects: 'There's no point in my changing one religion that doesn't mean much to me to one that doesn't mean anything to me.'

7. RELIGION

Josephine Bruegel scarcely feels Jewish at all: 'I have very little to do with Judaism... We had very little to do with Jewish matters, we had more to do with non-Jewish matters. We never really had any contact, you see.' Though her husband was 'a good Jew', Klary Friedl also assumes a resolutely secular stance: 'I believe in being honest and decent and this is my religion.' Seven of the twenty-five fully Jewish interviewees – Hilde Ainger, Mimi Glover, Josephine Bruegel, Lotte Berk, Helga Reutter, Renée Hubert and Margarete Hinrichsen – married non-Jews; in the case of Margarete Hinrichsen, this was the decisive factor which stopped her from emigrating to Palestine, belonging to any Jewish organisations or going to synagogue. Such rates of 'marrying out' and lapsing from Jewish religious observance indicate how rapidly the refugees from Central Europe, unlike their co-religionists who had come from Eastern Europe at the turn of the century, would integrate into secular British society. The refugees founded very few religious institutions, the best-known being the New Liberal Jewish Congregation, based at Belsize Square Synagogue. They did not create an identifiable and lasting community of their own based on religious observance, and certainly nothing to compare with the synagogues and other distinctive institutions which Anglo-Jewry founded and through which it constructed for itself a religious/cultural self-image that make it an identifiable, discrete group.

However, the picture overall is not one of complete dissociation from Judaism, even though the refugees' sense of their Jewish identity is often more cultural than religious. At least one, Eric Rose, seems to have strengthened his attachment to his native faith in England, thanks to his involvement with Jewish student organisations, through which he met his wife, to his career with Marks & Spencer, and his family connections with Israel. He is proud that his grandchildren, born in Israel, feel equally at home in Jerusalem and in London – as he does himself. Ernst Flesch, who was placed on arrival in a Jewish orphanage in Glasgow, had contact with a number of Jewish institutions and gravitated naturally to working for a Jewish photographer who specialised in East End Jewish weddings. He does not, however, share Eric Rose's enthusiasm for Zionism:

> I didn't think [Zionism] was the solution to the Jewish problem, really. . . I thought, if we were against Nazi nationalism, why should we be for Jewish nationalism? After all some wings of the Zionist movement are very extreme. Even in Vienna, the Revisionists they were called, that was the Irgun lot, the Jabotinsky lot, were very unpopular, even with the other Zionist kids. They walked around in jackboots, you know, in uniform.

Elizabeth Rosenthal was brought closer to her ancestral faith by adversity. After being brought up in Germany totally unaware that she was Jewish, her experiences as a child refugee in Oldham awakened her to what she was:

> [My foster family] went to church every Sunday. C of E, and I said, 'I am not going to church. I am Jewish.' And they said, 'Then you must go to the synagogue.' There wasn't a synagogue in Oldham and I never went to the synagogue. My Jewishness was very liberal. I didn't know I was Jewish until I was told I was 'ein Jude'. And I had Jewish education in Caputh [her school] but very little as I mentioned. So I didn't think I ought to go to the synagogue. But I knew at that moment, aged eleven, that I was Jewish and I was loyal to the Jewish people. And there was no way that I was going into a church.

This attempt to impose a certain type of religious behaviour on her rekindled in her

> . . .the whole emotion of having all the people behind me right back to . . . not Adam and Eve but the people of Moses. It was my people and they I knew had been driven out of Nazi Germany for the sake of being Jewish. That was my identity. Never kept secret or never . . . no doubt about it, even though one doesn't have to believe in everything. But it's a very deep feeling.

The same sense of underlying allegiance to the Jewish people, largely shorn of any religious dimension, is movingly expressed by Nelly Kuttner, for whom observance has become a private ritual of memorial to the loved ones she has lost:

> When I came here to this country, I felt very Jewish, but I am not religious at all, only when I was working here in the household [as a domestic], I kept the fast day and had a seat in the synagogue in

7. RELIGION

> Hammersmith, and when I was with Stefan [her husband] for the first year, the second, third, fourth year, I had an operation and he said, 'I won't allow you to fast. You have lost your parents, you have lost all your relatives, finish with that.' So I finished, and on the fast day, some people observe that day, maybe not fasting the whole day, but still I just light two candles, 24-hour candles in memory of the dead, and I lead a normal life. I go to the office, I have no restrictions, it's a normal day for me. For me, there is no need to fast to think about the dead, because I think about them every day. It is not a formal thing for me any more. And the two candles were lit even when Stefan was alive, I lit one for his daughter he lost and I lit one for my parents, that's all. He didn't ask me to do it, but I did it.

Her identification with Jewry, though typically indifferent to strictly religious matters, comes across in her feelings about giving a proper Jewish burial place to her husband, who had converted to Christianity:

> I couldn't care less about afterwards [i.e. after death], people can put me in a dustbin, I couldn't care less, but in the end Stefan was Jewish by birth, he only later converted to Presbyterian. He liked it, but I mean, he went to the church just to go to a club. He was not religious at all, he just went as a tradition and sometimes I went with him as well, but he still felt very Jewish inside.

Nelly Kuttner is one of the very few to mention attending a synagogue in England, the Reform Synagogue in Berkeley Square, though she has long ceased to go there. Even the Liberal Synagogue in Belsize Square, in the heart of the area of refugee settlement in London, appears only as the venue for Club 1943, for which Hans Seelig acts as chairman and Ernst Flesch as treasurer. Mimi Glover attends the Liberal Synagogue in St John's Wood regularly, and also goes to synagogue when in Vienna, although during her husband's lifetime she dutifully tailored her Jewishness to his Anglicanism: 'He was very Church of England, but I was still Jewish, I never changed my religion, I fasted on Yom Kippur and cooked his lunch and when he died I joined the synagogue.' Even at school, she had shown a surprising aptitude for Christian religious education, though this could be explained by her reluctance to sit outside the classroom in a cold corridor during religious instruction: '[The teacher] said that I was his best pupil, because he allowed us to stay in the room, because it was too cold in the corridor. Well, it was interesting, you learnt something else and religion is religion, even if it is Catholic.'

Such a relaxed attitude to religious orthodoxy is only to be expected from those who, like most of our interviewees, were brought up with little firm attachment to Jewish beliefs and practices. The majority of them accordingly distanced themselves to varying degrees from those beliefs and practices and integrated into secularised British society. Adelheid Schweitzer, largely non-practising in exile, recalls the pattern of her life, which has developed in a way not untypical of the Jewish interviewees:

> My husband came from a much less assimilated home than I came from myself, but dropped almost everything by the way. He still wanted a Jewish household and a kosher household when he first knew me, and I said 'You've got the wrong woman'. We never had a kosher household. We go to synagogue – they call it schul here – from time to time and on the high holy days.

Both her children, British and non-religious, 'married out'; she did however feel it incumbent on her to transmit to them something of their Jewish heritage, by giving them their respective bar and bat mitzvah, and she is pleased that her grand-daughter wears the Star of David which she gave her.

Renée Hubert turned more sharply against religion, finding the manifestations of religiosity on an English Sunday alien and ridiculous and preferring 'non-religious' France. In the small English towns where she taught during the war, she was in any case totally cut off from all things Jewish. Peter Singer had been an active member of a Zionist youth group in Germany, but in Britain he joined the Communist-organised Free German Youth, where Jewishness played no part. Later, it was through a contact on the refugee network that he built his career, but there was no renewal of any specifically Jewish dimension to his life. Peter Johnson soon cast loose in Britain from such Jewish roots as he had had: he first lived with a group of entirely unreligious Jewish boys from Germany; the

7. RELIGION

chief attraction that caused him to join the Jewish club founded by the West London Synagogue seems to have been its good, cheap food. Connections with Jewish organisations often arose from thoroughly secular motives: Hans Seelig was sent to a Jewish private school soon after arriving in Britain, but only to overcome his language problems, and he soon returned happily to the British education system. Similarly, Elizabeth Rosenthal made contact with organisations like London Jewish Graduates purely for social purposes. At the far extreme is Hans Brill's father, who turned triumphantly native, adopted the image of the pipe-smoking Britisher and took pride in joining the Home Guard. His son's life in Britain predictably shows no trace of Jewishness.

This leads on to the important question of the refugees' identity, a difficult and problematical area. Gertrud Wengraf, who describes herself as 'not religiously inclined', was never a religious or practising Jew and consequently lays no claim to a Jewish identity in Britain: 'I'm not an Englishwoman, I don't think I am. On the other hand, I'm not an Austrian either; I'm not a Jewess either because my religion doesn't come into it. So I'm a bit in the middle of nowhere.' Josephine Bruegel, a German-speaking, non-practising Jew born in Czechoslovakia when it was still part of the Habsburg Empire, likewise has difficulty in defining her identity; asked whether she feels herself to be English, Czech, Austrian or Jewish, she can only respond by denying that she is Jewish. The Jewish refugees who had seen themselves as well assimilated into German or Austrian society, and had therefore largely laid aside their religious faith and adherence to Judaism, suffered very keenly the loss of a sense of identity that had been secure until the advent of Hitler. Unlike the observant descendants of the earlier wave of Jewish refugees from Eastern Europe, they had no real sense of Jewish identity on which to fall back.

With the brutal death of her father, the living embodiment of the strategy of combining German patriotism with loyal Jewish observance, Margarete Hinrichsen also suffered the loss of the main pillar of her identity: 'After '38 I really didn't feel German at all, ever, any more.' But neither could she assume the religiously-based identity of the observant Jew and, *faute de mieux*, has acquired a vaguely

British identity, adopted partly vicariously, through her British-born children, and partly as a means of emphasising her rejection of her previous German identity:

> Having married someone who wasn't Jewish, my children are both baptised, because I felt it was better if they wanted a religion to have a religion. I couldn't give them a religion because I had lost whatever belief I had because of what had happened in the world... Once you have children your life changes. In a different country your life changes very much. I made a lot of friends through the children and I feel far more British. I don't feel German at all.

Jewish refugees like her are most reluctant to define themselves as German or Austrian, understandably in view of the treatment they endured at the hands of their erstwhile countrymen.

Yet at the same time their assimilated and non-religious upbringing ensures that they cannot see themselves fully as Jews. Peter Johnson was brought up to feel prouder of his long German ancestry than of any religious affiliation:

> We called ourselves 'Germans of the Jewish faith'. We were Germans first and Jews second. We weren't religious. We were very conscious that we had been Germans for generations on our mother's and on our father's side.

He was a member of a German-Jewish youth organisation which stressed its allegiance to German values and society, with strong overtones of Germanic nationalism. Ilse Wolff and Margarete Hinrichsen were members of similar groups. Of her time in the 'Deutsch-Jüdische Jugendgemeinschaft' Ilse Wolff recalls: 'We thought of ourselves as being German Jews, not Jewish Germans.' In Britain, those refugees who had been brought up as Germans first and as Jews only second were to overcome their rejection by Nazi Germany by assimilating into the society of their adopted homeland, not by reverting to the Jewish faith. If as a group they kept a discrete identity of their own, it was not defined by their religion, but rather by the culture they brought with them.

Some of our interviewees appear very distant from any sense of a religiously-based Jewish identity. Dorothea Galewski's brief

7. RELIGION

acquaintance with Judaism ceased with her emigration in 1939, and Ernst Flesch lost his religion in his early teens when it was rammed down his throat. Tellingly, Hanna and Peter Singer married at a registry office, because she felt that it would have been hypocritical to go to a synagogue. Margarete Hinrichsen has cut herself off completely from her German-Jewish origins, though at the cost of losing her former closeness to her 'old' family. The memory of her previous, partly Jewish identity remains with her, in that she still accuses herself of 'straying from the faith' by having lived with her future husband before marriage and feels a sense of guilt at having abandoned her father's religion: 'I never belonged to any Jewish [organisations]. I didn't even go to synagogue in England, though my father would have been heartbroken that I didn't.'

The relationship of the interviewees to their Jewishness is indeed more complex than a simple process of progressive and inevitable separation from it. A sense of Jewish identity remains with all of them, even when they seem to have moved a long way from the religiously based lifestyle of their forefathers. The key element here appears to be what one might best call a cultural sense of Jewish identity. Eva Sommerfreund, almost completely unreligious, is not concerned about the fact that both her daughters have married non-Jews, but she is very insistent that they should remain conscious of being Jewish. Although she has negative feelings about religion, believing it to lead to fanaticism, she stands firmly by her own Jewish identity. That identity is clearly assimilated as well as secularised: she disapproves of the refusal of the more orthodox Jews to assimilate, and believes that she has by now much in common with the native English in the externals of her lifestyle, though she has preserved her own identity in the private sphere, and especially in her cultural and artistic heritage from Central Europe.

There is also a marked tendency for Jewish interviewees to return to their roots in their later years. Lotte Berk is one who feels herself to have become more Jewish with age. She still does not mix easily with religious Jews, citing two of her students:

> They don't want to speak German. They are much younger than I am, they are 56 or something, they are not really my cup of tea, I'm

not [comfortable] with religious people, it somehow kills my sense of humour.

Nevertheless, she is one of several interviewees who with advancing age mixes increasingly with Jewish friends from similar backgrounds. Her defiantly individualistic creed combines secularised humanism with a deeply-felt, personal sense of religion: 'I always say, God is within me, I make my life. Everything else is not true.' Stella Rotenberg has also become aware in later years of the importance to her of her Jewish identity, which is above all that of the victim of persecution, the refugee forced to flee abroad: 'I am a Jew because I am persecuted.' The lesson that she has learnt from her experiences encompasses Jewry in the wider community of humanity: 'You should not be a friend to the Jews, you should be a friend to all humankind.'

A particularly clear case is that of Hans Seelig, who, after a phase when he thought of himself as British, rediscovered an interest in his origins in his middle years. Later, after his mother's death, 'I grew back into Jewishness, I started attending our synagogue, over in St Albans at the time.' This new religious dimension to his life does, however, have its limits: his new awareness of his Jewishness is closely linked to his work with Club 1943, to cultural and intellectual pursuits, and he expressly ranks music above all else as a source of religious inspiration:

> But the things I've got very active in are – first and foremost Club 1943 – in other words, returning to my background, rediscovering the Jewish religion, although in many respects I'm very unorthodox even from the Liberal point of view – sometimes I'd go so far as to say I'm little more than a positive agnostic – but a very positive one, I get more religion out of music than out of. . . I mean, quite seriously, more religion out of music than out of anything else.

Here again, the cultural component in the refugees' Jewish identity emerges prominently.

7. RELIGION

3. Attitudes to unassimilated Jews and relations with Anglo-Jewry

Before they went to Britain, the assimilated Jews among our interviewees were aware of a gulf between them and their more orthodox fellow Jews who had kept the religiously-based customs and appearance of the East. Hanna Singer remarks on the lack of contact between her family and Orthodox Jews, between those who were Jewish only by birth and those who were so by religious faith and observance:

> And on the whole we didn't seem to meet, I don't remember meeting Orthodox people. So when Halle had invited its ex-citizens, the Jewish ones, for some great reunion, because it was 300 years of the Jews in Halle a few years ago, I was really surprised to hear there were all sorts of people that I'd never, never heard of because they were Orthodox . . . there wasn't a lot of contact, didn't seem to be any overlap.

In internment on the Isle of Man, Peter Gellhorn too sensed the gulf between assimilated and Orthodox Jews: 'The Orthodox Jews, they were given one boarding-house alone for themselves and when you went there it was just like going abroad. They said: "Oh good morning, Mr Gellhorn, nice to see you," but you belonged to another world, they had their own.' Mimi Glover is unsettled by the contrast between the Jews who had attended her synagogue in her youth and the Orthodox Jews with their prayer shawls who go there now. A good indicator of the distance between the assimilated Jews and those from the East is their attitude to Yiddish: whereas the eastern Jews spoke Yiddish, and at least some passed it on to their Anglo-Jewish descendants, families like those of our Central European refugees had long dropped it as a relic of the ghetto. Those that mention it in their interviews do so only to profess ignorance of it: Elizabeth Rosenthal, for example, 'didn't know there was such a thing' as Yiddish.

In Austria relations between the assimilated Jews and the 'Ostjuden' had long been strained:

> The westernised Jews usually regarded their eastern co-religionists with suspicion if not outright contempt and rarely intermarried with

them. They saw the Ostjuden as loud, coarse, dirty, immoral, and culturally backward. As in Germany they were seen as apparitions from an earlier period of Jewish history the assimilated Jews wanted to forget. Well-established Viennese Jews even held them responsible for arousing anti-semitism.²²

The religious Jews from the East were seen by middle-class German and Austrian Jews as lacking the culture and education which they had gained and prized so highly, and as posing a standing threat, through their appearance and customs, to the successful assimilation of the Jewish community into modern society.

Helga Reutter, already very assimilated in Vienna, married a non-Jew and brought up her daughter as an Anglican and 'completely British', to avoid her becoming a member of an exposed minority (though she is perfectly content that her daughter then proceeded to marry a husband from another ethnic minority). This strategy may have in part reflected her pre-emigration fear of the hostility from the native population that the Jews from the East might have brought down upon the heads of the precariously assimilated Jews settled in Vienna:

> I had some relatives in the Second District where many Jews lived, I personally felt slightly uncomfortable when I saw them with the payes [ringlets] and the kaftans. It was most unfair, because probably my great-grandfather did exactly the same, but I still felt just as uncomfortable as when I go to Golders Green now and see it. . . There's no reasonable explanation for it. My husband who was purely 'Aryan' didn't mind at all, but I do. I don't know, perhaps I don't want people to look at them, because personally I hate it. And people talk about Jew-boys and so on.

She found the British Jews clannish and unwelcoming, and suspects that they in turn found the new arrivals from Central Europe arrogant, on account of their sense of cultural and educational superiority, a point that is picked up by Eva Sommerfreund:

> I think, our lot that came over this time, as compared to the ones that came at the turn of the century or before that even, were rather more

---

22. Bruce F. Pauley, *From Prejudice to Persecution. A History of Austrian Anti-semitism*, Chapel Hill / London, 1992, pp. 66f.

7. RELIGION

intellectual, more educated, we didn't push anybody, we learnt English very quickly. We adopted English habits as we should. . . I don't know if I'm supposed to say this, but I get rather angry with anybody, whether it's Italians or Jews or whatever, who do not conform to the English.

The desire to assimilate and to leave the old habits behind, a tendency already clear in the refugees' native countries and reinforced by the rupture of forced emigration, comes across clearly here. The refugees found little common ground with any of the existing groupings within Anglo-Jewry, whether traditionalist or secularised, middle- or lower-class. Several of the interviewees record a dislike of the ultra-Orthodox strain in Jewry, bred of the mistrust of any fanaticism, religious or political, that they had learnt under Nazism. Helga Reutter regards the 'super-Orthodox' as 'no better than Islamic fundamentalists', a sentiment forcefully echoed by Eva Sommerfreund:

> I don't like the fanatics, and they are mostly fanatics because they inflict their own [beliefs on others], they get angry when their children marry out of the faith, but if Christians get angry when their child marries someone not of the faith, namely a Jew, then they call them Nazis. But they're doing exactly the same and that makes me angry.

This uneasiness about religious Jews who keep to a traditional lifestyle is a principal cause for the failure of the interviewees to develop close relations with the existing Jewish community in Britain, who were the descendants of immigrants from Eastern Europe at the turn of the century and who had retained the religious observance and related customs from the East. The virtual absence of any mention of organised contacts with established Anglo-Jewry, whether social or institutional (through synagogues, clubs, etc.), is one of the more surprising findings to emerge from analysis of our interviews. Some of our interviewees found the gulf between their middle-class backgrounds and the working-class background of many British Jews unbridgeable: when Hans Brill was boarded out as a child with a Jewish tailor's family in Islington, he was greatly disturbed by the wife of the house beating her son with a clothes-hanger; and Elizabeth Rosenthal in Oldham felt unable to take up a Jewish family's offer of hospitality because 'they were very Jewish and very poor and [led] sort of a different life altogether'.

As we saw in Chapter Four, several of the interviewees who worked as domestic servants after arriving in Britain record unpleasant experiences with Anglo-Jewish employers; these include Eva Pollard and her sister, Helga Reutter and Nelly Kuttner, whose employers, an Anglo-Jewish barrister and his American wife, would not let her leave until she had scrubbed the floor of her room, a task which, as she remarks bitterly, she had escaped performing for the Nazis in Vienna. There were of course many instances of kindness and charity towards the refugees from British Jews and Jewish organisations: Eva Pollard received help from a Jewish organisation and her parents from an Anglo-Jewish family, and Stella Rotenberg feels very much at ease with British Jews, who accept her as a Jew regardless of her country of origin. Nevertheless, relations between the two groups were strained from the start and, for the majority of the refugees from Central Europe, remained cool at best.

This significant feature appears to be historically determined by the interviewees' pre-emigration attitudes to Eastern Jewry, above all by the inbred fear of behaving in any way that might trigger anti-semitism. Margarete Hinrichsen had been brought up to avoid any appearance of extravagance for that reason:

> An absolute point was made, as long as I was still at home in Pomerania, not to live an ostentatious life at all. On the contrary. Never, never, never was there any ostentation in our life. Never. . . it seems to be a Jewish trend to show off and this was what was absolutely not done in our family. No way. My mother didn't have a fur coat. My mother had a fur coat where the fur was inside, just so as never, never, never to be conspicuous in any way. It was drummed into us children absolutely, especially in a small town in Pomerania where there was always inherent anti-semitism.

Such behaviour may be seen as contrasting with the perceived tendency of British Jews to flaunt their material wealth and success more conspicuously.

The fear of arousing anti-semitism, however, also operated in the

7. RELIGION

reverse direction, with the British Jews resenting the newly arrived refugees, who might draw unwelcome attention to them. An incident recounted by Eva Sommerfreund illustrates this vividly:

> I remember in Anson Road [Willesden] there was a house next to us which belonged to some English Jewish people. I don't want to say their names because it wouldn't be fair perhaps, but they had some friends in one evening and we were also invited, Andrew and I, and we had a rather unpleasant conversation, because they told us they didn't want us. They, the Jews, didn't want us to come in here... He explained to me: 'My family came from Poland or Russia, I don't know [which], at the beginning of the century.' He described it rather sort of picturesquely, he had to walk in the street right by the wall, you know, slink along by the wall and then as he grew up and made his way, he was by now proudly walking in the middle of the road. Now we came and pushed them back to the wall... Because we didn't speak English, we were not English... our habits [attracted bad publicity] for the Jews... That's how we pushed them back to the wall and they held this against us.

Given this history of mistrust, fear and resentment between the two Jewish communities, the lack of contact between them becomes more readily understandable. Although there were of course instances where refugees married into the existing Anglo-Jewish community and participated in its activities, there is with the exception of Eric Rose little evidence of this among our interviewees, and that is a significant pointer. Unlike Anglo-Jewry, which has remained closer to inherited, religiously-based traditions and social patterns, our interviewees, even when Jewish, have developed an identity as a distinct social group which owes less to religion for its internal coherence than to the cultural values discussed in earlier chapters.

4. The non-Jewish refugees

As already indicated, it makes little sense to classify the six non-Jewish refugees as 'Christian'. The three radical left-wing activists, Alfred Dörfel, Eugen Brehm and Alec Armstrong, were adherents of parties opposed ideologically to Christianity as a pillar of the established order and as the natural foe of revolutionaries. This, one might add, divides them sharply from the Austrian Catholic refugee Erika Young, whose distaste for Nazism and its anti-semitic excesses was inspired by the religious-conservative values of her parents. Before emigration, when they were politically active, the three left-wingers had shown a commitment and a loyalty to their respective movements which dominated much of their lives and led them after the Nazi assumption of power to face imprisonment and the risk of death, until they were forced into exile. As the detailed account of their political experiences in an earlier section has shown, politics arguably played the central role in their lives that religion did in the lives of the committed Christians.

Christian values played a decisive part in the lives of Christel Marsh and Ruth Herring. Christel Marsh's father was a devout Lutheran who passed on to his daughter the high moral standards that made it impossible for her to conform to the demands of the National Socialist regime. Her instinctive revulsion against the lies, denunciations and violations of basic moral standards that characterised life under Hitler emerges plainly from her interview. The opposition to Nazism she learnt from her parents was moral, not political – she emphasises that they never joined a political party. Refusing to compromise with the regime's requirements, she joined the Confessional Church at a time when the Nazis were firmly in control of Germany, an act of great courage for a young woman. This led to her being denounced and to the ordeal of a Gestapo interrogation. She still reproaches herself for denying under interrogation that she was a member of the Church. No other interviewee made religion a matter of life and death to the extent that she did; in the parents' generation, only Margarete Hinrichsen's father consciously put himself in the position of risking his life for his faith. Christel Marsh's decision to emigrate was, however, taken as a result of becoming engaged to an Englishman, not directly as a result of religious opposition to Nazism.

Ruth Herring, a keen churchgoer since her youth, came from a solidly Protestant background and had a priest as both her religious and her musical mentor. However, a middle-class Protestant background was by no means a guarantee of opposition to Hitler, which

7. RELIGION

leads one to conclude that Ruth Herring's refusal to behave according to the standards current in Germany after 1933 was motivated by ethical qualities personal to her; there is no evidence that her family felt in any way uncomfortable in Nazi Germany. Christel Marsh provides a fairly detailed picture of her family in this respect: her parents were liberals (see Chapter Two), and she was, as a schoolgirl, very open about her opposition to Nazism and considers that her family's support of this attitude (which her sister shared at the time) was her 'backbone'. She, however, became an exception among the three children, in that her brother, a Luftwaffe pilot in the war, and her sister, who changed into a Nazi zealot, developed along very different lines. Ruth Herring left Germany much earlier than Christel Marsh, and her confrontation with the demands of National Socialism occurred under circumstances that did not involve such acute personal danger. On her first visit to England in 1934, her stay at a Quaker college had a lasting impact on her, giving a qualitatively different dimension to her sense of religion: 'It seemed to give life to all the faith I'd ever had and ever been taught.' Consequently, when she refused, on a visit to Germany, to become complicit in a scheme to incriminate the professor who had supervised her dissertation, and thereby jeopardised her standing in the eyes of the authorities and her academic career, emigration to Britain was a natural choice. Her religious faith as a Quaker has become a pillar of her life, influencing her in both thought and deed. This is, however, untypical of the refugees overall, Jewish or non-Jewish.

In the case of most of the Jewish refugees, the process of secularisation, already far advanced in their countries of origin, continued apace in exile, where it was arguably accelerated by their failure to establish close relations with Anglo-Jewry. Their sense of their Jewish identity owes more to their experiences of racial persecution under the Nazis than to religious devotion. The non-Jewish refugees are divided between left-wing political opponents of Nazism, for whom religion was unimportant, and those who opposed the regime on moral grounds, whose stance, by contrast, was largely underpinned by Christian values.

CHAPTER EIGHT

Facing the Facts:
Relations with the 'Heimat'

Charmian Brinson

1. The prewar years: from the Reich to Britain

As Peter Gellhorn was leaving Germany for Britain in September 1935, he was both captivated by the beauty of the Rhine Valley and convinced that he would never see it again. Yet he was clear, even as early as 1935, that there was no other course of action he could take: 'It is a question of staying alive or not. There was no reason to be homesick... It was a fantastic picture, but you knew very well it was absolute death to try and stay there.' Others, though not all, of our interviewees adopted an equally pragmatic approach towards their changed circumstances: Eva Pollard, for one, who in April 1939 was engaged in her uncongenial domestic job in London, could nevertheless describe herself as 'happy because one was so pleased to be out of Germany'.

Peter Gellhorn was not the only interviewee to have taken a clearsighted view, even in the early exile period, of the political situation in Germany and the threat it posed. Thus Adelheid Schweitzer, arriving in Britain in June 1933, had 'no intention of coming back for good until this Nazi period was over. I wasn't going to spend a year or two or three while it worked itself out, as all the older people did.' And while she did, in fact, return home occasionally during the 1930s to attend to family matters, she would on no account allow her husband-to-be to do likewise, being well aware that 'it was much more dangerous for men than it was for women'.

Similarly, Hilde Auerbach was clear from the start what Nazism meant:

8. RELATIONS WITH THE 'HEIMAT'

> From the beginning... I felt there was no life for me in Germany under Hitler. I said that from the very beginning, from the very first years, very strongly... I felt this was something very evil, I don't know whether many people felt that from the beginning, but I was very strongly aware of it.

She attributes her prescience to the fact that before 1933 she had already spent much time out of Germany 'and that gave me perhaps a wider horizon'. Meanwhile Lotte Berk, equally clear-sighted, had assessed the National Socialist threat to the Jews from her reading of *Mein Kampf*. She recalls how she rejected a non-Jewish suitor – even before the Nazis' assumption of power – with the words: 'You're crazy [to want] to marry me, I'm Jewish and you're not Jewish. We are dirt, we are gypsies.'

From 1938, of course, the future developments both in Germany and on the international scene were plain to see. Ilse Wolff arrived in Britain in April 1939 with no expectation of returning home in the foreseeable future:

> In the first years of Hitler we all expected it not to last long. But in '39 we already felt that there will be a war. And at that time we were not so optimistic any more. Because Hitler had done so much without war, going into the Rhineland, etc., and over-running Austria and annexing it. So we saw and felt what a menace this was; and we did not expect to come back quickly.

Remarkably, even though still a child in 1938, Erika Young was equally aware that war was on the horizon – and she welcomed the prospect: 'I knew, I was utterly convinced, as were my parents, that a war would come. It had to come and the Nazis had to be got rid of.'

For interviewees like Ilse Wolff and Peter Gellhorn who viewed their emigration relatively positively, there were aspects of life in their new country that epitomised the distinction between Britain and Germany at that time. For Ilse Wolff, a significant moment arrived when, as described in an earlier chapter, the Hyde Park deck-chair attendant was content to take her at her word, thereby displaying a basic human trust that she felt she would not have encountered in Germany. Peter Gellhorn was impressed by the freedom of speech he experienced in Britain; he in any case did not take long to feel at home here: 'You know, in Berlin I had come to feel that I had a wristwatch with too many different times from all the clocks everywhere around, and coming to England I found plenty of people with the same kind of watch.'

Yet, for other refugees, misgivings and regrets were very much in evidence. Renée Hubert, initially taking refuge in France, recalls fellow exiles there 'who wanted to go back to Germany and my father would spend hours persuading them: "You're going to regret it. Stick it out here. It's tough but you're not going to go back to the life you had in Germany." But a lot of people went back.'[23] Hilde Ainger, who arrived in Britain in September 1934, was still able to visit her parents in Germany up until 1937. Then her father was warned that if she re-entered the Reich she would have her passport impounded: 'That was actually very hard, because there wasn't a home any more, you know, I knew that was final . . . and that was hard to take.'

Significantly, it is two of our non-Jewish interviewees who describe feelings of the greatest ambivalence towards Germany in the 1930s. Ruth Herring, who in hindsight condemns her own 'ignorance' and 'inexperience', initially found it difficult to deal with the questions about conditions in Germany that were put to her at Woodbrooke, the Quaker College, other than by informing her interlocutors that Germany was no business of theirs. A visitor to Britain at this stage rather than a refugee, she became confused and upset, too, by the stories told by the German-Jewish refugees at Woodbrooke:

> I felt very divided because what they were talking about was clearly true, but it also seemed to me that they were making the most of it to gain sympathy and attention. What rather grated was that they were very ready to run down Germany and the Germans and that I was determined never to do.

23. It was indeed not uncommon, in the early exile period in particular, for refugees to return to the Reich, often with very serious consequences. On this, see for example Rudolf and Ika Olden's account of the first year of emigration, *In tiefem Dunkel liegt Deutschland: Von Hitler vertrieben – Ein Jahr deutsche Emigration*, ed. Charmian Brinson and Marian Malet, Berlin 1994 (but written between November 1933 and April 1934), especially pp. 131ff. (chapter entitled 'Zurück! Zurück?').

8. RELATIONS WITH THE 'HEIMAT'

Yet, as Ruth Herring herself goes on to say, she was neither blind nor deaf to what was actually happening, observing, for instance, on her visits back to Glogau, the brutality of the treatment afforded the Jewish train passengers, as already quoted in Chapter Three. Her parents, to whom she related stories told her by Jewish refugees in England, reacted tellingly: 'Poor Ruth, she's fallen victim to foreign propaganda!'

The second, Christel Marsh, arrived in Britain not long before the outbreak of war. While her reasons for emigrating were more obviously compelling than those of Ruth Herring – she had been a member of the oppositional Confessional Church in Halle and had fallen under official suspicion, moreover she had come to England to marry her British fiancé – she too experienced enormous ambivalence about leaving her country:

> I was very torn, I was in a terribly torn mind. Quite appalling. If I had realised I would never see my mother again, or my sister, I don't know whether I would have done it. . . Also, although I've always been a fanatical anti-Nazi, you might say, I've never been anti-German as such.

As a further parallel, it is interesting that back in 1934, at around the same time as Ruth Herring had encountered German atrocity stories at Woodbrooke, Christel Marsh suffered a similar experience in Sweden and reacted remarkably similarly:

> I read the Swedish newspapers and got the idea of how Germany looked from the outside. And it was a very different picture from what it was on the inside. I felt very torn. Fortunately my Swedish friend and her family were very quiet people and I think really quite unpolitical, so I wasn't tempted to [hold] long diatribes against Germany, because my mother had made it quite clear to me that you don't foul your own nest when you are outside. . . So I didn't, but of course I seethed inwardly when I read what the world thought about Germany.

In the England of the 1930s, there was a body of informed anti-Nazi opinion, principally to be found in liberal and left-wing political and intellectual circles, that attempted to support the refugees from

Nazism and to promote the idea of the 'Other Germany'. As a political refugee, Eugen Brehm, for one, had access to such circles, to prominent figures such as the politician Fenner Brockway. Christel Marsh was fortunate to find in her British husband Norman, a comparative lawyer, an Englishman who was 'better informed than I was' on what was happening in Germany.

More commonly, however, on arrival in Britain, our interviewees encountered worrying misapprehensions and prejudices concerning Germany and the German situation. One of the crudest was exhibited by Eva Pollard's young charge who addressed her as 'Hitler'; 'he didn't realise that there is a different Germany', she adds. Different – and far more serious – misjudgments were displayed both by British supporters of appeasement and by British fascist sympathisers, as Peter Gellhorn recollects:

> The rest of the world did not always take notice of what happened in Germany. The English King was said to have sent a telegram to Hitler congratulating him on his birthday. You had to be careful what you said here because people said the refugees are spoiling the relationship between Germany and England. . . Hitler had a lot of sympathisers in England. There is no question about that. I met some.

Ruth Herring stayed with a Quaker couple in Bentham who 'thoroughly disapproved of the propaganda which was probably fuelled by lots of the Jewish refugees in this country'. Even the Jewish Refugees Committee took its time in arriving at a realistic assessment of the situation, as Adelheid Schweitzer, who called on them for help in June 1933, remembers: 'I was advised by Mr Davidson, one of the managers or directors, to go back home. I told him what my parents were doing and so on and he thought I should go back home and it would all blow over.'

Even as the interviewees began to adjust to their life in British exile, their anxieties concerning conditions in the 'Heimat' – not only Germany, of course, but also Austria and Czechoslovakia – by no means abated. The final prewar years were overshadowed for many by concerns about family and friends in the Reich and by efforts to bring about their emigration. Despite much advice to leave

8. RELATIONS WITH THE 'HEIMAT'

Germany, Margarete Hinrichsen's father was deterred from doing so by a reluctance to start life again from scratch; he was killed on Kristallnacht. 'After 1938,' his daughter remembers, 'I really didn't feel German at all, ever, any more.' Stella Rotenberg tells of her brother's attempts to bring their parents to safety in Sweden: by the time he had obtained the permits, it was too late for them to leave Vienna. They were subsequently deported and killed. Nelly Kuttner blames herself to this day for her own tardiness in leaving Vienna which, as she sees it, left her with too little time to arrange for her parents' emigration; they, too, perished in the Holocaust. One of the most chilling stories in this respect is that of Gertrud Wengraf who not only was unsuccessful in arranging her parents' emigration but also had the misfortune to fall victim to a confidence trickster:

> I couldn't get my parents out because they were too old, although . . . at the time in Britain there were some people who made a profession . . . out of luring people's money – refugees' money – out of them and promising to get people out of Austria. And there was this man somewhere in Kent who advertised that he could find jobs even for older people. . . But he was pretty much a fraud. He collected so much money. . . And then when I had paid that . . . he said that they were too old. . . I never got my money back! It wasn't a lot, but it was a lot for me then. But I was . . . so very disappointed and upset about it.

The episode so distressed her, in fact, that she went into premature labour as a result. Her parents were later deported from Vienna and never heard of again.

Others among our interviewees, fortunately, had happier experiences. Hilde Ainger was successful in obtaining the necessary British financial guarantors for her parents, thus enabling them to emigrate (though her sister, who was left behind, perished in Auschwitz with her husband and children). Lotte Berk, who failed to persuade her father to come to Britain, nevertheless succeeded in saving her sister by passing her off as her servant. With the help of the Jewish Refugees Committee, Helga Reutter brought her parents to Britain not long before the outbreak of war, as did Hilde Auerbach through the Society of Friends' Germany Emergency Committee.

Adelheid Schweitzer, whose mother happened to be visiting England at the time of Kristallnacht and decided not to return home, then found a guarantor for her father, in the form of an ex-patient of his, and for her parents-in-law in her husband's departmental head (a well-known friend to the refugees, Professor Samson Wright of the Middlesex Hospital).

However, even with a fortunate outcome of this sort, the personal anguish involved should not be underestimated. The eleven-year-old Elizabeth Rosenthal, for example, who had only a short time to wait before her mother could join her in Britain, nevertheless went through torments:

> I suffered so much waiting that I can't explain how dreadful it was. . . And I felt as deeply and as tragically as anyone could. I must say it was the worst time of my life. I never had anything worse than that waiting for that month because I was terrified that she wouldn't come out and I would never see her again.

So scarring was this experience, she concludes, that 'it lasted all my life'.

2. *The war years*

After war had been declared, of course, contacts with the homeland were almost totally severed. Such correspondence as could still be maintained was severely limited. Ernst Flesch's parents maintained contact with him in Scotland for a while by writing via an address in Holland but their correspondence came to an end with the fall of the Low Countries. Christel Marsh, too, managed to keep up communication with her mother, firstly by writing to her via contacts in Switzerland and Sweden, and then through the twenty-five-word message scheme operated by the Red Cross; however, mother and daughter were each intensely fearful about their continuing correspondence, on the grounds that it could prove damaging to the other. Similarly, Peter Gellhorn's mother, who endeavoured to keep in touch with her son through the same scheme, did not dare to reveal in her letters that his sister had been put into prison: 'She wrote that Liesl is ill. Quite incurable. This was as much as she dared

8. RELATIONS WITH THE 'HEIMAT'

to say. I could not guess what it was. I heard later what it was, after the war.'

While everyone in Britain was undoubtedly affected to a greater or lesser degree by the outbreak of war, the situation was a particularly poignant and difficult one for the refugees. Christel Marsh, who had already married her British fiancé in a civil ceremony, seems to have felt the need to add spiritual reinforcement to her new British ties:

> When the war broke out we were in Bath for the weekend and when we heard Chamberlain announcing it we took the next train back to London and went to the vicar of Christ Church Woburn Square... and said would he give us a service of blessing... after which we considered ourselves married properly.

For Gertrud Wengraf, isolated with a young baby, it was ironic that this particular day should bring her a unique – if fleeting – sensation of unity with her British neighbours:

> The day when war was declared was the only day when I had some contact and some friendship from my neighbours in that block of flats. Everybody came together, everybody talked to each other, and they knew that I had a baby. I didn't know that they knew, because nobody ever talked to me. And that was the only time I had some contact with other people.

For Nelly Kuttner, however, the war, even at the outset, augured terrible personal loss: 'It is now 3rd September... the war started at 11 o'clock. At 11 o'clock the first siren and from that moment, I know I will never see my parents again. I had to give up that hope. I collapsed and I was lying on the floor.' And for Ernst Flesch, too, in the orphanage in Scotland, the outbreak of war signified an absolute separation from his parents. Though still young, he, like Nelly Kuttner, was remarkably far-sighted about what would follow: 'I remember saying at the beginning of the war – I was only eleven – "Now the Jews have had it in Europe".'

An active member of the Young Austria organisation (one of whose articles of faith was the existence of the 'Other Austria'), Ernst Flesch was able, even in wartime, to retain a positive image of his homeland: 'In spite of everything ... we knew even then, there was a great deal of affinity with Austria. After all, this was our country, that's where we were born, where our childhood was.' In the circles in which he moved – Austrian circles 'quite distinct from the Germans' – the Austria that mattered was the 'free, independent, democratic Austria' towards which all present activities and future planning were directed.

Several of the interviewees, however, remember the conflict with regard to the 'Heimat' that they experienced at the time, with Christel Marsh recalling how her longing for scarce German books proved a source of annoyance to her husband: 'And then sometimes Norman got a bit impatient: "You are English now, you know."' He had, she lamented, failed to grasp the continuing significance to her of her native language. Stella Rotenberg, as a writer, draws a clear distinction between her wartime feelings for Germany and Austria, on the one hand, and for the German language, on the other. Certainly she distanced herself completely 'from the Germans and Austrians, yes, that's for sure, I wanted to have nothing at all to do with Germany and Austria, nothing, nothing, but the German language, yes, that's the most important thing for me.' Gertrud Wengraf, however, reflects on a more practical wartime accommodation as between her old and new countries:

> Well we certainly didn't want to go back to Nazi Austria, Nazi Germany, and of course the more the war progressed, it wasn't very likely that we were going to be able to go back, so I really felt that particularly with my children being born here... I felt that I settled in.

3. The end of the war

i. Revelations of the Holocaust

The end of the war was marked for almost all the interviewees by the horrific disclosures from the concentration camps and by the personal consequences these brought with them. Many had, of course, been conscious from early on of the existence of the camps: Adelheid Schweitzer recalls that by 1935, certainly, she and others had been

8. RELATIONS WITH THE 'HEIMAT'

aware of the internment of political prisoners, while Ernst Flesch, who 'knew all about concentration camps from the very beginning', had had relations in both Dachau and Buchenwald in the early days. Indeed, Helga Reutter's father had spent several months in Dachau before emigrating to Britain, an experience from which he never fully recovered. Yet such camps, terrible as they were, were merely forerunners of the later extermination camps. Though little could be established for certain in wartime Britain about the conditions in these camps, rumours abounded, as Klary Friedl recalls: 'Oh we did know, you know, you did know it, everybody did know a little, maybe a little more, because people told you and ... you know.'

Nothing could prepare one, though, for the losses that many of our interviewees had to face. Thus Klary Friedl, informed by her brother-in-law of the death of her entire family and much of her husband's, was literally stunned by the enormity of the news:

> Ernst's brother ... came to England to a World Jewish Congress ... And he arrived one Saturday ... We lived at that time in Chiswick and we had tea and he said, 'My goodness, nice china and laid table and good food – it's marvellous and wonderful.' Then he looked at me and he said: 'But I must tell you something. Your father is dead, your mother is dead, your brothers are dead. Ernstl – ... your sister is dead, her husband is dead and the child is dead.' So I looked at him and I said to him: 'Help yourself, have another cup.'

It was, she recalls, as if her whole past had been wiped out at a stroke: 'Do you know, ... from one minute to the other, your yesterday collapsed. I can tell you [anything I like about my past]. I can tell you I was a queen, and you can't contradict me because there is nobody to contradict me, to say I am lying.' Eva Sommerfreund had to learn from a friend that her father had been shot in Theresienstadt – there was no documentary evidence of this – while Stella Rotenberg's brother was given only an extremely inexact account of the circumstances of their parents' deaths. And Gertrud Wengraf, as already mentioned, does not know to this day what became of her parents after their deportation from Vienna.

Understandably, for those of the interviewees who were able, it became a matter of paramount importance to establish how their relatives met their fate. Thus Nelly Kuttner returned to Vienna in 1946 to see what traces could be found of her vanished family and friends. One harrowing incident followed another: at the former home of some friends, both the flat and the furniture – which she still recognised – had been expropriated by the porter who informed her, with complete indifference, of the previous occupants' death. At the house of her aunt and grandmother, she was met with the blithest of greetings from the caretaker – 'Oh, you are here, look, Vienna is so lovely, are you coming back?' – and the inevitable news that 'they are all gone'. She also succeeded in discovering the circumstances of her parents' deportation in 1942: a man, an 'Aryan', who had twice before managed to help them avoid such a fate, arrived too late on this third occasion. When she attempted to seek the man out, she learned that he, too, had died: 'One after the other. After this we left, you can imagine in what state.'

Similarly, Peter Johnson set out after the war to investigate details of his father's internment in Nazi-occupied Holland and subsequent deportation from Westerbork transit camp to Auschwitz (where he perished). Adelheid Schweitzer would later visit Theresienstadt to search out the exact particulars of her uncle's death, demonstrating a similar need or desire to grasp the realities of the situation. And Hanna Singer, too, who suffered years of uncertainty as to her father's wartime fate, welcomed the opportunity finally to establish the facts:

> After the war [we heard] from my father that he was at the Camp de Gurs [an internment camp in south-west France] . . . and then nothing, and then a letter from the Red Cross saying that he had definitely died in Auschwitz . . . but I'd feel compelled to watch every programme about . . . it could be [about] Belsen and I'd look for him although I knew he wasn't in Belsen. And then there was a notice in the monthly bulletin of the Association of Jewish Refugees that the French equivalent of that association had brought out a book which named . . . all the German and Austrian Jews who'd been deported from France . . . and I got that book and it . . . [had] the names of the people, the year of birth and where they were born and then a page reference, and it told you what actual transport and where they were

8. RELATIONS WITH THE 'HEIMAT'

gathered up, what date they left and what date they were killed. It's like this business that you need a grave [in order to come to terms with a death] and that was a great relief in an odd sort of way because it took away this, you know, having to watch all these programmes just in case you saw him somewhere.

However, even if Hanna Singer has finally managed to achieve a degree of relief, the same cannot be said of Lotte Berk, whose father's fate and that of others in occupied Holland continues to haunt her:

And that's where they got him. . . But every day I can't get over it, what they have done. I imagined the families – I watched this Anne Frank portrait, I fell asleep and I woke up in the morning and in my dream the Nazis were in England. And I had the same fear. The fear is really my whole problem.

And there are others among our interviewees who found, and continue to find, their losses too painful to articulate or even to contemplate. Helga Reutter describes how her father could not speak of the deaths of his siblings, then considers her own reluctance even today to confront these issues: 'You know it's a long time ago, but I don't know, in spite of not being all that close to them, I still hate to talk about, you know, sort of delve into what might have happened to them.' Klary Friedl recalls how she, too, adopted silence as her survival strategy:

And then I decided that I won't talk any more about my. . . I have an imagination, and that's why I told myself you must put a blank on it. . . I agreed with Ernst we won't talk about it. . . You must build a wall, otherwise you can't live, otherwise you can't breathe, you otherwise can't laugh or eat or work because of this terrible tragedy, because you ask yourself why.

A few, a very few, of the interviewees were fortunate in that, against the odds, their relations survived the war. Thus Ernst Flesch would learn that his mother had survived Belsen; she arrived in Britain in 1946 and lived out the rest of her life here. Peter Gellhorn's mother who, while not in a concentration camp, endured 'a terribly, terribly hard life' during the war as the former wife of a Jew, also came to Britain after the war – 'terribly thin, almost half starved' – while his half-Jewish sister, who survived her imprisonment, succeeded in emigrating to the United States. And with great ingenuity Klary Friedl's mother-in-law, though Jewish, managed to live through the war on false papers and arrived in 1946 to join her son and daughter-in-law in Britain.

Finally, with regard to the Holocaust and our interviewees' relationship to it, it is noteworthy that a number of our sample went on to become professionally involved in the aftermath of these terrible events. Those most directly concerned were the refugees employed as interpreters in occupied Germany: thus Peter Johnson, as already mentioned, was employed by the British army to assist camp survivors returning to Germany, a job he found engrossing. Dorothea Galewski, too, at the age of nineteen, was working as a linguist in Germany, first in carrying out a census of the civilian population and then as a translator-reviewer at the Nuremberg courts, where she was dealing with documents relating to the IG-Farben trial:

> I was really far too young, it upset me greatly, because IG-Farben was prosecuted under several headings, one of which was the use of slave labour and experiments on human beings, and there was very graphic information in these documents and I really was very deeply unhappy... The papers that we worked on were so harrowing that I became quite depressed.

In addition, on a more academic level, both Josephine Bruegel's husband and Ilse Wolff would find themselves professionally engaged with Holocaust materials, the former as a scholar in the area and the latter as the librarian of the Wiener Library, an institution devoted to the study of this field.

ii. To stay or to return?

For most of our interviewees, a return to their homeland after the war, whether to Germany, Austria or Czechoslovakia, was scarcely an option. Some, like Hilde Ainger, Christel Marsh and Mimi Glover, were married to British partners;[24] others, even without formal British ties, already felt settled in Britain. Hilde Auerbach,

---

24. However it should be noted that, had it not been for her British-born daughter, Mimi Glover would have considered a return to Vienna after the death of her husband in 1971.

8. RELATIONS WITH THE 'HEIMAT'

asked whether she had considered returning to Germany, answered 'No, never!' while Alec Armstrong was even more emphatic: 'No, of course, never! Never! Absolutely never!' Klary Friedl, who was posed the same question with relation to Czechoslovakia, replied: 'It's an unwritten law, you can't go back.'

For Ruth Herring, there was literally nowhere to go back to: Silesia had been ceded to Poland and the German-speaking population expelled; moreover, her hometown of Glogau had been razed to the ground. And some of our Jewish interviewees were equally adamant that there was no home for them to return to either in Germany or in Austria after the wrongs done to the Jews there. Hanne Norbert-Miller, speaking of Vienna, contends that 'there were still the same people there, weren't there?' Similarly, Stella Rotenberg maintains not only that 'I wanted to have absolutely nothing to do with either Austria or Germany' but also, despite her enduring love of the German language, that 'where German is spoken, I can't live, for I know about the things that have been done where German is spoken'.

Where refugees did return, their decision could well cause a split in the immediate family: thus Helga Reutter remained in Britain, despite her parents' return to Vienna which, in her opinion, proved 'a strangely ghetto-like place to be in because there were [only] one or two non-Jewish people that my parents were very friendly with'. While Ilse Wolff's journalist husband, to take a further example, went back to Germany for professional reasons, she herself chose to remain in Britain, partly because of family ties here, partly because of her commitment to her work at the Wiener Library. As a result their marriage foundered. And most saddening of all in this context, perhaps, is the story of Hans Brill's sister: as an activist in the London-based Free Austrian Movement, she was determined to return to Austria to take part in its reconstruction, a decision that necessitated leaving her baby behind in Britain. Although the child was in the care of a loving grandparent, the problems caused by the four-year separation have never completely been resolved.

Peter Gellhorn, too, had the opportunity to return to Germany, in his case as second conductor in Düsseldorf, but for personal and above all professional reasons – he had recently agreed to join

Covent Garden – he decided to refuse it. He is clear, however, that had he been unhappy with his professional prospects in Britain, he would have gone back to Germany without hesitation:

> Had I been dissatisfied with my work and had an offer, I would go anywhere, it doesn't matter, I mean Germany, had I been unhappy with what I was doing I would have gone. My home country is where my work is really, I mean music is a life sentence you know, you can't choose any more, you must do what you must do.

Generally speaking, though, it was the political refugees – like Hans Brill's sister – from among the German-speaking emigration in Britain who, once the war was over, would consider whether there was a role for them in the erstwhile 'Heimat'. Josephine Bruegel and her husband, who had served as a member of the Czech Exile Government while in Britain, returned to Czechoslovakia shortly after the war but, falling victim to the prevailing anti-German policies there, had to seek refuge in Britain for a second time, arriving back in November 1946 in a state of near poverty. Their story is paralleled by the slightly later experiences of some friends of Adelheid Schweitzer's, a Communist exile from Czechoslovakia and his wife, who returned home to Czechoslovakia in 1948 'and were actually quite welcomed to start with'. Later, however, having fallen out of favour with the Czech Communist authorities, they lost both the husband's job and the family flat and saw no alternative but to come back to Britain (where the husband suffered severe psychiatric illness).

Nelly Kuttner's husband Stefan, a Social Democrat, contemplated returning to his native Austria to play his part there; Nelly, however, who had lost both her parents in the Holocaust, was implacably opposed to such a plan and her husband acceded to her wishes, remaining with her in Britain. Similarly Ernst Flesch who, though arriving in Britain as a Kindertransport child, grew up here to embrace the role of young political exile, and Eugen Brehm, a political exile from the start, both anticipated a return to Austria and Germany, respectively. As things turned out, though, Ernst Flesch was unable to follow the example of his comrades in the Free Austrian Movement owing to the fact that his mother, the Belsen

8. RELATIONS WITH THE 'HEIMAT'

survivor, came to join him in Britain. And in any case, with the onset of postwar political disillusionment, he soon abandoned his plan to return:

> As time went on, we heard... that what we had thought might happen in Austria didn't. In fact I went to the World Youth Festival in Budapest in '49 and I met some of my old mates there and one of them said, 'When are you coming over? When we're a People's Democracy?' Anyway, by then I'd dropped out. There was no point. I was staying here.

The year before, in fact, Ernst Flesch had already been back to Vienna, both to visit a friend, a returner, and 'to see what it was like' for himself. He found his friend to be sadly disenchanted with politics while he himself suffered a chastening experience:

> There was a 'Jugendtag' of some sort with Ernst Fischer [a leading Austrian Communist who had returned from Moscow] speaking on the Rathausplatz. I remember, the chap whom my friend was staying with was of course still organised [in the Party] – we went back by tram and I heard some young fellow say, 'They're all Jews anyway,' even in '48! So I thought, 'Don't let's overdo it!'

Eugen Brehm, too, had initially hoped to go back to Germany and considered that, had he agreed to join the postwar SPD, he could have succeeded in doing so relatively quickly. As it was, his efforts to return had to be channelled through his Anglo-American rather than his German contacts and in fact failed, leaving him 'very downhearted for the first year or two'. By 1947, he records, he had decided 'not quite happily' to remain in Britain. Yet it is noteworthy that, when looking back nearly fifty years later on this turn of events, he would conclude: 'I would have been very unhappy if I had returned to Germany, I would not have fitted into anything, I think, certainly not into a party or any political movement... Anyway, the atmosphere in Britain had spoiled me for good for Germany.'

In any case, Eugen Brehm, like nearly all of our interviewees, applied for and obtained British nationality after the war, an act which marked one of the most significant steps in the break with the old 'Heimat' as well as in coming to terms with the new situation.

Interestingly, only Alfred Dörfel and Ernst Flesch, both former Communists, as it happens, have retained their original German or Austrian nationalities throughout the years that each has lived in Britain. Yet surprisingly, Alfred Dörfel, unlike most of his fellow political exiles, never entertained the plan to return to Germany, for reasons that included the unwillingness of his Jewish first wife to consider such a course of action. This was compounded by the fact that, when his wife subsequently grew ill and he was obliged to devote less time to his political commitments, he was expelled from the Party. At the same time, however, Alfred Dörfel could not, and cannot, contemplate the idea of applying for British nationality, a fact he attributes to the series of unpleasant experiences he suffered at the hands of the British authorities during his first years in Britain (above all, at his Knightsbridge tribunal and aboard the *Ettrick*) as well as to his postwar dealings with Home Office officials. These and other factors have led him to conclude that 'the upper class, the ruling class in this country, did not accept us [the refugees] as such in the country', and have persuaded him of a profound official hostility that for him far outweighs the friendly reception he has received from other sectors of British society.

For some years, he had no alternative but to travel on a rather unsatisfactory British travel document. In the end, however, Alfred Dörfel, who admits to a 'love-hate [relationship] with Germany', was persuaded by his friends to reapply for German citizenship: 'Fred, you aren't betraying yourself... Germany has changed. There are a lot of other things now.' And asked whether, more recently, he has ever reconsidered the question of British nationality, he replies that his aversion to applying for citizenship of a country whose officials regarded the refugees as 'scum' and 'outcasts' remains 'deeply ingrained'.

As for Ernst Flesch, his first visit back to Vienna was on an Austrian passport (which was obviously in keeping with his early desire to return to Austria). Not until the late 1950s did he apply for British nationality – and his application was turned down. He himself sees the probable reason for this as lying less in his former political allegiances and more in the suspicion, voiced by a Special Branch Officer at the time, that he had deliberately delayed his application

8. RELATIONS WITH THE 'HEIMAT'

in order to avoid British national service (a charge which he denies). The situation could doubtless have been rectified in more recent years; however, in the event, Ernst Flesch, who has retained his largely positive view of Austria, remains untroubled by the fact that his home and his nationality have not been brought into formal accordance with one another.

4. Postwar encounters with the 'Heimat'

By and large, by the end of the war or soon after, the majority of our interviewees had decided with varying degrees of enthusiasm that their future lay in Britain. Nevertheless, for some, the first visit back to Germany, Austria or Czechoslovakia after the war is remembered as a particularly critical event in their lives and not infrequently in terms of a harrowing ordeal. Elizabeth Rosenthal offers an unforgettable description of just such an experience when she recalls her 1953 visit to Cologne, her first back to Germany since childhood:

> I woke up in the bus and there was a frontier guard speaking German and asking for our passports. It was penetrating... and it went right through me in a physical way and I realised I was going back to Germany which I had left and escaped from and I was so physically revolted that I was in a bus going back into that hell... It was very emotional... I thought, 'What am I doing here and why am I going back?' If I could have jumped out and run back I would have done, but I couldn't.

And this was just the beginning of what she perceived as an extended nightmare: Cologne still lay in ruins; she and her travelling companions were housed in a bunker without natural light; worst of all, perhaps, since no one was aware of her background – she chose never to speak of her origins at that time – nobody realised that she was suffering. The fact that the Cologne Carnival, which struck her as grotesque and surreal, was in full swing further intensified the threatening nature of the experience for her, such that she underwent what may have been a kind of temporary breakdown:

> We went out into the street and there were people dancing and they were all dressed up in costume with masks and drunk. It was so

dreadful. All these vulgar Germans who were drunk... I was horrified and frightened... I just couldn't bear it. I didn't go on dancing. I don't know whether I danced at all. I just went back into the bed in the bunker. I don't know what else happened. I don't even know how many days we were there, but I know I didn't sleep and when we went to Lille again, a night journey, I was so relieved. Again a frontier guard, I was so relieved I had a British passport.

It was to protect herself against this sort of experience as well as out of a certain defiance that Hilde Ainger, who admits to some curiosity regarding her birthplace, has never revisited Germany:

Some pride comes into it: we've been treated so badly. I'm not going back to them and also, quite apart from that, I don't know what good it would do to my... emotions, whether it would churn things up which I can leave alone, the way I live. I mean, I can talk perfectly happily about everything without it upsetting me, but if I actually go there, I have no idea what it would do. But quite apart from that, as I said, there is pride and knowing the anti-semitism there. So I've no desire to go back.

Eva Sommerfreund only revisited Austria for the first time eight years ago and experienced great ambivalence in her feelings towards the old 'Heimat': 'I was determined not to get sentimental before I left here and I didn't really, but I loved it. I must admit that I loved it, I didn't want to. Intellectually, after all, they've thrown us out but emotionally I feel at home.' Following a second visit, during which she was torn by a similar mixture of emotions, she resolved to avoid such conflicts in the future: 'I don't want to go there any more. I have a feeling that they've taken something from me – where I belong, in a way.'

Lotte Berk was initially determined never to visit Germany again: 'After what they did, I said we will never touch the German ground again.' She later relented – if on one occasion only – and returned to comfort a dying friend and found it 'not ... so bad'. Similarly, Hanne Norbert-Miller felt no desire to revisit Austria and only did so in 1970 in order to meet an elderly Czech aunt (who could travel to Vienna but not to London). 'I decided my aunt was more important to me than my feelings towards Austria,' she explains. As it was,

8. RELATIONS WITH THE 'HEIMAT'

she chose to spend most of her visit in the Austrian countryside, for Vienna was altogether too disconcerting and distressing: 'It was a completely strange town, with familiar street names... It was nothing to do with the town where I grew up... There wasn't a single person left... It just had nothing to do at all with my youth.' Indeed, Adelheid Schweitzer, who first revisited Bad Nauheim at the end of the 1940s, experienced such intense feelings of alienation and rootlessness – at the loss of 'the childhood home' – that it overwhelms her even today to recall it.

Obviously, one of the most painful aspects of the 'homecoming' was the forcible reminder of the events of the Holocaust that this presented. Certainly a substantial part of Hanne Norbert-Miller's distress in Vienna in 1970 can be attributed to this:

> You see, there was not one person left, family or friends. You mustn't forget that. They had all disappeared in the Holocaust... My grandfather, my mother's father, was taken to Theresienstadt when he was ninety-one. My father's mother and sister disappeared... There was an enormous family of aunts and cousins but nobody, nobody was there.

In a more generalised but no less disturbing manner, Stella Rotenberg's view of present-day Vienna is similarly overshadowed by the city's sinister past:

> I find it painful when I am in Vienna because you see I have other memories of it and I see the houses, for instance, and I know what happened there. For instance the cellar in the Karajangasse, this school in the Karajangasse, which was a Gestapo cellar, a torture chamber...

And Nelly Kuttner expresses this same feeling most forcibly when she laments of her former street in Vienna that, though beautiful, 'it is for me like a cemetery'.

Both Lotte Berk and Alfred Dörfel, when revisiting Germany after the war, were oppressed by an almost obsessive perception of Germans in their role of former Nazis. Indeed, for Alfred Dörfel, 'everything which came in or out of Germany was Nazi-tainted'. He recalls his first journey back to Germany in 1959, in order to visit his second wife's family in Worpswede, near Bremen, as intensely upsetting for all concerned:

> I hated all of it. My wife was in tears all the time. Everywhere I saw officials. There was the forester standing there... She [my wife] said: 'Look, there's the forester, he was of course a Nazi.' I would have killed him. I was in trouble wherever we were. On the bus, when I saw a uniform, they were all Nazis.

This was, he concedes today, not correct, and it is an obsession that over the years has lost most of its hold on him. (For others, however, in whom such preoccupations still persist, see below.)

If Alfred Dörfel's account of his first visit back to West Germany makes for gripping reading, then the parallel account of his initial encounter with the German Democratic Republic (GDR) is still more compelling, all the more so since it constitutes one of only two reports on this subject from among our sample. Of course, on the face of it, as a Communist, moreover as a man actually hailing from Leipzig, Alfred Dörfel might be expected to have viewed the GDR as his spiritual, if not his physical 'Heimat'. On the other hand, it should be recalled that he had been expelled from the Party some years before. Nevertheless, since he had retained his Marxist convictions, one might have imagined that his first visit back to Leipzig during the 1960s would have struck some sort of chord in him. But in fact he disliked it intensely, missed the freedom and wealth of the West and was irritated by the 'stupid little forms' he had to fill in. He was disappointed, too, by his former comrades who appeared to him to have been 'brainwashed', leaving him with the feeling that he himself was now 'the only really deep-minded Communist' among them. The final straw occurred when he took his wife to visit a childhood haunt just outside Leipzig, attempted to photograph it and was severely reprimanded for taking a picture of a 'Volkseigener Betrieb' (state-owned concern). He could never, he maintains today, have returned to the GDR after the war, as many of his former comrades did, since he was 'already too anglicised'.

The second exposure to the German Democratic Republic is described by Elizabeth Rosenthal who, despite her ordeal in Cologne and subsequent difficulties in Düsseldorf (see below), nevertheless

8. RELATIONS WITH THE 'HEIMAT'

elected to cross the Berlin wall in the late 1960s to visit a friend whose family had supported hers during the Nazi period. The border crossing, she recalls, was 'another horrible experience' during which her papers were confiscated and she was locked in a room: 'And I thought: "Heavens, now I shall have to stay in the Eastern bloc. How am I going to get out? My father was kept there for ever[25] and I will not see England again, my friends or my mother." I felt this was really the end. What am I doing in Germany?' Once through, however, and despite the inescapable stress of being in Germany again – 'How old is he? How old is she? What did he do? What did she do? That lasts forever' – she could feel 'at home' at least in the company of her old anti-Nazi friends. When in East Berlin, she also took the opportunity to revisit her former home and school – but from these, interestingly enough, she felt completely dissociated: 'I wasn't coming back. The past was another place, another time. It wasn't me because I was gone... I wasn't coming back at all and there were certainly no roots and no connection.'

While detachment can in no way be said to characterise Elizabeth Rosenthal's complex and troubled relations with the former 'Heimat', any more than it can for the majority of our interviewees, there are nevertheless a few who, on returning after the war, were apparently able to distance themselves more or less entirely from the whole situation. Ilse Wolff's description of her first re-encounter with Berlin is remarkable for its coolness: 'I was detached ... and interested in the change. I did not have any people there. I found one school friend after the war again, but otherwise it was so different that again I can't say I reacted violently in any way.' Likewise Erika Young, while experiencing a sense of alienation in Vienna in 1961, claims not to have been disturbed by this but rather to have found it 'interesting': 'I was no part. I felt more or less like a tourist... I didn't feel emotional about it, not in the least... I didn't feel that I had any loss personally, particularly because I was just so glad that I'd landed in England.' However, it is perhaps noteworthy – in the face of such studied detachment – that it was to Austria that Erika

---

25. Elizabeth Rosenthal's father, who went to work as an engineer in the Soviet Union in 1931, had been arrested on a 'spying charge' in one of the purges and died in Russian captivity in 1943.

Young chose to return both for her honeymoon and to conceive her first child.

In any case, if detachment remains the exception rather than the rule in the interviewees' attitudes to the 'Heimat', some have arrived at a kind of compromise position. Thus Gertrud Wengraf, while clear from the outset that she had no wish to return permanently to Austria, unreservedly enjoys the Austrian countryside[26] on her return visits there. And Peter Gellhorn, asked how he felt when re-entering Germany, adopts a pragmatic and indeed broadly positive view of his former country:

> Well, you know, it's like an old pair of slippers, they still fit you, even if you have different ones now. So many things were familiar and all the nightmares had gone. Now and then you heard people talk in the way that made you feel, well, they hadn't learnt much, but generally I have a good feeling about Germany.

Most of the interviewees still retain certain contacts in their original countries, whether these be of a personal nature, such as Hilde Auerbach's brother in Germany and Hans Brill's sister in Austria, or of a professional kind, such as Peter Johnson's customers in the fur trade. Both Ilse Wolff and Stella Rotenberg make the point that the sort of people with whom they have come into contact through their work in Germany or Austria since the war hold, as one might expect, very different views from the people from whom they originally fled. On a personal level, and exceptionally, Mimi Glover maintains that those Austrians – Catholics and Socialists – who were her friends before her emigration and with whom she has since remained in contact have never behaved badly towards her; on the contrary, she feels more comfortable with these people, even now, than with her British acquaintances. Margarete Hinrichsen recalls being introduced to her husband's family and friends in Germany after the war and finding them 'all very nice, obviously anti-Nazis who had suffered a lot themselves'. Yet, despite this, her initial visit back in 1949 'was not very easy for me', while subsequent visits have had their difficulties as well: 'Every time, actually, I go back to

---

26. The native landscape continues to hold a strong attraction for a number of the ex-Austrian interviewees and often constitutes an added cause for ambivalence towards the former 'Heimat'.

8. RELATIONS WITH THE 'HEIMAT'

Germany, I usually get an hysterical illness. I cough or I start a nosebleed. All subconscious.'

Helga Reutter, too, admits to unease, even today, though more particularly with regard to her former compatriots, the Austrians: 'We've got some, two, very good friends who have definitely never been Nazis. But the general population I feel uncomfortable with.' Ernst Flesch cites the line, 'Wie schön wäre Wien ohne Wiener' (How lovely Vienna would be without the Viennese), though countering this with: 'But of course that doesn't mean to say there are not a lot of very good people there.' Meanwhile Eva Sommerfreund laments of present-day Austrians: 'I have the feeling that they don't want me or they didn't want me.'

In connection with this, a number of the interviewees express their awareness of the continuing presence of anti-semitism in German and Austrian society. Austria fares particularly badly on this score: Erika Young, Ernst Flesch, Hanne Norbert-Miller and Helga Reutter, among others, all deplore the level of anti-semitism currently prevailing there. Helga Reutter recalls being greeted on one occasion with a 'Heil Hitler!' salute while Ernst Flesch has similar experiences to relate:

> If you go to Austria you hear many horrific things. You can't walk around in Austria without hearing nastiness. . . We had some horrible experiences and so I've never gone back for good although I've often been back on holiday. I even had a girlfriend in Vienna for a time and I went with her to Steiermark [Styria] a few times on holiday in the summer. You sit in a pub and somebody suddenly starts singing the 'Horst Wessel', you know, and things like that.

Understandably enough, the figure of the right-wing Austrian politician, Jörg Haider, looms large in our interviews, with Ernst Flesch assessing him – coolly but with all due seriousness – as a 'shrewd operator' and a 'good demagogue' who 'has got more influence than he should have'.

Of course, Germany, too, comes in for criticisms of this sort, with Hilde Ainger pointing to the anti-semitism she feels is prevalent in Germany as well as in Austria. Elizabeth Rosenthal, who has had a number of unfortunate brushes with fascism in postwar Germany, describes attending a Socialist Education conference in Düsseldorf, in 1967, which was attacked by neo-fascists with CS-gas canisters. Nevertheless, it is noteworthy that, unlike Austria, when Germany comes in for criticism in the course of our interviews, this generally relates less to its present record than to its past history. Significantly, it is the former Germans among our interviewees who articulate the profoundest suspicion, even today, of any German in their own age group. As Peter Johnson puts it: 'I see behind everyone who is of my generation someone who has worked in a concentration camp.' Similarly, Hilde Auerbach records: 'I always sort of wonder what has this elderly person done under the Nazis.' And Adelheid Schweitzer expresses much the same sentiments when she explains why her present-day German contacts are strictly limited:

> I'm extremely suspicious of anybody I meet in my age group that I don't know a lot about. I have met people and they've all told you that they weren't Nazis, and oh no, and they were pushed into it, and they couldn't help themselves, and so on and so forth.

She does take pains, however, to draw a distinction between the older and younger generations of Germans and she speaks movingly of her sustained contacts with and positive feelings towards the latter: 'I have visits from the children of the people in Nauheim. They have all been with me and my children have been there on exchanges. I do not feel that one has any right or need to carry this terrible burden into the next generation.' Lotte Berk, too, despite her self-confessed anti-German feelings, is prepared to distinguish between the 'parents . . . or grandparents', on the one hand, and the 'newly-born ones', on the other, as are others of our interviewees. Elizabeth Rosenthal, indeed, made it her business on a return visit to another former school, the celebrated Caputh (by then an East German school for the underprivileged), to 'talk to the present generation' on her experiences during the Nazi period. 'The young people,' she maintains elsewhere in her interview, 'well, they were young and they couldn't be blamed, they were born afterwards.' Interestingly, Hanna Singer recalls how, for her, a measure of reconciliation was achieved through the younger generation when, in recent years, she visited her student daughter in Mannheim:

8. RELATIONS WITH THE 'HEIMAT'

> It was the first time we stayed in Germany as opposed to maybe a quick overnight stay if we couldn't avoid it, but I never fancied the idea of going to Germany on holiday or something like that and so we met some of her friends, people her age, and I think that was quite good.

However, even if Hanna Singer's daughter enjoyed positive experiences in Germany, the same cannot be said of Eva Sommerfreund's daughter whose pre-existing anxieties about Germany were compounded by the fact that 'she fell in love with someone whose parents were so obviously Nazis... that [it] ended... there and then'.

It is perhaps germane to record here that in recent years both Adelheid Schweitzer and Walter Wolff have accepted invitations back to their original home towns, issued in the name of reconciliation. The former, admittedly, was initially reluctant to accept Bad Nauheim's hospitality: 'I avoided that for years, I thought I don't need that, but eventually I accepted it.' Walter Wolff, for his part, was invited by the Berlin Senate to meet fellow pupils from his boyhood and he succeeded in renewing a number of former contacts there.

5. Apportioning blame

Several of our interviews, especially with the Austrians, contain discussion of the relative parts played in the Third Reich by Germany and Austria. Nelly Kuttner is not alone here when she contends that 'the Austrians were worse than the Germans'; nevertheless, other former Austrians, Gertrud Wengraf and Ernst Flesch, do lend a certain support, the former obliquely, the latter explicitly, to the idea of Austria's 'victim status'.[27] Gertrud Wengraf, as already noted, was anxious to arrive at some sort of *modus vivendi* in her relations with Austria:

> I loved the Austrian countryside, you know, and I didn't feel this antipathy towards the Austrians. And the Austrians actually at that

27. Proceeding from the Moscow Declaration of 1943, the official Austrian position was established after the war whereby the annexation of Austria by Germany in March 1938 was an act of aggression comparable to Hitler's later attacks on Czechoslovakia, Poland and the other occupied countries of Europe.

time seemed to say or said they had never been Nazis ever... I don't know whether I believed it but I was quite happy.

Ernst Flesch's formative wartime experiences in the Free Austrian Movement, which took pains to draw a clear distinction between Germany and Austria, plainly still predispose him towards the idea of Austria as victim; he discusses the issue thoughtfully and at length:

> Yes, Austria could say it was a victim, which is true up to a point. Don't forget the Nazis were not the majority in '38... No, I would say a third roughly. A third Social Democrat, a third Catholic – Schuschnigg – and maybe a third Nazi sympathisers. And of those only a minority were active, of course... Sure, the Austrian Nazis were worse, if anything, than the Germans, but the Germans were in charge, very definitely. We had Gestapo people from Germany coming to run the country. The Austrians, the ... Nazis got the good jobs and they got the Jewish flats and businesses, etc., but they didn't run the country. Baldur von Schirach ran the country... Of course, mind you, they sent [the Austrian] Seyss-Inquart to Holland and [the Austrian] Kaltenbrunner became the Head of the Sicherheitsdienst. In Austria itself they didn't have Austrian Gauleiter, they had Germans. They made sure of that.

In so saying, he also acknowledges that a large number of Austrian refugees do hold their former countrymen responsible for what happened in Austria and, where the postwar period is concerned, he freely concedes that denazification measures, though 'not all that thorough-going' in Germany, were nevertheless more effective there than in Austria. His assessment of the negative side of Austria's showing is echoed by Eva Sommerfreund:

> I feel they [the Germans] are fairer . . . in terms of after the war. In terms of Israel . . . Wiedergutmachung [restitution], not only that. Young people actually went there and worked in the kibbutz and I have the feeling I've got less of a grudge against the Germans than against the Austrians.

In the course of their interviews, Erika Young, as a former Austrian, and Elizabeth Rosenthal and Peter Gellhorn, former Germans,

8. RELATIONS WITH THE 'HEIMAT'

all take the opportunity to consider how fascism was able to take hold in their respective countries. Erika Young recollects the poverty following the defeat of 1918, and sets the National Socialist popular appeal in this context, while recording her own antipathy to mass movements of any kind:

> If somebody does come and promises you jobs and all that – and most people don't think politically – that had something to do with it. People are inclined to 'follow my leader'. That's something I learnt about. I can't bear joining things, I can't bear pressure groups, I can't bear any kind of leadership business, not being my own person, an independent thinker. I suppose one can see how this can escalate.

Elizabeth Rosenthal, for her part, considers both the Prussian ideal of obedience and the concept of 'evil' to be relevant aspects here, together with the fact that 'there wasn't enough active goodness' which she amplifies as follows: 'If good people do nothing then evil people win and that happens elsewhere, I mean not only in Nazi Germany.' Characteristically, Peter Gellhorn makes music his starting-point, registering his perplexity that Hitler and other National Socialists could display sensitivity to music while otherwise behaving 'in the most beastly way'; then he ventures to set the anomaly into a wider framework:

> It is almost more frightening than if they had simply been brutes. But it was a twisted sophisticated brain that went wrong. I always say it is like in physics. Every action has a reaction. If you live in a primitive society somebody might hit you on the head but they won't do anything very remarkable either. But if . . . the standard is very high, a nation that has contributed to arts, literature and music as much as any other, or even more in some things, if they go from high [to low] . . . they sink much deeper. Which they did. There is not much comfort in that explanation but I think it is like that. . . Other people cannot understand it because they are not at that stage themselves. And they think Germans must be biologically different from everybody else. This of course is nonsense. I heard that said during the war sometimes and I said: 'It is very simple. When the war is over, just kill every German, woman and child and we will all get rid of this nightmare.' And – look at [Germany] now! When I go

[there], I don't have a bad feeling at all; though the world seems always to have the same problems.

Who, then, according to our interviewees, can be held responsible for the crimes of the Third Reich? It was noted above that some of our interviewees, Adelheid Schweitzer among them, tended to suspect any German or Austrian of the appropriate generation of complicity in the Nazi regime. She is also disinclined to accept the classic plea of ignorance here, citing the case of a German friend of her brother's: 'He told me that he had been stationed somewhere near Belsen and didn't know what was going on there... [But] I did not believe that.' Peter Gellhorn, on the other hand, considers that 'it is a hopeless pursuit to apportion responsibility' while Hans Seelig, in a sobering reflection, recognises that the pressures to conform must have been overwhelming: 'And I have to say to myself – if I'd not been Jewish, I can't guarantee that I wouldn't have fallen prey to that brainwashing.' Erika Young, who likewise pleads for an understanding of human frailty, is even prepared to extend this to include Kurt Waldheim, the UN Secretary-General subsequently exposed as a Nazi collaborator:

> Things happen because people are scared and they think if they attack the victim they won't be attacked themselves, which is why you'd got Jewish people who were anti-Semites themselves because they thought it might save them, but it didn't. All sorts of reasons. I wouldn't ever dream of judging Waldheim, for example... It's hard to know what pressure was put on him to collaborate up to the point in which he did. But I don't think anybody who wasn't there can judge that, or even has the right to judge it.

Peter Gellhorn, meanwhile, lights on another much publicised case of alleged collaboration with the Third Reich, that of the conductor Wilhelm Furtwängler, and suggests that there was another side to the coin, namely the latter's aid to persecuted Jewish musicians. As to the accommodation with the regime that enabled Furtwängler to pursue his career in Nazi Germany, Gellhorn is prepared to accept that 'he couldn't do without a German audience', thereby dismissing the case that is frequently made against Furtwängler and declining to condemn him:

8. RELATIONS WITH THE 'HEIMAT'

One doesn't know what collaboration means. Is a baker to stop baking bread because he doesn't like the government? Where do you draw the line?. . . People talk about civil courage. Most people want to live, they don't want to die. . . When people say he [Furtwängler] was a collaborator, it means nothing to me.

As Peter Gellhorn indicates here, the people courageous enough to resist were relatively few and far between. During the war, the Free Austrian Movement in Britain had propagated the idea of offering support to the resistance movement back in Austria; but as Ernst Flesch now concedes, the internal Austrian resistance did not amount to much:

There wasn't much resistance. There was some, it must be admitted. At the end of the war there was an Austrian battalion in the Tito army but I'm sure they were all Slovenes from Kärnten [Carinthia]. Pretty sure. . . There was some resistance, of course, but not a great deal. The majority went along. They may not have liked it, but they went along with it. . . . All honour to those who did [resist], as in Germany, but it was a small minority.

Elizabeth Rosenthal, like Ernst Flesch, pays tribute to the few who were willing to sacrifice themselves in the struggle against Hitler, while lamenting that 'there were not enough people who knew and there were not enough people who dared. . . The people who found out and who tried to stop it, they were too few and it was too late.' Peter Gellhorn, however, speaks up for those who, while disliking the Nazi regime, were afraid to show open resistance, which would, in his opinion, have constituted a fairly pointless act. As he describes his mother's experiences at the end of the war, he extends the conventional image of the 'Other Germany' to include these silent dissenters, members of what has elsewhere been called the 'inner emigration':

The Americans were coming and [people] put out the white flags and Eva [a friend] came to [my mother] and said: 'Frau Gellhorn, we have won, not the Nazis.' This is the Other Germany. There were plenty of those but some of them didn't have the courage to say so. This does not mean that they merely became accomplices because they did not want to risk getting killed the same day. That would not matter to the Nazis, just one more on the heap of millions. What impression do you think you could make by dying too? You would just be another corpse.

After the war, so he continues, many of these right-minded Germans not only 'had to pay the bill when Hitler was dead' but also, purely on account of their German passports, had to be 'ashamed for something they hadn't done' (the concept of German 'collective guilt' was widely promoted in the early postwar years). It is interesting to note, however, that Ilse Wolff, who recalls meeting 'those Germans who had not any feelings of guilt because they were not guilty of anything' on her first visit back to Frankfurt, demonstrates a very different perception of postwar German psychology in which any notion of collective guilt is well and truly rejected.

6. Views of present-day Germany and Austria

The interviewees, both because of their earlier experiences with the 'Heimat' and the length of time since spent in Britain, do not for the most part exhibit great interest in present or future developments in the old country. Indeed, as has already been documented here, a good number still demonstrate reluctance to have any dealings with it. Thus Hans Brill, for one, continues to avoid Germany and, though visiting his sister in Austria on occasion, abhors the materialism he observes there, as well as other aspects of present-day Austria. The concern expressed by many of our interviewees at any persistent anti-semitism in Germany and Austria, the latter particularly, as manifested by the popularity of Jörg Haider and his Austrian Freedom Party, has already been recorded. Ernst Flesch is one of the most trenchant on this. Yet it is he, notably the one remaining Austrian citizen from among our sample, who displays the greatest degree of engagement with and approbation of postwar developments in Austria. He was not disappointed, he maintains, that Austria failed to follow 'the Socialist direction' that he and his Free Austrian Movement comrades had so passionately wished for; indeed it was 'just as well it didn't after what we know now'. Rather, from today's

8. RELATIONS WITH THE 'HEIMAT'

standpoint, the somewhat different postwar political developments in Austria meet with his general approval:

> The Austrian state had a new beginning in 1945 and it was an anti-Nazi beginning and they've remained so ever since. One can't say anything against them... [Things] didn't turn out as we thought they would turn out but on the other hand Austria did go through a democratic development... It was a new start and it's been democratic ever since. There's a lot to be said for that. And I think nowadays the majority of the younger people are democrats, more or less.

It is illustrative of the disparities in the views encountered in our sample that Austria, so often a target of criticism, should receive such a positive endorsement. Conversely Germany which, in its postwar form, tends to evoke a lesser degree of apprehension from our interviewees, is perceived by Peter Johnson, in its post-unification state, at least, as worryingly fragile: 'I know that the political situation [in Germany] is very precarious at the moment and I don't know what the government can do now about it. It's a big problem.'

Peter Gellhorn's attitude to contemporary Germany is an essentially pragmatic one, though his pragmatism does not preclude a distinct dash of optimism. It cannot be claimed that his views are typical of the ex-Germans, any more than Ernst Flesch's views represent those of his fellow Austrians, from among the interviewees, for the viewpoints on the former 'Heimat' as represented by our sample are nothing if not diverse. What marks out Peter Gellhorn's sentiments towards present-day Germany – and, of course, as a musician of international standing, he has had occasion to revisit it more frequently than most – is his clear-headed espousal of the principle of reconciliation:

> I think they [the Germans] have learnt a lesson. Without wanting to be patronising, most of the people who live there now weren't born at that time; you can't really hold them [responsible]. And they have in the middle of Berlin a column on the Wittenbergplatz with all the names of all the concentration camps and to say that we must never forget. As one German minister at the time said: 'These things have happened, we can do nothing about it, we can only hope that the world may forget'; and he added: 'But the world can only forget if we

never forget.' And that is the attitude of many German people at the moment... I mean, let everybody look at their own backyard and see what has to be put in order there. We all have something that needs looking at, and on the whole, considering the terror of that time, I have a good feeling in Germany, I don't have any resentment or anything like that at all.

Like Peter Gellhorn, Hans Seelig, too, has arrived at a personal accommodation with Germany and its past; and he addresses the subject in strikingly similar terms:

> I go back happily. I go back without any feeling of resentment or whatever. People of an older age, I sometimes think – well, what were they yelling in the 1930s and '40s? – but I dismiss it from my mind. I don't forget, I don't forgive – you can't forgive, of course, and you certainly shouldn't forget – but you can become reconciled with the way people are.

For Nelly Kuttner, however – and by no means for her alone – such a stance remains out of the question. Movingly she describes being urged by a Viennese friend to claim entitlement to a flat on the site where her parents had lived and her absolute abhorrence of the suggestion: 'She said, look – you see the mentality of these people – [they told me to] take the flat and sell it. I said, Bertha, with the blood of my parents – they stayed till the last moment in that house – I should make a business and sell the flat? No!'

Nelly Kuttner, for her part, can still maintain that 'I am not a person to hate'. Not so others among our interviewees, however, who do not hesitate, even today, to express their feelings towards their former compatriots in terms of unqualified hatred. Thus Lotte Berk, for one, whose father was deported from Holland back to Germany, freely concedes: 'I have got such a hate for the Germans. I think all Jews have.' And Klary Friedl, whose whole family was wiped out in the Holocaust, harbours a hatred for the Germans that is 'like an illness because it hurts you and it eats your insides out'. The terrible wrongs perpetrated and suffering endured still persist, undiminished, in the hearts and minds of a number of the interviewees whose continuing grief most definitely does not admit of reconciliation.

CHAPTER NINE

Postwar

The Challenges of Settling Down

Marietta Bearman and Erna Woodgate

In Europe the long-awaited end of the Second World War finally came on 8 May 1945. This momentous day saw many festivities all over Britain and elsewhere, as has been amply recorded. However, as Stella Rotenberg recollects, there were also small-scale, intimate celebrations with friends: 'I really remember the celebrations afterwards, and I know that a friend invited me and two other women refugees and we went to a hotel and had a dinner there, a small party.'

As was the case for many in the population as a whole, our interviewees were busy rebuilding their lives, and the end of the war brought new opportunities in training, education and work: many refugees availed themselves of these with great energy, perhaps especially so because of their personal histories and the tremendous struggles they had already undergone. In the immediate postwar years naturalisation became possible and most of the interviewees took up the opportunity. This removed barriers and work restrictions, enabling refugees to operate under largely the same conditions as the indigenous population. Naturally, they followed a variety of avenues in their work and careers, not least because of differing social and educational backgrounds. However, some of the women did not pursue work outside the home, whether as a matter of choice or through force of circumstance. These women, as was also the norm among the indigenous population in those postwar years, put much of their effort into bringing up their children and supporting their husbands' careers. For all of the refugees who had decided to stay in this country there came, however, the additional challenge of integrating more fully into British society.

1. Aspects of integration: work and careers

i. Special opportunities in the postwar period

For a number of the interviewees the fact that they had German as their mother tongue in itself provided opportunities for work in the immediate postwar period, although this did not necessarily lead to permanent careers. The British and American occupying forces in Germany were in need of German speakers who could work as translators, interpreters, surveillance officers and in related areas, and they trained a number of refugees, some of whom were already serving in the British Army, to act in these capacities. This is how Peter Singer, Dorothea Galewski and Peter Johnson came to be back in Germany in 1945. Peter Singer spent six months on postal censorship and telephone surveillance in Southern Germany. He recalls: 'One of the first jobs I went out on was looking for Martin Bormann in Bad Tölz.' However, by no means all the surveillance work involved searching for such high-profile figures, but rather, as he says, 'most [of the calls] were very mundane and very local'. Dorothea Galewski's work for the US Army also involved surveillance, but she found her assignment to work as a reviewer, checking the accuracy and style of translations relating to the IG Farben trial in the Nuremberg courts, harrowing and depressing. Although working with a very congenial group of people, she looked forward to leaving Germany again and returning to London. Peter Johnson, having passed his British Army interpreters' examination on VE Day itself, was sent by the Army to Hildesheim, where he worked for seventeen months as an interpreter. He too was confronted with the horrors of Nazi atrocities but felt he was able to make a positive contribution by ameliorating the plight of many in those immediate postwar months:

> That was the most interesting... because my main work wasn't for the army. I was looking after people returning from concentration camps who were assigned to various... projects in Germany, doing social work. Through this... I was able to help many people.

Having German as his mother tongue provided Eugen Brehm with work too, but in his case this led to his life's career with the BBC Monitoring Service, as we have seen. He found the atmosphere there

9. THE CHALLENGES OF SETTLING DOWN

so congenial that he rejected a later opportunity to work in a similar capacity for the Germans in Cologne.

ii. Careers in teaching

A relatively large proportion of our interviewees followed careers in education, with language teaching being the most prevalent. Hilde Auerbach, Lotte Berk, Hans Brill, Ernst Flesch, Erika Young briefly, Mimi Glover, Ruth Herring, Renée Hubert, Elizabeth Rosenthal, Hans Seelig and Hanna Singer taught at educational establishments ranging from a private finishing-school to university. Among these, not surprisingly, several taught German, thereby finding themselves in a position to contribute to the preservation of the best of German and Central European culture, which they had experienced before circumstances forced them to leave their homeland.

As we have seen, Ruth Herring started teaching German at the prestigious Wycombe Abbey School before the war; after the war, she continued her long and distinguished career as Head of German at Wycombe High School, where she was an inspirational teacher. Hilde Auerbach's career took her along a similar path. She completed a second degree in French and German at Birkbeck College (University of London) in 1947. This led to her career as a language teacher at the Royal School of Bath, of which she reports: 'There we taught up to university level and I was the only one to teach German at that time. . . I also did some A-level, and it's good if you do the whole thing.' Even now, in retirement, she enjoys language-related activities, such as the Cercle Français and serving on the committee of the local German Society.

Ernst Flesch too became involved in a career in secondary education after the war, though by a more circuitous route, which took him from working in the field of photography to a Church of England training college where he says they were 'trying to produce English Christian Gentlemen, which wasn't exactly me'. Later he taught at Shoreditch Comprehensive School while studying at Birkbeck College, which eventually led to a lecturing post at Barnet College, where he taught mostly A-level courses. As a young refugee he had very much missed parental support in his early career endeavours. Indeed, his achievements are entirely due to his own efforts, since he had come from a very modest background, and his schooling had been severely disrupted by the war. He acknowledges, however, that employment opportunities were more readily available in this country after the war, particularly in the more flexible English education system. As he says: 'We were lucky really, the postwar generation here, that they needed teachers like a piece of bread.'

The desperate need for teachers in the postwar period is also reflected in Erika Young's brief career as a Latin teacher at a Brighton convent school immediately after she had taken her School Certificate in 1945, a position for which she did not really feel qualified:

> So I, aged seventeen or eighteen, taught Latin to the whole school, including A-level equivalent. . . Without any training, having only just done the exams myself, which was quite hard because I had to teach authors I didn't know myself. But I had my own Latin teacher not that far away, so when I got really stuck I just went back to Worthing and got some advice.

While teaching in Brighton, Erika Young also took a university correspondence course in English and eventually embarked on a career as a journalist.

An Oxford graduate, Hans Seelig taught in grammar schools for a number of years but ended up teaching in the higher education sector, at Hendon College, now the University of Middlesex. Here he was involved in developing German on the Humanities degree programme, 'so we had two degrees in which German was taught. I think it was the best thing I did in my teaching career.'

Elizabeth Rosenthal, too, taught in a number of different educational establishments, mostly as a French specialist. Like Ernst Flesch, she combined working as a teacher with further study: she enrolled for a part-time degree course in French at Birkbeck College and, happily, managed to secure a scholarship that enabled her to take a higher degree, with a focus on late medieval French romance. Perhaps partly through the influence of her mother, one of the first Montessori-trained teachers in Germany, she was interested in all aspects of education, which is reflected in the variety of positions she

9. THE CHALLENGES OF SETTLING DOWN

has held. At first she worked in primary schools, where she developed a special interest in children with learning difficulties. Interestingly, it was her spell as an English Language Assistant in France which to her confirmed that she was really accepted as an English person: 'So that was when I was fully integrated, if you ask when.' Her career in higher education started in the early 1960s, when she became a tutor in the French Department of the University of Wales, in Swansea. This was followed by a post at Gypsy Hill College, part of the University of London Institute of Education, where she founded and was Head of the Department of Modern Languages. She enjoyed 'a very happy time there', until her department fell victim to cuts in the education sector and she took early retirement in 1982, a hard blow to such a dedicated teacher: 'I thought it was the end of the world.' But showing the resilience and adaptability of so many of our interviewees, she continued to work in a variety of roles: as a part-time German teacher at Imperial College London, for instance, and as an interpreter and translator at conferences of the International Union of Social Democratic Educators.

Somewhat surprisingly, considering German is their mother tongue, two of our other interviewees also taught English. Hanna Singer, who had a degree in English from Royal Holloway College, made teaching this subject her career. She explains it as follows: 'I think, really because I liked learning English so much, I thought I'd like to teach others English.' She had chosen to study at Royal Holloway because it was a residential college and her family did not have a home of their own until shortly before she graduated.

In Mimi Glover's case, English was one of a number of subjects she taught in a variety of schools during the war and for a short time afterwards, until the birth of her daughter. The fact that in later life, aged sixty, she trained as a guide for English Heritage and then took visitors on tours around the House of Commons is a further indication of the flexibility displayed by many of our refugees. This trait can also be discerned in Hans Brill's career. He is one of the youngest of the interviewees and, although he left school at sixteen, his whole life seems to bear witness to a very positive attitude to learning and new ideas. Having trained for a career in the Navy, eventually becoming a submarine commander, he completely changed direction and studied Modern History at Oxford, followed by a postgraduate diploma in History of Art at the Courtauld Institute. The renowned art historian Ernst Gombrich had advised him: 'If you want to become an art historian, for heaven's sake become a historian first.' Hans Brill certainly enjoyed 'the excellent scholars' with whom he had contact, such as Isaiah Berlin and the mathematician Harry Pitt. In his subsequent career, as a lecturer in art history and librarian at Wimbledon School of Art and at the Royal College of Art, he developed innovative approaches by teaching art contextually. Although officially retired, he now works freelance, emphasising that he still teaches 'passionately whenever I can'.

This section should not be concluded without a mention of the career of Renée Hubert who, it will be recalled, left England to join her family in the USA during the war. She obtained a PhD from Columbia University in New York and enjoyed a very varied and successful university career teaching French and Comparative Literature in different establishments in the USA such as Sarah Lawrence College in New York City, University of Illinois and University of California at Irvine. She has always been, and indeed still remains, very active in research in her fields: in the last thirty years the relationship between painting and poetry has been a particular interest and, more recently, the nature of the book itself. She still regularly delivers papers at academic conferences in both the USA and Europe.

iii. Careers in publishing, the arts and related creative fields

The challenges and opportunities for those of the interviewees who tried to establish themselves and build up a career in these areas were varied. Some found that their highly individual talents were appreciated and in demand, while others felt that their new environment was less than encouraging.

As already noted in an earlier chapter, Ilse Wolff's successful career culminated in her position as Chief Librarian at the Wiener Library in 1947. Prior to this, whilst she was assistant to the then Chief Librarian Gustav Warburg, she had followed courses in librarianship and had taken the Library Association Examinations. She was very much involved in the development of the library as an

9. THE CHALLENGES OF SETTLING DOWN

important source of information about the Jewish situation during and after the war:

> We went on collecting Nazi material and also built up the library... It started being used by members of the BBC and Foreign Office, and especially the Central Office of Information, and later, after the war, when the Nuremberg Trials began, we were very important suppliers of material.

Not only did Ilse Wolff feel deeply involved in her work in the library, she also experienced the sense of community in the area where it was then located. This was in Manchester Square, home also to the Jewish Agency. She recalls that when the Jewish state was founded in 1948, 'the whole square ... was celebrating. That was one of the memorable events there.' She mentions that the library became 'a very important part of my life... I was married to the Wiener Library.' She met many well-known personalities there, such as Thomas Mann and his daughter Erika and, in 1955, the first president of the Federal Republic of Germany, Theodor Heuss. With a sense of achievement, she tells how she had, purely on her own initiative, started a series of printed catalogues which 'found their way into all university libraries and public libraries and were reviewed in various papers'. Her career at the Wiener Library ended in 1966 when she left for reasons of ill health. Yet her resilience and ability to cope with all kinds of challenges revealed itself once again when in 1968 she became, in her own words, 'a publisher overnight', after the sudden death of her second husband Oswald Wolff, the publisher and head of the book importers Interbook. 'The publishing got me', she says, and in her distinguished second career she published books about Max Frisch and Dietrich Fischer-Dieskau, among others, as well as Willy Brandt's autobiography *In Exile*, which became her bestseller.

It was through personal contacts that Erika Young got the opportunity to work in a field of special interest to her. After her short foray into teaching she met the owners of the British/American Catholic publishing house Sheed and Ward, who took her under their wing and offered her work. She was subsequently able to fulfil her ambition to become a journalist when she secured a post on the

Norwich Evening Press and *Eastern Daily News*. After establishing a family, she continued to work as a freelance journalist.

The architect Alec Armstrong also had to rely on the intervention of sympathetic employers, the architectural partnership Powell and Moya, to find career opportunities. He had, like many other émigré architects, been refused membership of the Royal Institute of British Architects, although his educational credentials were of the highest order since he had attended the Bauhaus, the famous German school for arts, crafts and architecture in Dessau, as well as the Technische Hochschule Berlin and the Humboldt Universität Berlin. He comments: 'I have never been a member [of the RIBA] and therefore as an architect I was an assistant for other people.' In the early postwar years Powell and Moya were struggling to establish themselves and salaries were of necessity low. Alec Armstrong recalls that he was 'very, very hungry because I got £4 a week at the time ... and they had no money themselves'. However, in spite of financial hardship he enjoyed his work. 'It was wonderful there', he says, as he felt he was working with people whose cultural values he shared. His career subsequently took him to a lecturing post in Nigeria, positions with some of the London boroughs, and finally a professorship in History of Art and Architecture at the then Hammersmith College of Art and Design (now part of the University of Greenwich).

While refugees often had difficulties in the then rather restricted field of architecture, the world of music was perhaps traditionally more welcoming to talents from abroad. Peter Gellhorn's career seems to bear this out. By 1941 he had joined Sadler's Wells Opera, and although at that time not yet naturalised, he was able to get a work permit because: 'I had operatic experience even very brilliant musicians couldn't provide at that time. I wasn't taking anything away. On the contrary, I could claim that I enabled English artists to do their job more efficiently.' After the war, he became a conductor of the Carl Rosa Opera Company and also conductor and Head of Music Staff at Covent Garden. It is certainly a tribute to Peter Gellhorn's talent but perhaps also to the open-mindedness of the English musical establishment that he, a German, was able to obtain such important posts so quickly. He himself was aware of this situation:

9. THE CHALLENGES OF SETTLING DOWN

It was a risky thing after the war with Germany and Austria to have an Austrian as musical director [Karl Rankl, then musical director at Covent Garden] and the assistant director born in Germany . . . of course I had to be careful and not overstep the mark.

Peter Gellhorn moved on to other prestigious positions such as conductor at Glyndebourne Festival Opera and Director of the BBC Chorus. Through his teaching and performances he continues to be an inspiration to many musicians.

Like Peter Gellhorn, two more émigrés amongst the interviewees, the dancer Lotte Berk and the actress Hanne Norbert-Miller, succeeded in establishing themselves in the performing arts. After their emigration in the 1930s Lotte Berk, together with her dancer husband, performed with the Ballet Rambert as well as at Covent Garden. In the postwar period she developed her influential exercise and fitness method, for which she is now perhaps best known and which is described in the book she co-wrote with Jean Prince, *The Lotte Berk Method of Exercise*.

The actress Hanne Norbert-Miller was soon performing at the Austrian Centre's theatre, the 'Laterndl', after she arrived in Britain. At the same time, she acted for other refugee organisations such as the theatre of the Free German League of Culture, and she later gave frequent readings at Club 1943. Like many other refugee actors, she also worked for the BBC, gaining a staff position in the Austrian Section as an announcer and translator which, as she emphasises, was regarded as war work. During this time she established friendships and contacts which she valued throughout her life: 'I suppose through these little theatres and the BBC one became very much a close group of friends. . . That was probably my closest circle of friends.' After the war there was still a great deal of demand for her work and she continued with the BBC both in their German and Austrian Sections. She recalls: 'You see, directly after the war we did a lot of plays. Erich Fried translated plays, because in those days the Germans didn't have those plays. So there were still quite a lot of acting possibilities.' In 1946 Hanne Norbert-Miller married the well-established refugee actor Martin Miller. After the birth of their son in 1951 she mainly worked freelance. In spite of her work for refugee theatres and the BBC, she feels that her career might have taken her further if circumstances had been different: 'I missed what I originally wanted to do. I didn't have a career in the theatre, which I started with great hopes.' These feelings of regret are understandable, considering her promising start before emigration, but she emphasises that there have been compensations: 'I've got a lovely son who cares about me... well, I've had a good life.'

The writer Stella Rotenberg echoes Hanne Norbert-Miller's sentiments about emigration preventing the development of full personal potential. She states this clearly when she says: 'I am aware of the fact that I lost a lot. I think if circumstances had been different, I could have achieved more in life.' Her work as a writer would have profited from the stimulus of the German language environment and of critical interaction with fellow writers; she emphasises how helpful this would have been, especially as she lived in Leeds after the war, far away from other German-speaking writers: 'Had I had any contacts, not necessarily always encouraging ones, sometimes also critical, hostile ones... If, for instance, let's just assume I had known Erich Fried... I had nothing at all, not a sound, nothing.' Nevertheless, three collections of her poems have been published, *Gedichte* (1972), *Die wir übrig sind* (1978), and *Scherben sind endlicher Hort* (1991). For the latter she was awarded a literary prize by the Austrian Ministry of Education and Art in 1992, and in 1996 the Austrian Republic conferred on her the Austrian Cross of Honour for Science and Art, First Class. Even though it seems that writing is closest to her heart, it will also be recalled that she had to abandon her potential career as a doctor when her medical studies in Vienna were curtailed because of the necessity to emigrate. Although she reconciled herself to this, she still has some feelings of regret: 'I've come to terms with it, but I think I would have made a sympathetic doctor.'

iv. Careers in the medical, social and scientific fields

A relatively small number of the interviewees worked in these fields, where they managed to build satisfying careers, albeit not without having to overcome difficulties arising from their particular circumstances.

9. THE CHALLENGES OF SETTLING DOWN

Josephine Bruegel who, as we have seen, almost completed her medical studies in Prague before emigration, was eventually given the chance to finish her medical training and obtained work at the Royal Marsden and Princess Elizabeth Hospital almost immediately after qualifying in 1942. As a graduate of a British medical school, she was more fortunate than her counterparts with German and Austrian qualifications; they were subject to the restrictions imposed by the British Medical Association, which proved most reluctant to admit refugee doctors onto the register of licenced practitioners. Josephine Bruegel enjoyed a successful and varied medical career, which took her from working in, and eventually being in charge of, the Accident and Emergency Department of the Whittington Hospital to doing pioneering work in family planning and finally to setting up her own surgery as a general practitioner. The conclusion she reaches on her life and career is: 'In any case it has been a very satisfying life, a very interesting one.'

Adelheid Schweitzer certainly encountered difficulties when she was looking for work, on one occasion precisely because of her German background and name. After her husband's death in 1952 she had been obliged to find employment, but her application for a post as administrative secretary to the child analyst Margaret Lowenfeld was rejected, although she had worked for her before: 'They said they couldn't employ me because there were already so many people on the notepaper with foreign names, they couldn't have yet another one.' She was thus forced to settle for a less interesting job with an import/export firm where she had been employed before the war. While she appreciated this much-needed employment opportunity, she knew that she was really looking for a greater challenge, which eventually led her to train as a psychiatric social worker. This was by no means an easy choice and initially it involved voluntary welfare work. She describes her work at the London Care Committee, an organisation set up to look after London schoolchildren in deprived areas:

> They had one paid worker for every office and the rest were volunteers. I worked as a volunteer, going down one evening a week, visiting families in the Oval area, living out here... I really don't

know how I did it. Once I was nearly hit by a man who interrupted an interview. He didn't like me there. Some of the interviews were conducted on the doorstep because people wouldn't let you in.

After a preliminary social science course at the London School of Economics, Adelheid Schweitzer was finally able to enrol on the mental health course. She recalls that 'it was very hard going, very hard going. Physically hard going because of the distances one had to travel'. She did, however, qualify in 1957. Her career choice was perhaps not entirely surprising, since her father had been a cardiologist and her husband an academic and doctor. Hilde Ainger, on the other hand, feels that she would have liked to have been a social worker, but that emigration prevented her from fulfilling her ambition: 'If I'd had a chance to get any sort of training I would have been incredibly interested in social work . . . you see, if I'd stayed in Germany, I would have gone to university.'

Although Walter Wolff had a long and successful career as a chemist, he too did not have the opportunity to realise his initial ambition of becoming a doctor: 'My early hopes had been to study medicine, but the course in medical studies would have been far too long and also expensive, so I had to choose an alternative.' This alternative was to work as an assistant to an eminent biochemist, Dr Synge, at the Lister Institute while at the same time studying at the Chelsea Polytechnic and becoming an Associate of the Royal Institute of Chemistry (ARIC). His diligence paid off, since he was able to secure an excellent position with Glaxo where he worked for forty-six years, including a spell in East Africa. He considers that he has been involved in the pharmaceutical industry at an interesting time:

> There was a certain element of luck, in so far as when I came and worked for the pharmaceutical company – which now, incidentally, is the largest in the world – I came there with the experience I previously gained at the Lister Institute, which was unique and quite revolutionary in analytical chemistry. . . It was also a time of great change and advance in the pharmaceutical industry, and I happened to be around at the development of penicillin, which of course was the first antibiotic and virtually revolutionised all treatment of bacterial diseases.

9. THE CHALLENGES OF SETTLING DOWN

v. Careers in business

Those of our interviewees who forged their careers in business also displayed impressive talents. Klary Friedl, who after her husband's death in 1984 continued to run the successful import/export business Orientex they had set up together during the war, had previously proved her indefatigable spirit in a number of varied enterprises even before she left Slovakia, as we have noted earlier. After emigration, while faced with the need to earn a living without a work permit, she turned her talents to making cheese, which her husband sold to establishments like Marks & Spencer, Lyons' Corner House and even Fortnum & Mason. In their import/export business, which included dealings with Eastern Europe (mainly Hungary), the Friedls made use of their prewar background, not least their knowledge of Hungarian. Klary Friedl sums up her life: 'Well, I had a very, very good life in England. In a way very successful because we worked and we managed to achieve something.'

After his time as an interpreter in the immediate postwar period, Peter Johnson returned to his career in the fur trade, which he continues to pursue. He is also very active in the field of voluntary work, with a particular interest in the Australian branch of the *Dunera* Organisation. Nelly Kuttner, after having to do domestic work for some years, was finally able to return fulltime to her original profession of milliner, having started again in a small way by altering the hats of fellow-refugees on her days off. Her millinery business, Fleurette Fashion, became very successful.

Two of the interviewees, Peter Singer and Eric Rose, whose careers took them to high managerial positions, had emigrated in their teens and completed their education in this country. Peter Singer's headmaster had a high opinion of his pupil's abilities and recommended he should go on to university. However, circumstances were not in his favour. After taking his School Certificate in 1940, aged seventeen, he first worked as a farmhand but soon looked out for opportunities to follow his engineering interests and eventually managed to get a place on an industrial training course for aircraft production. Consequently, Peter Singer worked in the aircraft industry where he also involved himself in the Amalgamated

Engineering Union. He comments on his work: 'I felt I was doing something useful... That was my ... wartime effort.' While servicing and overhauling aircraft engines for D. Napier & Son he studied for a year on a part-time engineering course at London University, a vindication of his former headmaster's confidence in him. After his postwar work in telephone surveillance in Germany, Peter Singer returned to Britain and continued to pursue his interests in things technical, working in various small engineering firms. He soon moved towards management and eventually became a director while his passion for engineering was turned into the hobby of making model aeroplanes. Still fascinated by modern technology, he was pleased when electronic equipment arrived at his place of work. He sums up his working life as follows: 'We were, I felt ... reasonably happy doing a sometimes quite onerous job, but nevertheless you got a certain amount of satisfaction. I had a nice big office and finished up with a computer on my desk.'

Eric Rose's special interest was textiles. After he had finished his studies at the London School of Economics in the immediate postwar period, he was offered a lectureship there, which he rejected. Because of his interest in textiles, he became an apprentice at his uncle's firm in Bolton while also attending Manchester Technical College. Later, when looking for a job, he encountered some anti-semitism, although eventually being a Jewish refugee turned out to be helpful because, through a connection of his father's, he finally secured a job interview with Marks & Spencer. The interviewer, Dr Kann, was himself a refugee who held an important position in the company and Eric Rose was offered a management traineeship. This was the first step in a very successful career, taking him via production and merchandise development to senior management positions. Now in his retirement, he remarks on the strong ties his working life created for him: 'I am in very close touch with the LSE and with Marks & Spencer – they're my roots. Wherever I go in the world, somebody knows one or the other or both and I get an entrée everywhere through them.' In his retirement Eric Rose has taken the opportunity to follow yet another interest, art and dance, his studies reaching a very high academic level:

9. THE CHALLENGES OF SETTLING DOWN

> I decided to study History of Art. I got the diploma in History of Art at Birkbeck College and then I did a Master's degree in Arts Criticism at City University, and I am now starting on a PhD, also at City University, researching at the Laban Centre for Movement and Dance on modern dance: German influence on British dance.

In this pursuit Eric Rose combines aspects of the culture of his country of origin with that of his adopted country. Like so many refugees, he contributes to the cultural and intellectual enrichment of this country.

2. Aspects of integration: language, naturalisation, identity

While an active working life may to an extent be an indication that a reasonably settled and financially secure state has been achieved in the country of emigration, it does not necessarily reflect how much a person really feels integrated into the new environment. Mastering the new language, but also a continuing emotional attachment to the mother tongue, or even a pronounced rejection of it, all affect the integration process. Some of the interviewees, however, feel that having once been uprooted, they never managed to feel completely rooted again.

i. Challenges presented by the new language

As has already been established, the ages of the interviewees on arrival in this country ranged from eight to thirty-four, and their knowledge of English likewise varied widely. Most coped impressively with being thrown into a completely new language environment.

The youngest arrived between the ages of eight and fifteen and were most directly exposed to the new language in their schools in England. For Elizabeth Rosenthal, who already had some English and who felt she had had very good language teaching at Caputh, the experience of having to move to this country was given a positive dimension by her enthusiasm for the new language, as we saw in Chapter Three. She recalls: 'I was thrilled to come to England. Absolutely what I'd wanted more than anything else, to try out my

English.' Hans Seelig, too, coped very well with the challenge of learning English. He had arrived at the age of nine and, as we have seen, initial language difficulties at his first school were soon overcome after he changed to another school. He felt that after six months in England, he 'was perfect in English'. He even passed the 11-plus examination and won an essay prize. Erika Young, who had no English on arrival, fared similarly well: 'I came in September and by the end of that term, the winter term, I was first in the class in every subject except English, where I was about third.' She ascribes her speedy acquisition of the language to the need to communicate which, she says, makes any child 'learn very, very fast, because I did, and I'm certainly not exceptional'.

Only one of this youngest group, Eric Rose, who was very competent in French but had little English, was initially more troubled by having to cope with the new language at school, in his case Holloway Boys' Grammar School, where he was obliged to catch up with Latin at the same time. It is perhaps of some significance that he was already a teenager when he came to England and had to deal with the new language:

> My English was very poor. Because my German and French were very good, my English had been neglected ... well, by the time we realised I was going to come to an English-speaking country I was already too ... well, quite old, really, I was twelve or thirteen ... And the thing that shook me most, apart from the fact that they were all boys and no girls, was that they were doing Latin, which I had never even touched on.

Quite a few of the young adult arrivals amongst the interviewees also took the challenge of the new language in their stride. Indeed, some arrived already confident of their language skills, acquired either at school or at university. Both Josephine Bruegel and Ilse Wolff express their positive attitude. 'I loved the English language. I always loved it', is how the latter puts it. She had on a previous visit gone to Speakers' Corner, to 'improve my English'. However, it was not 'love at first sound' for everybody. Ruth Herring had first heard English spoken by a native speaker at university in Munich, and she comments: 'I thought English was awful.' But she was later

9. THE CHALLENGES OF SETTLING DOWN

converted to the beauty of the language on hearing John Gielgud on stage.

Others who felt confident about their language skills, having learned English previously, were Christel Marsh, Eugen Brehm, Hilde Auerbach, Hanne Norbert-Miller, Adelheid Schweitzer and Peter Gellhorn. Eva Pollard, who had been working as a translator for a chemical firm in Berlin, had had the foresight to take lessons to ensure that she would be able to cope with the language of the new country, and Hanne Norbert-Miller states that: 'English was the only useful thing I ever learned at school. We were taught very well because the Head was fanatic about English.' Her school experience is echoed by Peter Gellhorn, who refers to his 'very good English teacher at school'. Even so, he was surprised when on arrival he could not understand everybody, 'because they did not enunciate like an English teacher does'. He relates an experience on the Underground when, having asked for directions, he received an answer that sounded like 'change bikes' but, as he eventually realised, meant 'change at Baker Street'.

Peter Gellhorn found this amusing. However, not everybody had an untroubled time as far as the new language was concerned. A simple linguistic misunderstanding could reveal a deep cultural difference, as with an incident that Helga Reutter experienced as very upsetting, since offence was taken where none had been intended. She had a document which required the signature of a policeman, so she took it to Harrow Road Police Station:

> I went in and I said to the policeman like a good girl: 'I read, you must sign that for me.' He said: 'I must nothing,' and 'Perhaps you're used to talk to your policemen in your country like that.' I had no idea what I had done and I nearly... I don't cry easily and I didn't cry, but I must have looked as if I was going to start any minute.

Equally the new language environment presented a difficult challenge for Gertrud Wengraf. Although eventually, after about two years in this country, she was to feel comfortable with English, she initially found, arriving from Austria with just one year of school English, that the new language was more difficult than she had expected:

> I thought when I came that I was quite good, because I had been reading [English] and been able even to write, but when I came here, I was quite, quite lost. It was very, very difficult for me. I didn't understand a word, because people spoke too fast, I thought.

In her case the experience of being unable to cope was exacerbated by the task given to her in her first – unpaid – job here: answering telephone enquiries for the support organisation Austrian Self-Aid. Hilde Ainger also recalls a hurtful experience soon after her arrival in this country. She arrived in 1934 aged seventeen, and had her first au pair job with a rather unpleasant wealthy family who saw fit to laugh at her for her less than perfect grasp of English:

> They were incredibly unkind, also about my English... I listened, and I remember on the second day or so, she asked me to go to the baker's and buy sixpenny-worth of buns. I didn't know what buns were, nor did I catch the sixpenny-worth. Then she explained, and I gathered buns were cakes and I said: 'How much will they cost?' She then amused herself by telling her friends how stupid I was.

This family was quite unwilling to take the trouble to help her constructively to learn the language or to explain anything about her new environment:

> I had quite a while there without ever being corrected, and also I realised afterwards that actually they spoke with a much smaller vocabulary than friends I made later... nothing was explained to me... There was nobody really to help me with any of this.

Other interviewees, such as Nelly Kuttner and Peter Johnson, felt that they too could have done with some constructive correction in order to speed along the learning process, but English reticence would often prevent this. Peter Johnson states: 'The silly thing is that in England no one ever corrects you.'

For some, improving their English was seen as a task to be tackled together with fellow émigrés. For example, the strategy of Peter Johnson and his friends was to pay forfeits whenever one of them slipped into German:

> There was a group of four of us, four boys, and we had agreed that we would put a farthing into the kitty for every German word we used,

9. THE CHALLENGES OF SETTLING DOWN

and I think in this way we got nine shillings together, and with this money we went to the cinema and had tea. That was a very good thing, because I was told that in the beginning I used to speak German at night in my dreams. Then I spoke a mixture of German and English, and then I dropped German altogether.

Peter Johnson initially always carried a dictionary with him. But eventually he felt confident enough to accept the advice, given to him by a bus conductor, to throw the dictionary away and just say what came into his head, 'and of course he was quite right'. With the passage of time and owing to the demands of life, English eventually became the preferred language of communication for most. Gertrud Wengraf's account bears this out: 'I always spoke German to my husband. And to some of the friends I had. I still had some friends from Vienna then. I still have one, but by now we only speak English.' Only when they have visitors from Austria or Germany do they revert to their mother tongue: 'Suddenly it seems quite normal to speak German!'

ii. The personal view: attitudes to German and English

Feelings and attitudes towards both the new and the old language are closely tied up with the individuals' sense of identity, with their personality and creativity and their degree of integration into their adopted country

German may be rejected as too painfully connected with the past, or it may be carefully guarded and nurtured as something too precious to lose. Elizabeth Rosenthal was invited to teach German classes at Imperial College, but initially she was not keen to take up this opportunity: 'I did not want to teach German, I wanted to teach French.' However, when she eventually decided to accept the offer she found that she was enjoying her work. Ruth Herring's chosen career, on the other hand, was to teach German: 'I have been privileged to teach German all my life.'

Expectations as to the possibilities and limitations of the language the interviewees chose to use also vary. Thus even Hans Seelig, a professional linguist and creative writer whose competence in both languages is of a very high standard, feels that he might not have surmounted the language barrier entirely: 'Yes, this language thing – I find it actually quite interesting. I struggle with German and I struggle with English when I want to work more creatively.' Others, however, feel very much at ease about their use of German. Peter Gellhorn who, as an eminent conductor and pianist, expresses his creativity through music, says about his German: 'One doesn't forget how to swim.' Ilse Wolff, too, feels comfortable with either language: 'I like to think that I can switch from one language to another easily... I don't choose it, it depends on whoever I am with.'

The emotional attachment that some have to their mother tongue is revealed very clearly in Josephine Bruegel's efforts and those of her friends to keep the German language alive. They felt a commitment and a duty to maintain a high standard in the language – which was perhaps, for her, a continuation of a practice already established in German-speaking circles in Prague.[28] She states: 'Throughout the war we strove to maintain our German language and to make it more beautiful... Those amongst us who felt that it was our duty to maintain the German language and literature were very active in this respect.'

Ruth Herring seems to have thought along similar lines when she helped to set up a small school for children of internees in her Isle of Man internment camp, where most of them had problems with both English and German. She felt it was important to use 'one language or the other and not a "speak", which was neither English nor German'. She says: 'I have no patience with people who start stuttering and mixing it [German] all up with English.' As a teacher of German, she valued the opportunity to maintain her German at a high level, yet she admits that having spent so many years outside the German language environment has affected her: she does not always have immediate recall of all her German vocabulary when visiting the country, and some modern expressions are unfamiliar to her.

Not all of Ruth Herring's fellow émigrés had the opportunity to keep using their mother tongue. Right from the beginning of her life in England, Christel Marsh, married to an Englishman, missed being

---

28. A particularly pure form of educated German without local overtones was used in Jewish German-speaking circles in Prague, as exemplified by the writings of Franz Kafka, Max Brod and other authors of the 'Prague Circle'.

9. THE CHALLENGES OF SETTLING DOWN

in close contact with German: 'The language was a major loss, a very major loss... I was very reluctant ... to let the German drop... I hankered after German books.' Eva Sommerfreund also makes an interesting observation regarding language. She keenly feels the loss of German in one particular respect. As she had no English on arrival in this country, she could not cope with English verbal humour and felt deprived of the comfort that a humorous exchange in one's mother tongue can bring, especially in hard times: 'I never laughed for years.' Even now German jokes are a bond with her friends: 'It is funny that we still sometimes remember the old jokes in German.' This is of course a wider issue than simply not being able to share a joke. Language and culture are closely bound up, and not being able to fully understand the language bars one from fully appreciating the culture, and vice versa, thus contributing to a feeling of isolation and not belonging. And yet, in spite of these feelings, the use of English eventually took over.

During the war, the incentive for many of our refugees to use English, either in public or even amongst themselves, was particularly strong, as German was, after all, the language of the enemy. Hans Seelig's parents spoke mostly German at home and he remembers: 'I was terrified in case my parents spoke German in the street, especially during the war. I would sort of crawl away – "I don't belong to them" sort of thing.' He is of course describing the attitude he had as a child, when the need not to appear different is often felt particularly keenly. He goes on to relate that his parents soon gave up speaking German in public because 'both of them wanted to integrate here'. Gertrud Wengraf also recalls a general reluctance in the refugee community to use their mother tongue: 'Somehow, particularly in the street, it wasn't very well looked on to speak German.' Not to speak in a foreign language was regarded by the established Anglo-Jewish community as a sign of politeness and loyalty towards the host country and was indeed advised in a booklet entitled 'Helpful Information and Guidance for Every Refugee', issued by the Jewish Board of Deputies in December 1938, and intended to be handed to every refugee on arrival in Britain.

For Elizabeth Rosenthal, adopting the new language so eagerly was part of coping with the émigré situation and the separation, albeit brief, from her mother. Consequently, when they were reunited a few months later, Elizabeth Rosenthal could not bring herself to speak German, and from then on they continued to use English, even in the home. She recalls: 'We went to Manchester and I met her at the station. And I couldn't speak German... And she spoke German and I spoke English.'

Concerns among some refugees about keeping the German language alive in the next generation led to the question of bringing up the children to be bilingual. Hanne Norbert-Miller attempted to use German with her son, born in 1951, but feels:

> We weren't very successful in making him bilingual. There were so many theories. Whenever a refugee child was born when we were at the BBC, the German Section usually had an enormous table in the canteen and all the intellectuals were discussing whether one should speak German to them first.

Erika Young, while never speaking German in the home nor emphasising her Austrian background, was nevertheless keen for her two daughters to learn some German, which they mostly picked up on holidays in Austria. She explains: 'So we always went skiing to the Semmering [mountain near Vienna] which did not have foreign tourists... hoping that they might pick up German.' Bilingualism in the next generation is not the usual pattern among our interviewees, and there is, indeed, some retrospective regret about German not being used in the home. Thus Gertrud Wengraf, who avoided speaking German with her children during the war, says: 'Perhaps I should have done. I often think I did the wrong thing.' Hans Brill, too, regrets that the use of German was not maintained within his family, stating that 'as a result my children were not brought up to be bilingual; they are sorry about that and so am I'.

On the domestic front, the matter of language was certainly not always straightforward. Christel Marsh's English husband who, as a lawyer, had spent some time studying in Germany, had initially been keen to speak German at home with his wife. Eventually, however, he grew impatient with her continuing attachment to her mother tongue, thinking that she should identify more strongly with English. She feels that he was unable to appreciate her

9. THE CHALLENGES OF SETTLING DOWN

emotional ties with German. The writer and poet Stella Rotenberg encountered a similar attitude in her husband, a refugee from Czechoslovakia for whom German was, above all, Hitler's language: 'You and your Hitler-language', he would say to her. However, while admitting that the language had been tainted, she rejects most vehemently the idea that the whole German language was nothing more than the debased, violated version used by the Nazis. German for her is:

> The language I love, Thomas Mann's language... Hitler couldn't even speak German, not proper German, just a German full of lies. He ruined the German language too, but not my German, not the language I like. He was not able to touch that.

The German language is part of her essential being: 'It is where I am at home, something that belongs to me... Apart from my son, the German language is really the most important thing in my life.'

Although, as has been stated, English is now the language of habitual use for most of the interviewees, borne out clearly by the fact that the majority chose to be interviewed in English, most think that their origin is still discernible because of their accent. Christel Marsh found English vowels difficult to pronounce: 'We weren't taught very well in that respect at school. For instance, the difference between "bad" and "bed". It took me years before I really began to be aware of it.'

Feelings about having a German accent vary, however. While Elizabeth Rosenthal's German accent is virtually undetectable, she herself is aware of a small residue of German interference. She had arrived at a young age, as had Ernst Flesch, who now speaks with a 'semi-London accent... but always keeping my foreign intonation. I've never lost it. I think at ten you don't lose it any more.' Evidently, Gertrud Wengraf does not entirely agree, since she observes that some of her younger émigré friends did manage to lose their accent. She herself was a little older on arrival, and although she feels confident that she uses good English, people still ask her where she comes from because of her accent. This happens also to Klary Friedl, somewhat to her irritation. She says: 'And if I open my mouth, they ask me: "Where do you come from?" Now I am so tired of it, I say:

"Oh, I come from Kew Gardens."' Hilde Ainger still experiences similar reactions to her accent and manages to make light of it: 'I still don't like it much that a few minutes after I meet somebody they'll say to me: "Do I detect a German accent?" or "When did you come to England?" or something else. But generally I have got greater worries than that.' Helga Reutter mentions that such an accent can have a distancing effect. Even though it is often seen as charming, it still sets her apart: 'It [gives] you the feeling that you don't quite belong.' Stella Rotenberg's statement also bears this out when she talks about: '...the distance, it does not necessarily have to be a hostile distance... When I meet people, when they hear me speak, they know I am not from here. They are friendly, interested, and I am quite sure they bear me no ill will, but I am not one of them.'

iii. Naturalisation

Applying for and receiving citizenship of the country of immigration marks a definite stage in the integration process. However, it is a deliberate step, whereas, as already noted, integration as such is more gradual, more bound up with feelings and attitudes that become internalised.

Only a few refugees achieved naturalisation before the war, usually because they had emigrated in 1933 or soon after and thus fulfilled the requirement of having resided in Britain for a minimum of five years. Most of the interviewees became naturalised British citizens after the war, some by their own choice, whilst the younger men, such as Hans Brill and Hans Seelig, were included in their parents' naturalisation procedures. In the case of women who married British-born husbands, such as Christel Marsh and Hilde Ainger, citizenship was conferred automatically, providing them with at least some sense of security. The former states: 'We went to the Registrar's Office and bought a special licence. And after one week we could marry and that gave me the nationality immediately, and all this was finished, not being able to stay. That was that.' Refugees who joined the British army during the war, like Peter Johnson, were given the privilege of citizenship immediately after the war. However, at this point it was not extended to their wives.

Not many of the interviewees mention naturalisation as a special

9. THE CHALLENGES OF SETTLING DOWN

event. For Klary and Ernst Friedl who came to this country on Czech passports, it was particularly easy to be naturalised, and consequently they did not even bother to apply for citizenship until 1954. When asked whether they had any problems with the application, Klary Friedl's answer was an emphatic 'Not at all, not at all', and she emphasised that she felt accepted by British society. For Adelheid Schweitzer, however, acquiring citizenship was 'a wonderful relief'. The whole family – husband, brother, and mother-in-law – were naturalised in 1948, and she describes how she felt when she returned with a British passport from abroad for the first time: walking proudly through the gate marked 'British Citizens' seemed to her 'wonderful, wonderful. It was a great, great moment. Unforgettable.'

Finally, two of our interviewees, Alfred Dörfel and Ernst Flesch, never became British citizens, as discussed in the previous chapter. Whilst the former did not wish to do so, the latter was refused. Ernst Flesch feels in any case that the official granting of citizenship does not necessarily reflect how much the émigré truly feels integrated into the new country: 'I've never become British. I like it here, I've stayed here, it's my base, I've had a career here, but I don't think you ever really become English. You could become British naturalised, certainly, but no, you don't become English.'

iv. Feeling at home in the new country

Is it possible to discern from the observations of the interviewees those factors which have contributed to their perception of belonging to their adopted country? As Ernst Flesch points out, work and career are clearly important elements in the integration process, and Eugen Brehm, too, speaks of this. He considers that the excellent relationship he had with his colleagues during his long career at the BBC Monitoring Service in Caversham helped to make him feel socially integrated. A number of the interviewees do indeed mention the wider social groups to which they were introduced through their own or their spouses' work. Hanne Norbert-Miller is a case in point. She says that both she and her husband 'felt very welcome and at home in this country... Especially through my husband being really part of the theatre establishment.' His work seems to have made such an impact that she has continued all her life to feel connected to the English theatre world. For a few, there were opportunities to be included in the gatherings of the British Establishment. Erika Young, although she herself did not set much store by social events, relates: 'My husband worked in the House of Commons – so we did things like going to the Speaker's parties... I didn't care much for social life... but I had it. It was there for the taking.'

Klary Friedl and her husband also enjoyed contacts with Establishment figures, in particular after the war with members of the Labour Government. She describes their friendship with Barbara Ayrton Gould MP: 'We [were] very friendly... we went to her house, she came here a lot and I liked her very, very much.' She later came to know the Director-General of the BBC, Huw Wheldon, who introduced himself as a near neighbour when he saw her sweeping outside her house; he may well have been intrigued by this typically Continental habit. Subsequently the two families became very good friends.

Such fortuitous encounters which may well have helped with the integration process did not arise for everybody. Margarete Hinrichsen was acutely aware that the impetus for achieving successful integration in the new country had to come from herself. She says: 'I had to make my own life... You make a conscious effort to get on with the other life. You certainly go under if you don't.' Many émigrés, on the other hand, were drawn together by their shared experiences and looked for friends among other refugees. Eva Sommerfreund confirms this tendency, 'not because I don't want to move in other circles, but it happened like that'. This point is echoed in almost identical terms by Gertrud Wengraf, who says of her friendships within refugee circles: 'It wasn't my intention and I certainly haven't done it deliberately, but somehow that's how it happened – I feel more comfortable with them.' Helga Reutter also mentions that she has more contact with people of a similar background, adding: 'I can't even say why.'

Such friendships continue to be much valued by many of the interviewees. They had often come about through involvement with official refugee organisations, which for some became an important focus point – even later on in life – through which they could keep up the link with their refugee experience. This was certainly the case for

9. THE CHALLENGES OF SETTLING DOWN

Ernst Flesch who, as we saw in Chapter Four, had been a very active member of Young Austria, the youth section of the Austrian Centre, during the war. Later in his life he became involved with Club 1943, eventually becoming its treasurer: 'It's a good organisation. Some of the talks are very interesting, marvellous many of them, so I do enjoy going there. It's very nice and pleasant,' he comments warmly.

Hans Seelig feels the refugee club reconnects him to his roots. For him, Club 1943 means 'returning to my background, rediscovering the Jewish religion, although in many respects I am very unorthodox'. He tells how after the death of his mother he became increasingly active in the club, where he often gave talks. When later a new chairman was needed, he stepped into the breach. He feels strongly about his continued involvement: 'In many respects I think of Club 1943 as probably the most worthwhile thing I have ever done.'

A slightly different function was fulfilled by 'The Hyphen', a social club co-founded in 1948 by Peter Johnson. As the name implies, the club's role was to be a link between the Continental and the English worlds, 'the connecting link between our former . . . state of being refugees and becoming full British naturalised citizens', as Peter Singer puts it. Elizabeth Rosenthal, too, mentions being part of this organisation, whose members arrived in England as children or young adults. On the whole, this age group was reasonably well integrated into the majority culture of this country, but they still felt the need for a gathering point for younger people who shared the experience of emigration from the Third Reich. Peter and Hanna Singer in fact met through The Hyphen, and married in 1955.

The process of integration was assisted by the refugees' children growing up in this country. For Helga Reutter, contacts with English people certainly intensified as a result of meeting the parents of her daughter's schoolfriends and Margarete Hinrichsen observes: 'I made a lot of friends through the children, and I feel more British.' Emigration can, however, in some cases preclude a sense of definite identification with any particular culture. Thus Gertrud Wengraf feels settled to an extent because her 'children are pretty well integrated and that makes me feel comfortable if you like'. However, as we have seen, she also states: 'I am not an Englishwoman, I don't think I am. On the other hand, I am not an Austrian either. I am not a Jewess either because my religion doesn't come into it. I am a bit in the middle of nowhere.' Even after having lived in this country for fifty years or more, the feeling of not being firmly rooted in one particular culture is shared by some of our other interviewees. Klary Friedl comments:

> It's a very interesting question. If I go to Central Europe, I'm crying out for England. If I am anywhere else, I am so happy to come back, come back to my home, as the English say, my home is my castle. I like to be here, but I am different from the English people, my language, my food, all sorts of things, but we are such good friends, because we tolerate each other.

The interviewees express a range of perceptions about the role and place of the original culture in their lives. Thus Margarete Hinrichsen declares quite bluntly: 'I don't feel German at all.' Elizabeth Rosenthal, whose complex relations to her former 'Heimat' are described elsewhere, now feels no particular affinity with Germany as a country or with the German language, 'but the music and the literature and the culture, that is part of one's background'. Hans Seelig read Modern Languages at Oxford, thus reconnecting with the first language he had learned. He states that: 'As an English Germanist . . . [I] seemed to connect with my early experience . . . especially as my mother was very literary in her tastes.'

For Ernst Flesch, the original culture appears still to exert a strong pull. He sees himself, even now, as an 'Auslandsösterreicher' (expatriate Austrian). This is not only because he has retained Austrian citizenship, but also, as he says, 'emotionally one still feels Austrian . . . in spite of everything'. Ernst Flesch and Adelheid Schweitzer both draw a distinction between the concepts of Britishness and Englishness, the latter being seen as a more completely integrated state which can never be fully attained by émigrés. Adelheid Schweitzer states: 'I call myself British. I would never call myself English. You can't become English.' Mimi Glover does not even go as far as to consider herself British, in spite of holding a British passport. She sees herself as being too 'different . . . because I am a stranger here still, and there [Vienna] I'm at home'. This sits some-

9. THE CHALLENGES OF SETTLING DOWN

what oddly with her enthusiastic voluntary work as a guide for English Heritage at St Paul's Cathedral and the Houses of Parliament. Like Mimi Glover, Nelly Kuttner does not see herself as English either; however, she seems to accept this with equanimity. Although she says 'I have no true homeland', she emphasises that she is not concerned by this: 'No, not a bit, I feel here . . . I can never be English. I try, I live here, I change myself to the English way, you see, but I can't do it. I haven't been born here. I can't be expected to be English, but I try my best. I am very happy.'

The absence of a strong sense of belonging is seen positively by Eva Sommerfreund, who grew up in Austria and Czechoslovakia before emigration. She agrees with Peter Ustinov's proposition that it is preferable to stand above patriotic sentiments, quoting his statement: 'I am happy to say that my foot does not start tapping at any national anthem.' Josephine Bruegel, with a similar background, emphasises the advantages gained from the different cultures that play a part in her life: 'I live in German, Czech and English literature, and I see that as an advantage. I have never really considered what I feel myself to be.' Ruth Herring also finds that emigration has given her a wider perspective. Indeed, she feels privileged that her outlook has broadened through coming to Britain:

> I hope I have grown in maturity, in understanding human nature, in seeing the world rather than the country and/or just Europe. Because it struck me that in this country you have the chance of acquiring a global perspective, albeit an English-speaking global perspective.

For Hilde Auerbach, too, there have clearly been positive gains which, although unspecified, are firmly implied in her assertion that 'I still like being here best'.

Whether the interviewees see themselves as firmly integrated or whether they still have an acute sense of foreignness, they frequently, and often movingly, express their gratitude to this country and its people. 'I feel extremely loyal to this country, even if I criticise it sometimes,' is how Eva Sommerfreund puts it. At times, feelings of gratitude are mixed with a sense of obligation, as Hanna Singer says, but she adds that 'now I'd stress the gratitude much more and the awareness of what was done for us'. Stella Rotenberg also feels deeply indebted to Britain for giving her the chance to survive, as she expresses poignantly:

> I know that England, that is to say Great Britain, saved my life. And not only mine but that of others as well. Naturally, there are things one could criticise, and everybody is free to do so. . . But I don't want to forget that I am alive because I am in England.

Afterword

It must already be clear from foregoing chapters of this volume that not only do the interviewees have reason to be grateful to their host country for offering them a refuge at a time of danger and distress, but that Britain, too, has every cause for gratitude to the refugees from Nazism for their exceptional contribution to the life of the nation. Not for nothing was a 1995 article on this subject in the *Sunday Telegraph* entitled 'Hitler's Gift to Britain', a phrase so apt that it was adopted the following year for a conference on the German-speaking exiles in Britain, organised by the Research Centre for German and Austrian Exile Studies. In the sixty-odd years that have elapsed since their arrival, former German-speaking refugees have made their way to some of the highest positions in the country, have made an invaluable contribution in more or less every profession and walk of life, and have indeed been duly honoured for their achievements.

British science, for instance, has been enormously enriched by the presence here of practitioners of the calibre of Sir Hermann Bondi and Sir Rudolf Peierls or of the Nobel prizewinner Sir Hans Krebs. Similarly, British artistic life has been greatly enlivened by the painters Lucian Freud and Frank Auerbach, to take two outstanding examples, or by that felicitous combination, the Amadeus String Quartet (which traces its origins back to a wartime encounter in a British internment camp). Emigré historians such as the late Sir Geoffrey Elton and Francis Carsten are among the most prominent in their field, whilst it is hard to imagine the British publishing scene without the contributions made to it by Lord Weidenfeld, the late André Deutsch and others. And as for intellectual areas like psychiatry and art history (which were already comparatively advanced in Central Europe by the 1930s), their practice here has literally been transformed by the efforts of refugees from Nazism like Anna Freud and Melanie Klein or Sir Nikolaus Pevsner and Sir Ernst Gombrich.

We do not, of course, intend to suggest that very many of the men and women fleeing Hitler and taking refuge in Britain were in a position to achieve this degree of eminence. Nevertheless, it is our contention that the experiences of the people recorded in the present volume take their place alongside those of their more famous former compatriots and together go some way towards building up an overall picture of an unusually gifted and resourceful group of men and women, albeit one whose emigration was marked by great loss and suffering. This book, then, set out to explore and elucidate these experiences, both in relation to the thirty-four interviewees, whose achievements lie in a great variety of fields and professions, but also, beyond them, to the wider population of German-speaking refugees who managed, often only with the greatest difficulty, to make their way to Britain during the 1930s and to rebuild their lives here. As far as Britain was concerned, the immigration of the refugees from Hitler's Reich turned into an overwhelmingly positive experience – though whether Britain has learned very much from its past good fortune in this respect remains open to question.

Glossary and Abbreviations

Anschluss: Annexation of Austria by the Nazis on 12 March 1938.

Austrian Centre: Organisation founded by Austrian refugees in London in 1939 to provide social, educational and cultural services for refugees from Austria. Dissolved 1947.

Austrian Freedom Party (Freiheitliche Partei Österreichs): Far-right party in Austria often associated with proto-Nazi elements; leader Jörg Haider. Partner in coalition government since early 2000.

Austrian Self-Aid: One of the precursors and then constituent parts of the Austrian Centre (q.v.), founded in 1938 by Austrians to provide assistance to fellow-countrymen already resident in Britain.

Bekennende Kirche: see *Confessional Church*.

Bloomsbury House: Premises in Bloomsbury Street, London WC1 of Central Office for Refugees which housed the offices of most of the leading organisations working on behalf of the German-speaking refugees from 1939 onwards.

Caputh (i.e. Jüdisches Landschul- und Kinderheim Caputh): Mixed, progressive, largely Jewish boarding school situated in village of Caputh near Potsdam, overlooking Havel River. Founded 1931/2 by Gertrud Feiertag and closed by Nazis after Kristallnacht (q.v.).

Club 1943: Social and literary club set up in 1943 by refugees opposed to the more politicised Free German League of Culture (*FDKB* q.v.). Still meets regularly.

Confessional Church (Bekennende Kirche): Movement within German Lutheran church which openly opposed Nazism. Founded May 1934. Leading figures were Pastor Martin Niemöller, Professor Karl Barth and Dietrich Bonhoeffer.

CRTF (Czech Refugee Trust Fund): Originally 'British Committee for Refugees from Czechoslovakia', set up in September 1938, after Hitler's invasion of Sudeten Czechoslovakia, with a British Government fund of four million pounds for the support of refugees coming from that country (Sudeten Germans, Reich Germans and Austrians who had fled to Czechoslovakia and exiled Czechs and Slovaks).

FAM (Free Austrian Movement): Umbrella organisation founded in December 1941; aimed at bringing about united political front of all Austrian antifascist groups in exile.

FDKB (Free German League of Culture/Freier Deutscher Kulturbund): Founded 1938 as a social and cultural centre for German refugees and as a forum for refugee artists. Its lively programme of cultural activities included a Free German University.

Free German Youth: youth organisation of *FDKB*.

Gauleiter (= District Leader): Highest-ranking Nazi party officials below top Reich leadership; usually appointed by Hitler. Administered the Gauen, the Nazi administrative regions. In 1938 there were 32, by 1942 there were 42.

GRP (Gruppe Revolutionärer Pazifisten): Radical German pacifist group, founded by Kurt Hiller in 1926 and attracting a high-profile left-wing intellectual membership. Aimed to promote pacifism within a Socialist world order.

Gymnasium: Academic secondary school similar to British Grammar School.

Heimat = 'home' in sense of place where one feels at home at deepest level.

Jewish Agency [for Palestine, later *for Israel]:* Executive and representative body of World Zionist Organisation which, after playing major role in establishment of Israel (1948), took on responsibility for immigration, land settlement, youth work and other functions financed by voluntary Jewish contributions from abroad.

Jewish Refugees Committee (also known as *German Jewish Aid Committee*): Main casework committee for Jewish refugees, it was founded 1933 at instigation of Otto M. Schiff. Offices both at Woburn House and Bloomsbury House (q.v.). Still in existence today.

Kindertransport: Humanitarian action carried out 1938–1939 as a result of Kristallnacht, whereby over ten thousand unaccompanied children were sent from Germany and Austria on group transports to be educated and/or trained, mostly in Britain. The Movement for the Care of Children from Germany organised this initiative and over one hundred local committees were responsible for maintaining the children whilst they were awaiting placement in families. The 'foster parents' agreed to maintain and educate the children.

Kristallnacht: Pogrom of 9–11 November 1938, organised by Goebbels and Heydrich with Hitler's blessing. It consisted mainly of destruction of Jewish businesses and synagogues and wholesale arrest of Jews.

Laterndl: Popular Austrian exile theatre which ran under the auspices of Austrian Centre (q.v.) in London between 1939 and 1945.

'Machtergreifung' (= seizure of power): Term used by Nazis to indicate assumption of political power in Germany by Hitler on 30 January 1933 (although the Party did not yet hold a majority in parliament).

Mittelstand = middle class.

Nuremberg Laws: Laws promulgated in September 1935 which legitimated anti-semitism; laid down definitions of 'Aryanism' and forbade marriage between Germans and Jews, amongst other measures.

Ostjuden: Jews coming from eastern Europe who were Orthodox, retaining traditional dress, customs and language.

Reinhardt-Seminar: Drama school for actors and directors founded 1928 in Vienna by Max Reinhardt, eminent Viennese director who, somewhat against the fashion of the times, favoured an actor-centred theatre and ensemble playing.

Schutzhaft (= 'protective custody'): After Hitler's seizure of power many Jews and political opponents of the Nazis were summarily imprisoned without trial . Although the Nazis called it 'protective custody', it was in reality preventive detention.

SAP (*Sozialistische Arbeiterpartei*): Radical German Socialist party, founded October 1931 following a split in the SPD; despite its small size, particularly active in organising resistance against Nazism.

SD (*Sicherheitsdienst*): Nazi Party's intelligence and security body under control of Himmler and Heydrich. Held wide range of functions including protection of the Reich against enemies of the state.

Toynbee Hall: First Universities Settlement, founded 1884 in the East End; actively promoted practical social reform and evolved a significant social welfare and education programme, including the Workers' Educational Association. Provided some living accommodation also. Still flourishing today.

Wiener Library: Library which came out of Jewish Central Information Office, set up by German Jewish refugee Dr Alfred Wiener in Amsterdam in 1933, to collect and disseminate information about events taking place in Nazi Germany. Collection transferred to Manchester Square, London in 1939 and heavily used by British government departments in and after the war. Currently in Devonshire Street, London W1.

Young Austria: Youth organisation of Austrian Centre (q.v.).

NOTES ON CONTRIBUTORS

MARIETTA BEARMAN is a lecturer at Imperial College London and researches in the field of exiled Austrians; CHARMIAN BRINSON is Director of the Humanities Programme at Imperial College London; ANTHONY GRENVILLE is Senior Research Fellow at the University of Bristol and a freelance researcher; STEFAN HOWALD is a journalist, author and researcher; MARIAN MALET is Deputy Director of The Diplomatic Service Language Centre in London; JENNIFER TAYLOR is a freelance researcher; IRENE WELLS is a former refugee and lecturer; ERNA WOODGATE is a lecturer at Imperial College London. All have published in the field of exile studies.

Index

Acol Club 121
Aliens Act (1920) 127
Almas, Josef 143
Amadeus String Quartet 144, 247
Amalgamated Engineering Union 229–30
Amnesty International 119
Anderson, Sir John 149
Arandora Star 140, 148
Ardrey, Robert 143
Association of Jewish Refugees 194
Attlee, Clement 117
Auerbach, Frank 247
Auschwitz concentration camp 188, 194
Austria, Ministry of Education and Art 226
Austrian Centre 116–17, 121, 124–5, 225, 243, 249, 251–2
Austrian Freedom Party 214, 249
Austrian Self-Aid 91, 234, 249
Auxiliary Fire Service 156

Ballet Rambert 225
Barth, Professor Karl 249
Barthel, Kurt (KuBa) 142–3
Bauhaus 30, 224
BBC 101, 106, 155, 223, 226, 242
    Austrian Section 225
    Chorus 225
    German Section 225, 238
    Monitoring Service 95, 134, 218–19, 241
BDM (Bund Deutscher Mädchen) 29
Becker, Alfred 147
Bedales School 72
Beethoven, Ludwig van 18, 22
Bekennende Kirche (Confessional Church) 2, 53, 64, 115, 182, 187, 249
Beller, Steven 18

Belsen concentration camp 194, 195, 198–9
Belsize Square Synagogue, London 169
Benson Harrison, Rev. J. 146
Bergner, Elisabeth 19
Berlin, Sir Isaiah 222
Berlin Philharmonic Orchestra 19
Bloomsbury House 98, 249
Bohr, Niels 6
Bondi, Sir Hermann 247
Bonhoeffer, Dietrich 249
Bormann, Martin 218
Brahms, Johannes 20
Brandt, Willy 223
Brecht, Bertolt 24, 142
Breslau Philharmonic Orchestra 20
British Army 101, 155
British Committee for Refugees from Czechoslovakia (later Czech Refugee Trust Fund, CRTF) *see* Czech Refugee Trust Fund
British Library, National Sound Archive ix
British Medical Association 227
Brooke Bond 13, 98
Brooke family 13
Brüning, Heinrich 39
Buchenwald concentration camp 158, 165, 193

Camp de Gurs, France 194
Camp N, Quebec 143, 147
Camp News 142
Caputh school (Jüdisches Landschul- und Kinderheim) 24, 27, 62, 80, 170, 208, 231, 249
Carl Rosa Opera Company 224
Carsten, Francis 247
Caruso, Enrico 20
Central Office of Information 223
Centralverein deutscher Staatsbürger

INDEX

jüdischen Glaubens (Central Union of German Citizens of the Jewish Faith) 165
Chamberlain, Neville 48–9, 59, 64, 113, 191
Chelsea Polytechnic 228
Children's Inter-Aid Committee 69
Church of England 219
Churchill, Sir Winston 127, 134
CID 151
Club 1943 125, 176, 225, 243, 249
Comedian Harmonists 32
Communist Party, Communism 24, 33, 35–6, 40, 115–18, 161, 198, 200, 204
Confessional Church *see* Bekennende Kirche
Conway (training ship) 109
Covent Garden Opera House 224
Crossman, Richard 95
Cruickshank, Dame Joanna 146
Curie, Marie 6, 26
Czech Red Cross 87
Czech Refugee Trust Fund (CRTF) 48, 59, 76, 86–7, 95, 99, 105, 116, 156, 249
    German Communist group 99
Czech Socialist Party 115

Dachau concentration camp 58, 66, 128, 193
Daniel, Captain O.H. 142
Dante Alighieri 26
Deutsch, André 247
Deutsch-Jüdische Jugendgemeinschaft 174
Deutsche Arbeitsfront 45
Dickens, Charles 120
Dollfuss, Engelbert 35, 37
Dunera 138–40
Dunera Organisation 229
Dunera Statement 138

Eastern Daily News 224
Elton, Sir Geoffrey 247
Emergency Powers (Defence) Act (1940) 154
Emerson, Sir Herbert 49–50
England, Detective 155
English Heritage 221, 245
Ettrick 140, 200
European Committee of the Federal Union 116
Evesham police station 133–4

Fechenbach, Hermann 143
Feiertag, Gertrud 249
Fischer, Ernst 199
Fischer-Dieskau, Dietrich 223
Fleischmann, Peter 143
Fleurette Fashion 32, 229
Foreign Office 95, 223
Fortnum & Mason 97, 229
Franco, General Francisco 47, 148
Der Frauenruf 146
Free Austrian Movement (FAM) 116–17, 197–8, 210, 213–4, 249–50
Free German League of Culture 116, 121, 143, 225, 250
Free German University 250
Free German Youth 116, 172, 250
Freud, Anna 247
Freud, Lucian 247
Fried, Erich 225–6
Friedl, Ernst 72, 88, 155, 157–8, 193, 195
Friends' School, Great Ayton 132, 153
Frisch, Max 223
Fürnberg, Louis 142
Furtwängler, Wilhelm 212–13

Gál, Hans 144
Galsworthy, John 120
German Democratic Party (DDP; later Staatspartei) 33, 116
Gielgud, Sir John 233
Girl Guide Headquarters 93
Glaxo 228
Glyndebourne Festival Opera 225
Goebbels, Josef 251

Goethe, Johann Wolfgang von 18
Goldstein, Julie 19
Gombrich, Sir Ernst 222, 247
Goodman, Kirstin Mary 99
Gould, Barbara Ayrton 117, 242
GRP (Gruppe Revolutionärer Pazifisten) 115, 250
Gruber, Fritz 73
Gruppe Unabhängiger Deutscher Autoren (Group of Independent German Authors) 115–16
Grynszpan, Herschel 49

Habonim (Zionist youth organization) 168
Haider, Jörg 207, 214, 249
Hamann, Paul 143
Hammersmith College of Art and Design 224
Hay (internment camp), New South Wales 143, 147
Heartfield, John 143
Heckroth, Hein 147
Heller, George 143
Henlein, Konrad 48
Herring, Helmut 136
Herring, John 136
Hess, Dame Myra 159
Heuss, Theodor 223
Heydrich, Reinhard 251
Hiller, Kurt 115, 250
Himmler, Heinrich 251
Hindemith, Paul 23
Hindenburg, Paul von 45
Hinrichsen, Klaus 159
Hitler, Adolf 1, 8, 40–3, 45–51, 58, 59, 64, 81, 185, 211, 214, 249–51
Hitler Youth 29, 62
Hitler–Stalin Pact 156
'Hitler's Gift to Britain' (conference) 247
Hodgkinson Motors 154
Home Guard 173
Home Office 68–9, 127, 134, 150, 200
Hugill, Jim 118

Humboldt University Berlin 23, 224
Huyton (internment camp) 135–6, 142, 149
The Hyphen (club) 124, 243

IG Farben 196, 218
Independent Social Democratic Party (USPD) 35
International Union of Social Democratic Educators 221
Israelitische Kultusgemeinde (Jewish communal organization) 167

Jewish Agency 223, 250
Jewish Board of Deputies 73, 237
Jewish Central Information Office 69, 252
Jewish Refugees Committee 86, 104, 105, 153, 188–9, 250
Jews' Temporary Shelter, London 86
Joachim, Joseph 20
Jooss, Kurt 147
Jooss Ballet 147

Kaltenbrunner, Ernst 210
Kann, Dr 230
Kant, Immanuel 18
Kindertransports 1, 62, 69–70, 76, 80–1, 84–6, 124, 138, 144, 198, 250
Kisch, Egon Erwin 21
Klein, Melanie 247
Koenen, Wilhelm 142
Koestler, Arthur 34
Kraus, Karl 21
Krebs, Sir Hans 247
Kristallnacht (9–11 November 1938) 24, 27, 29, 49, 56, 59, 61–4, 66, 73, 75–6, 165
KuBa (Kurt Barthel) 142–3
Kushner, Tony 69
Kuttner, Stefan 171, 198

Laban Centre for Movement and Dance 231
Labour Party 115, 117

INDEX

Lagerlöf, Selma 21
Landauer, Walter 144
Laterndl theatre 116, 121, 225, 251
League of Nations 48–50
Lenin, V.I. 34
Lessing, Gotthold Ephraim 18
Liberal Party 116
Liberal Synagogue, St John's Wood, London 171
Library Association 222
Liebknecht, Karl 19, 34
Lister Institute 228
Locarno, Treaty of 47
London Care Committee 227–8
London Jewish Graduates 173
London School of Economics 153, 228, 230
Lowenfeld, Margaret 227
Lyons' Corner House 229

Madariaga, Salvador de 148
Man, Isle of 128, 135–8, 141–50, 177, 236
  Marine Biological Research Station 146
  Methodist Church, Port Erin 146
Manchester Guardian 73
Mann, Erika 223
Mann, Thomas 142, 223, 239
Marks & Spencer 97, 169, 229–30
Marsh, Norman 138–9, 188, 192
Mary Wigman School, Cologne 32
Masaryk, Tomás Garrigue 6
Miller, Martin 129, 225
Mooragh Times 142
Morrison, Herbert 148
Moscow Declaration (1943) 209n
Movement for the Care of Children from Germany 69, 250
Munich Agreement 56
Mussolini, Benito 47, 51

Napier, D., & Son 230
National Gallery, London 159
Nationalist party (DNVP) 33, 48
New Liberal Jewish Congregation 169
Niemöller, Pastor Martin 249
Norwich Evening Press 224
November Group 21
Nuremberg Laws 46–7, 54, 251
Nuremberg trials 196, 218, 223

Olympic Games, Berlin 47
The Onchan Pioneer 142
O'Neill, Lieutenant 139–40
Orientex 229

Peierls, Sir Rudolf 247
Perks, Dr Robert ix
Perutz, Leo 21
Pevsner, Sir Nikolaus 247
Pioneer Corps 100
Pitt, Harry 222
Pollard, Walter 130–1
Popular Front 116
Powell and Moya 224
Prager, Eugene 117
Prince, Jean 225

Quakers 59, 62, 73, 85, 183, 186, 188

Radek, Karl 34
Ramsay, Sir William 26
Rankl, Karl 225
Rath, Ernst vom 49, 65
Rawicz, Maryan 144
Reading, Lady 150
Red Cross 87, 190, 194
Redfern Gallery, London 143
Reform Synagogue, Berkeley Square, London 171
Refugee Club, Oxford 124
Reichsmusikkammer 31, 54
Reichsverband bildender Künstler (National Union of Fine Artists) 19, 54
Reichsvertretung der Deutschen Juden 63
Reinhardt, Max 251
Reinhardt-Seminar 32

257

Reininger, Lotte 73
Research Centre for German and Austrian Exile Studies (formerly London Research Group for German Exile Studies) vii, 247
Richthofen, Frau von 34
Riefenstahl, Leni 47
Röhm, Ernst 46
Rostal, Max 20
Royal Institute of British Architects 98, 224
Royal Institute of Chemistry 228
Royal Marsden and Princess Elizabeth Hospital 227
Rushen Outlook 146
Rutherford, Sir Ernest 6, 26

Sadler's Wells Opera 224
Sarasate, Pablo 20
Schiff, Otto M. 250
Schiller, Friedrich 18
Schirach, Baldur von 210
Schmidt, Heinz 99
Schuschnigg, Kurt von 34, 37, 48, 210
Schwarzwaldschule, Vienna 11
Schwitters, Kurt 141, 143–4
Scott, Lieutenant-Colonel W.P. 138–9
Seitz, Karl 34
Seydewitz, Max 36
Seyss-Inquart, Arthur 210
Shakespeare, William 120
Shaw, G.B. 143, 147
Sheed and Ward 223
Sherbrooke Camp, Quebec 150
Singing Babies 32
Social Democrats (SPD) 35–6, 40, 115, 116, 199, 251
Society of Friends: Germany Emergency Committee 189 *see also* Quakers
South Hampstead High School for Girls 26, 251
Sozialistische Arbeiterpartei (SAP) 36, 115
Spanish Civil War 45

Specht, Minna 145
Special Branch 200
Stacheldraht 142
Stalin, Joseph 8, 53, 116
Strauss-Pottlitzer, Margot 146
Der Stürmer 55
Sudeten German Party 48
Sunday Telegraph 247
Synge, Dr 228

Technische Hochschule Berlin 224
Theresienstadt concentration camp 193, 194, 203
Torberg, Friedrich 21
Toynbee Hall (Universities Settlement) 101, 125, 252

Uhlman, Fred 143–4
Ustinov, Peter 245

Versailles, Treaty of 47
Vienna Philharmonic 20

War Office 134
Warburg, Gustav 222
Warth Mill, Lancashire 134
Weidenfeld, Lord 247
Weizmann, Chaim 165
Wengraf, Paul 130
West Hampstead police station, London 131–2
West London Synagogue 173 Committee 86
Westerbork transit camp 194
Wheldon, Huw 242
Whittington Hospital 227
Wiener, Dr Alfred 69, 252
Wiener Library 95, 114, 196–7, 222–3, 252
Wigman, Mary 73
Wilhelm II, Emperor 34, 38
Wolff, Oswald 197, 223
Wolff, Peter 132
Woodbrooke College, Birmingham 73, 186, 187

INDEX

Workers' Educational Association 252
World Jewish Congress 193
World Youth Festival 199
World Zionist Organisation 250
Wright, Professor Samson 190

Young Austria 116–17, 125, 191, 243, 252

Zemlinsky, Alexander 21
Zimmering, Max 143